BEHAVIOURAL CONFLICT

Why Understanding People and Their Motivations Will Prove Decisive in Future Conflict

Andrew Mackay and Steve Tatham

with a chapter by Lee Rowland

✴ Military Studies Press

Military Studies Press
4 Dencora Park
Shire Hill
Saffron Walden
Essex, CB11 3GB
United Kingdom

First published in 2011
Military Studies Press, an imprint of Books Express Publishing

ISBN-13: 978-1-78039-468-8   paperback

ISBN-13: 978-1-78039-469-5   hardback

ISBN-13: 978-1-78039-389-6   eBook

DISCLAIMER: The views expressed in this publication are those of the authors alone and do not necessarily reflect the views of Her Majesty's Government.

100% of the Authors' Royalties will be contributed to Help for Heroes Trading Limited which Gift Aids all its taxable profits to Help for Heroes (Registered Charity Number 1120920).

Dedication

This book is dedicated to the men and women of HM Armed Forces, whom we both have had the incredible privilege and honour to command.

And to those who did not make it back home.

Help for Heroes is a registered charity looking after wounded and disabled members of the British Armed Forces.

www.helpforheroes.org.uk

Foreword

by *General Stanley McChrystal, US Army (retired)*

Former Commander ISAF, Afghanistan

It is an understatement of epic proportion, but every discussion of counterinsurgency should begin with the truism that it is complex.

On its grandest level, counterinsurgency is a struggle between a government and insurgents for the support of the people. Often described as an 'argument' where both sides make their best case to the population, it intertwines narratives of potential prosperity, freedom, equality, or other aspirations thought to appeal to the population. In today's age, much of the battle is waged in the media or in capitals far from the theater itself. It is examined and debated with almost clinical detachment, often by individuals woefully ignorant of the actual situation.

In reality, most counterinsurgency is local. Andrew Mackay and Steve Tatham never lose sight of this in their study on the role of individual motivation and behavior in conflict. Their subject is inherently difficult to treat, since there is no master template for how to fight insurgencies. There are proven principles, but, each community, tribe, or sect is new terrain. Victory begins in the village and the neighborhood by winning the confidence of those who live there. While this conclusion may *sound* obvious, it is not. In the last decade, the coalitions fighting in Iraq and Afghanistan have, through trial and error, and an ability to learn, made progress.

For the counterinsurgent, this complexity teaches humility. You read books, but more often you learn from mistakes. While commanding the International Security Assistance Force (ISAF) in Afghanistan, what I saw in the cities and countryside affirmed the importance of understanding local politics, individual needs, and communal motivations. We experienced repeated instances where what we initially assessed as Taliban actions were actually reflections of local frictions: an old blood feud, an unpaid debt, or struggles over all-important land. In a country torn by almost two generations of violence, the emotions behind such conflicts were easily mistaken for insurgency.

Our actions, although well intentioned, were often ineffective, sometimes even counterproductive. We reminded ourselves of cases where the construction of a road advantaged one community over another, or using outside contractors to build a school engendered resentment, and we found that sometimes even a positive effort made a situation worse.

Our intentions were good, but that is never enough. An inability to understand our surroundings often left a burned-out building or cratered road—a stark symbol of our shortcomings—and wasted precious time in the overall campaign. Waging such campaigns, designed to persuade people to behave in a certain way, is complex. Often, we do not know what the people want or how best to help them.

Sometimes, we are completely blind to a project's shortcomings, even though they are instantly obvious to locals. Gaining the right level of understanding is not easy. Actively communicating back to the population, and winning them to our side, is even harder. Sometimes it's impossible. But without the participation of the people, security won by the military won't endure. Even the most well-intentioned efforts can be counterproductive, leaving rancor in their wake.

In their study, Mackay and Tatham illustrate that counterinsurgency and information operations often exist in diverse environments. As the authors show, perspective is everything—a shared understanding of events is rare. Each village or neighborhood, religious group or tribal sub-set, has its own distinct history, grievances, allegiances, and aspirations. Therefore, no single strategy can ever be a complete solution. True understanding comes from saying, 'If I lived in this village, how would I react? Who am I to them, given what they have seen and lived?' We are tactically and strategically ineffective when we expect to win populations without trying to understand them.

Mackay and Tatham's work benefits from their personal experiences. In war, they have seen what it takes to alter individual behavior up close—and it shows. Between the two of them, they have served or commanded troops in conflict zones from Northern Ireland to Sierra Leone to Afghanistan over the last thirty years. Enriched by on-the-ground experiences with those varied populations, this book continues a broader, ongoing conversation about counterinsurgency.

The past decade has yielded many lessons—hard-won in long, bitter fights—and efforts such as this to capture even some of them, are worthy and necessary. True to their background as field commanders, Mackay and Tatham offer concrete recommendations for implementing robust theories. The next challenge, as the authors know well from their time in the service, is to translate the conclusions of the counterinsurgency conversation into reality on the ground.

Preface

Collectively, we have served in Her Majesty's Armed Forces for nearly fifty years. From Sierra Leone to Afghanistan; from Bosnia to Iraq; between us we have participated in seven military operations and countless training exercises. During the course of that time, despite being in different arms of the British military, we individually came to very similar conclusions about the fundamental nature of conflict itself. Whilst geopolitics, economics, religion and ethnicity all play crucial roles in starting and sustaining conflict, we are both firmly of the opinion that it will be people's behaviour, and 'our'[1] ability to understand and alter that behaviour which will become *the* defining characteristic of resolving armed disputes – be it before (and thus acting as a deterrence) or after. We believe that whilst behaviour is undoubtedly determined by a complex set of individual experiences, it may also be based upon a reality of perception (perception shaped by both the new frontiers of the information age, particularly the Internet and the so-called 'citizen journalist') and concurrently upon centuries-old constructs that guide and govern group behaviours. Today we can find just such an example in Afghanistan in the ancient honour code of *Pashtunwali* – a creed that predates Islam by some centuries and which curiously (to 'us') requires an enemy to offer hospitality and rest at one moment but enables, nay encourages, conflict and violence at the next. We say to 'us' because, of course, it is not curious to them, and so alongside our thinking on behaviour we will also consider the idea of rationality. We have often heard 'our' adversaries' activities described as being 'irrational'. We suspect that the only irrationality is 'our' ability to make a conceptual leap into the world that has shaped and formed their actions. Had 'we' done so, and had 'we' really understood what it was that drove people's behaviour, rather than judging it against 'our' own values and moral compass, we suspect that 'we' would not be talking about irrationality quite so flippantly and that the Afghan conflict, perhaps even the Iraqi one that preceded it, would not have cost 'us' so much time, blood and treasure.

We believe that Her Majesty's Armed Forces, and those of 'our' allies, will have to understand these concepts and then apply that understanding to military and diplomatic advantage in the future. Increasingly 'we' (and in particular the British Army) have started to generically refer to this as 'influence', but 'we' do so without any real understanding of what the word really means. This book then is the (incomplete) story of our journey in that understanding, a journey that takes us through seven military conflicts and through our, as military men, rather limited and perhaps even misguided attempts to apply our understanding of social science in practical military applications. We say 'incomplete' because the human condition has always astounded and amazed, and so will it always. It will be quickly apparent to readers, particularly those with backgrounds in

---

1   We use quotes, deliberately, around the personal pronoun 'we' to indicate collective groups – principally the West and its military and political class. We differentiate this from the use of the unquoted we, which is designed to reflect the personal views of the two authors.

psychology or anthropology, that neither of us are scientists and that our groping in the dark for answers, although at times successful, was by no means scientific. To help us understand the issue more fully, therefore, we have asked a real scientist, Dr Lee Rowland, formerly of the University of Oxford's experimental psychology department and now at the Behavioural Dynamics Institute, to write the final chapter for us. Lee is ideally placed to do so. Once upon a time he passed the gruelling Royal Marines Commando qualifying course and served as a marine for a few short years. As a psychologist he has studied and worked not just in universities and laboratories but, unlike many who theorise, proselytise and adjudicate on the subject from the safety of warm classrooms and lecture theatres, he has also worked in real, live, global hotspots – most recently Afghanistan. With his real-world practical knowledge and his theoretical and academic expertise, he is well qualified to help us understand what lies behind the often flippantly used term 'influence'. His work is free-standing; you do not need to wade through our work to appreciate his chapter, nor is it vital for you to read his in order to understand ours. But, we hope, both sections are mutually compatible and complementary. Dip in, and out, as you wish. And please, tell us what you think. Email us your thoughts and ideas, because no one has the monopoly on being right – and there is every possibility that we may be wrong. But until a debate is initiated, well, who knows? You can reach us via the book's website at www.behaviouralconflict.com

Andrew Mackay and Steve Tatham

November 2011

Table of Contents

About the authors

Andrew Mackay

In a 29-year career, Major General Andrew Mackay has seen operational service in Northern Ireland, Bosnia, Kosovo, Iraq, Lebanon and Afghanistan. In 2008 he was awarded the CBE for his command of 52 Brigade in Helmand Province, Afghanistan. Promoted to Major General in 2009, his last appointment in the British Army was as General Officer Commanding Scotland, Northern Ireland and Northern England. He is now Director of Strategy at Baobab Investments Limited.

Steve Tatham

Steve Tatham remains a serving Commander in the Royal Navy and has seen operational service in Sierra Leone, Iraq and Afghanistan. He holds an MPhil in International Relations from St John's College, Cambridge and has just completed a part-time PhD, also in International Relations. He is the author of *Losing Arab Hearts and Minds: The Coalition, Al-Jazeera and Muslim Public Opinion*.

Dr Lee Rowland

Lee Rowland is a senior scientist at the Behavioural Dynamics Institute. He holds a BSc in Applied Psychology, an MSc in Research Methods and a PhD in Experimental Psychology. A former Royal Marines Commando, he spent two years as co-director of the M.Sc in psychological research in the Department of Experimental Psychology at Oxford University. He has worked extensively on the ground in conflict environments.

Tim Harford

Tim Harford is a British economist and journalist. He is the author of four economics books, presenter of the BBC television series 'Trust Me, I'm an Economist', and writer of a humorous weekly column called 'Dear Economist' for the *Financial Times*, in which he uses economic theory to attempt to solve readers' personal problems. His other FT column, 'The Undercover Economist', is syndicated in *Slate* magazine.

Stanley McChrystal

General Stanley McChrystal is a retired four-star general and the former commander of US and International Security Assistance Forces Afghanistan (ISAF) and the Joint Special Operations Command (JSOC). General McChrystal is currently the co-founder of the McChrystal Group, a senior fellow at Yale University's Jackson Institute for Global Affairs, where he teaches a course on leadership in operation, and an advisor to the White House Joining Forces initiative aimed at assisting military families.

Books and articles by the authors

Andrew Mackay

Combating Serious Crimes in Postconflict Societies, edited by Colette Rausch (United States Institute of Peace Press, 2006).

Steve Tatham

Losing Arab Hearts and Minds: The Coalition, Al-Jazeera and Muslim Public Opinion (2006 Hurst & Co (UK), Front Street Press (US), 2006).

Strategic Communication: A Primer (Defence Academy of the United Kingdom, 2008).

Losing the Information War in Iraq: The Dynamics between Terrorism, Public Opinion and the Media (Centre of Excellence Defence Against Terrorism, 2007).

'Tactical Strategic Communication! Placing Informational Effect at the Centre of Command' (*Small Wars*, 2009).

'Al-Jazeera: Can it Make it Here?' (*British Journalism Review*, March 2005).

'Al Jazeera: Get Used to It, It's Not Going Away' (*Proceedings*, August 2005).

Terrorism, Security and the Power of Informal Networks, edited by David Martin Jones, Ann Lane and Paul Schulte (Edward Elgar Publishing, 2010).

Steve Tatham and Andrew Mackay

Behavioural Conflict: From General to Strategic Corporal: Complexity, Adaptation and Influence (Defence Academy of the United Kingdom, 2009).

Steve Tatham and Lee Rowland

Strategic Communication and Influence Operations: Do We Really Get It? (Defence Academy of the United Kingdom, July 2010).

Steve Tatham and Mohamed El-Katiri

Qatar: A Little Local Difficulty? (Defence Academy of the United Kingdom, August 2009).

Notes to the reader

Many people have contributed, directly and indirectly, to the publication of this book. Day in, day out, military officers, civilian officials, NGOs, academics and contractors wrestle with the very issues about which we write. We are grateful to the many colleagues, from across NATO, who contributed and who listened to our thoughts, giving us the benefit of their ideas and opinions. In particular, though, we would like to thank: Lieutenant General Paul Newton CBE, Director of Force Development and Training for the British Army, who sanely checked our work and pointed out where we had got it wrong, and right. Steve Rowland undertook much early background and preparatory research. Nigel Oakes and Ian Tunnicliffe of Strategic Communication Laboratories are truly expert in understanding behaviour and Target Audience Analysis and both of us have drawn extensively on their wisdom and experience; they gave freely of time and energy and we are very grateful. General (ret.) Stanley McChrystal (US Army) and economist Tim Harford readily gave up their time to write introductions to the work, and our reviewers, former soldier, journalist and MP, Martin Bell, General Sir Rupert Smith and TV presenter, and author, Nik Gowing, were all kind enough to read and comment. Andrew is also grateful to George Soros for taking the time to provide insights on his reflexivity theory and for accepting the drop in his net worth for the lack of royalties paid on his ideas. Finally, to our publishers, Duncan and John, who saw the value in what we had to say, and to Helen and Adrian Stenton, who diligently completed final production duties and made our words far more eloquent than we ourselves could ever manage.

A word about the photographs. The photo on the front cover is the view from Ireland sanger, British Military Base, Lashkar Gah, Afghanistan. The sanger overlooks the main gate of the camp and is placed at the intersection of three roads. For people-watchers it is absolutely fascinating, and for a surprising number of military personnel it is often the only view that they get of Afghan society. Whilst many combat troops interact with Afghans, on the ground, on a daily basis, many others in combat support elements do not. They may maintain vehicles, manage stores, pay, feed, care for and mount guard for combat troops. All provide invaluable service. But what they see from that guard tower is often their only, brief, view of Afghanistan before returning to their air-conditioned tents and British home cooking. We do not know the names of the man and woman on the motorbike, nor their backgrounds and circumstances. For a few fleeting seconds they passed across our field of view and they have intrigued us ever since. Who were they, where do they live, what are their jobs, their hopes, aspirations and fears? And how does our presence, in that military guard post, interact upon them and their future? Since the photo was taken responsibility for security in Lashkar Gah has now been handed back to the Afghans. In time, the sanger may well be occupied by a member of the Afghan security forces. Hopefully, over time, there will be no requirement for it to be occupied at all.

The back cover illustrates the expanse of Helmand's desert; It is hot, dusty, dirty, arid, inhospitable and, to us, utterly miserable. But it is also home to the people that we are working with and for. It is the environment that shapes the behaviours of so many of the Afghans with whom NATO forces work.

The rear cover photo of Andrew is by Robert Wilson; of Steve by Gary Morgan. Both are reproduced by kind permission.

Finally, to our personal friends, families and colleagues who have supported and encouraged us, we are very grateful.

Introduction

by Tim Harford

Bloodied by his counterinsurgency experience in Algeria, the French officer David Galula acidly remarked: 'If there was a field in which we were definitely and infinitely more stupid than our opponents, it was propaganda.' Andrew Mackay and Steve Tatham wonder if much has changed – and evidently feel passionately that the British military could be doing far better than it currently is.

By 'behavioural conflict', Mackay and Tatham have much more in mind than mere propaganda, of course: they are trying to take seriously Von Clausewitz's famous dictum that war is the continuation of policy by other means. There is little point in sending in the tanks without some clear vision of what effect may be achieved – and the key effects will often be political and psychological rather than physical.

Mackay and Tatham consciously nod towards behavioural economics – a newish discipline on the boundary between the rational-choice theories of economics and the laboratory work of experimental psychology. There is a risk here: that in looking towards academia, we tip over into the caricature of *The Men Who Stare At Goats*, hoping that in some unspecified way the latest psychological research will allow the West's Armed Forces to bewitch their enemies and capture the hearts and minds of the people. That temptation is firmly banished in the first paragraph of the first chapter. We learn, immediately, that 'influence' is not something that can be bottled, scripted or broadcast. It requires an on-the-spot appreciation of the incentives that are pressing upon the local population, many of which will be obscure even to the troops on the ground, let alone the wordsmiths crafting 'strategic messages' back at home. If an academic study of 'influence' can somehow assist the ordinary soldier on patrol in a complex and often baffling environment, it is good for something. If not, it is hard to see how it will help.

This book sets out several stark challenges, but three in particular stood out to this reader's eyes. The first is that war demands that young soldiers, sometimes with a limited education and little exposure to the wider world, are forced to make tough decisions in confusing environments. The desire for 'influence' calls for subtlety. Circumstances make subtlety elusive. Military doctrine and training must do the best it can to bridge that gap.

The second challenge, not unrelated, is equipping hierarchies to wield influence. Senior officers, and those with appropriate expertise in psychology, public relations, linguistics and anthropology, will often be far from the arena of battle when the decisions that count are taken. To make the situation worse, the subtleties of influence make it easy to mis-communicate – or even deliberately misrepresent – how things are going on the ground. If you've lost a helicopter, HQ will soon know. If you've lost a chance to win friends and influence people, nobody further up the military hierarchy need ever know. The soldier in question may not even realise the missed opportunity himself.

To some extent, this cannot be avoided. Yet it is alarming to reflect on how British and allied Armed Forces have passed up some simple opportunities to do better. Consider the notorious reluctance of the US military under Donald Rumsfeld even to use the term 'insurgent' to refer to the enemy in Iraq. As Andrew Mackay revealed, this was not limited to misguided spinning in press conferences (although that was certainly part of the problem) – British officers such as Mackay were admonished by US officials if they dared to speak the 'i' word. Nor are the British military blameless: when Mackay led a deployment to Afghanistan, he attempted to enlist the help of the Ministry of Defence's Directorate of Targeting and Information Operations in the fundamental business of winning over the population in Helmand. He found that not only were they unable and unwilling to assist, but that they did their best to prevent others from providing advice.

The final challenge sets the context for the whole problem: the world is changing rapidly, and information operations are perhaps changing faster than anything else. Tactics and techniques will have to adapt rapidly, and as Mackay and Tatham make clear, unconventional organisations such as Hezbollah appear to be able to adapt with ease. Can the West's Armed Forces do the same? I have no doubt that other readers will draw other lessons: this is a rich analysis, full of ideas and, as one might expect, heavy with the fruits of experience. It will not be a comfortable read for its target audience – but it will be a rewarding one.

1
Tomorrow's problems here today?

In late December 2007 a troop from 40 Commando Royal Marines were patrolling in the unpopulated area south of the Kajaki Dam in southern Afghanistan when they came across a lone farmer sowing seeds in a field. In the pattern of life prevailing in an area where the local population had long fled because of continual fighting, this was an event worthy of investigation. Doubly so, because the planting season was at the very end of its cycle, but curiously here was an individual apparently risking much to plant seed in the unforgiving and harsh Afghan soil. Yet the Royal Marines' initial assumption, that the farmer was planting poppy seed, could not have been further from the truth, for he was in fact planting not poppy but wheat seed, and he was well aware of how late in the planting cycle he was undertaking his task. His answer to the obvious question 'Why?' surprised the young Royal Marine patrol commander. The farmer informed him, through their interpreter, that as a result of the assassination of the Pakistani opposition leader Benazir Bhutto in Rawalpindi just two days earlier he, the farmer, had calculated that the price of wheat was going to soar and he wanted to take advantage of it. To the Royal Marines, and in particular to their commanders back in their HQ when they later relayed the story, this was astonishing. Here was an individual who probably ranked as being amongst the poorest in the world, making a strategic, in his terms, decision based on his knowledge of world events reverberating far away. This in a country where literacy is less than 30 per cent,[1] where communications are of the most basic form and where, traditionally, the extent of a farmer's horizon, both literally and metaphorically, was the valley or plateau in which he and his family eked out an existence.

Yet the story is more complex than even that, for there are other more fundamental lessons to be learnt from the incident. The first is that all of the Royal Marines' instincts and experience, drawn from days, weeks and months patrolling in the country, tour after tour, year after year, had led them to make the *wrong* assumption about the man's motives. They presumed he was engaged in illegal activity – that he might in fact be engaged in legitimate actions was not their first reaction. The second is that had those selfsame Royal Marines (or indeed the wider British Armed Forces they represented) actively set out to influence people in that region to grow wheat instead of poppy, almost certainly they would never have considered using the assassination of a foreign leader, and the associated microeconomics, as the lever for encouragement and persuasion. Quite simply, the Royal Marines, despite being some of the world's most highly trained troops,

---

1   Taken from the CIA World Factbook 2011, available at https://www.cia.gov/library/
      publications/the-world-factbook/geos/af.html

and with all their collective experience of operations around the world, stumbled only by accident upon an understanding of the motives of the people they were there to protect.

In March 2011, towards the end of her tour, Staff Sergeant Gaynor A[2] attended an Afghan women's conference in Helmand, southern Afghanistan. The conference was being held in the Blue Shura Hall in Gereshk under a fairly high-threat state. She recalls that:

> We duly clattered in, in full combat gear, to be faced with 350 burqa-clad women sitting facing us in solemn rows. We were able to talk to some of the women leaders, (who were the only ones with uncovered faces), whilst all waited for the guests who duly assembled on the dais. This included the District Governor, who, being under imminent threat of death, had brought his personal bodyguard of six ANP,[3] and who were armed with AKs[4] and wore body armour.

> Speeches duly completed, an Afghan traditional band mounted the stage. Ten minutes of music passed before the first bodyguard was overwhelmed with the desire to dance. Casting his weapon aside with enthusiastic abandon he proceeded to cavort in front of the 350 women and the invited guests. The kind of erotic dance which, anywhere else in the world – from Egyptian belly dancing to western lap-dancing – is only associated with women, turned out to be his specialty. This consisted of small pattering steps, hip-wriggling, shuddering, hand gestures running over the shape of his body and ending emphatically at his crotch. Meanwhile his eyes were closed in imagined ecstasy. Rather startled, we scanned the women for signs of reaction. The fact that most of their faces remained completely covered did present some difficulty. However, there was not a blip of reaction and nary a pause in the rhythmic clapping. This serene state of affairs continued even after the remainder of the bodyguard decided that joining in the fun was more important than guarding the Governor. They too put down their weapons and proceeded to dance in close pairs in imitation of the original dancer but this time with sinuous crotches shaking a couple of inches apart and staring into each other's eyes with 'come hither' looks and pouting lips. The men gave no sign that what they were doing was in any way unusual; indeed, despite its solipsistic nature it was performed with remarkable unselfconsciousness. And as for knowing what the women were really thinking – who knows? Metaphorically speaking, the curtain had

---

2   For security reasons the Staff Sergeant's full name has not been included.
3   Afghan National Police.
4   Avtomat Kalashnikova (Автомат Калашникова), the official name for the 7.62 assault rifle invented by Mikail Kalashnikov in 1947.

opened to give us a tantalising and revelatory glimpse of our own 'not-knowingness', then closed again.[5]

Both stories are illustrative of what our book is about. Both the Royal Marines and Staff Sergeant A were privy to events of which they had absolutely no understanding. Our book is not about the war in Afghanistan per se, nor is it about the conflict in Iraq or Libya. Nor does our book seek to provide great and insightful revelations about the location or the likely protagonists of future conflict; instead it seeks to focus upon one single thread that has, does and will characterise conflict, both now and in the future: people and their behaviour. More specifically, it considers how 'we' might attempt to influence individuals such as these, to positively influence their behaviour during conflict and, perhaps, even to use that understanding to deter future conflict.

In future, war will probably not be the same as Afghanistan – despite it taking up so much of our national effort, blood and treasure today. Events in Libya, Tunisia, Egypt and elsewhere are already causing 'us' to rethink what constitutes the nature and character of future conflict. Despite all 'we' think we know about the Middle East, and all of 'our' intelligence-gathering apparatus, critically no one saw the events of the first quarter of 2011 coming. What possible planning scenario would seriously propose the downfall of the Egyptian President Hosni Mubarak and his forty-year regime being initiated by the misfortune of a poor, hassled stallholder in Tunisia, slapped around the face by a female police officer? In Iraq 'we' planned, perhaps even expected, that Al-Qaeda would mobilise the Sunni majority in Iraq to fight once Saddam had fallen. 'We' never expected the previously oppressed Shia minority to coalesce and mobilise around a previously unknown cleric, Muqtada Al-Sadr. Who would ever have thought that in Afghanistan 'we' would be fielding female and religious engagement teams to win over a population, to be promoting a national sports policy as a means of diverting young men of fighting age away from the clutches of the Taliban insurgents? Yet all of this, and more, has come to pass, and the only defining characteristic is that it never, at any stage, figured in the advance military planning of the operations.

At best Afghanistan may perhaps offer only a passing template for the type of conflicts in which 'we' may become embroiled. At worst the next major conflict could find 'us' equipped, trained and orientated for the last conflict, unable to adapt to the demands and complexities that future conflict will throw up. For example, future conflict may not even exist geographically, in deserts, on plains or under jungle canopies, but instead, perhaps, in cyberspace, where its protagonists may not be soldiers but programmers, their weapons viruses and computer code. Former US Secretary of Defense Rumsfeld was pilloried for his 'unknown unknowns' speech, but we are inclined to think he was right. There are indeed

---

5   We have put some footage of this on YouTube for you to see for yourselves. Remember, these are security guards there to protect the Governor in a very dangerous part of the world: http://www.youtube.com/watch?v=C8zF0jgmYvQ

unknown unknowns – others may ascribe more elegant euphemisms such as 'Black Swans' and 'Outliers' – but regardless of terminology we think it is they that will cause the most seismic future events.

By their very nature, Black Swans[6] and Outliers[7] cannot be predicted, but we know that they are out there and that they are on the way. Their form, substance, characteristics and input will at best be figured out retrospectively and at worst not at all. 'Our' ability to react and adapt to these unexpected events will therefore be uppermost in the minds of the leaders and politicians of those nations whose domestic and foreign interests will be challenged and thrown into disarray. As a nation, and as an Armed Force, 'we' may not know the future, but 'we' do need to understand where to place the balance of future investment if 'we' are to maximise our chances of successfully navigating treacherous and fast-flowing events. The key to this is therefore to understand what might be common to the panoply of environments and circumstances in which 'our' Armed Forces might operate. If the potential geographical environment is removed then there are only two possible commonalities. These are people and information. First, wars do not start without the involvement of people. In the future 'we' will need an ever-greater focus on people and the rational and irrational behaviours that they either choose, or are compelled or tricked, to exhibit. Second, wars will be fought in an ever-growing information bubble whose characteristics of speed and availability now, paradoxically, can reach into the densest of cities or the emptiest spaces of desert and jungle. Ten years ago smart phones, Twitter, YouTube and Facebook were all largely unknown. Today these simple tools have seen revolutions seeded and dictators toppled. Who would bet upon what another ten years will bring?

And what of people? If there is one certainty it is that people are different. For a while a rather large international bank ran an advertising campaign that highlighted the differences in the way that its customers, in different parts of the world, behaved differently to similar events or circumstances. The bank sought to explain that whilst it was a global player, it could relate to people in a local manner – it understood people and their differences. 'Acting globally, thinking locally' ran the tag line. People can be divided in any one of a hundred or so different ways – nationality, ethnicity, race, religion, wealth, sex, poverty, age – the list is endless. Perhaps the only certainty is that they will exhibit behaviour in manners which, first, can have profound global effect; second, are conducted in ways which may appear utterly irrational and unpredictable to 'us'; and third, those same people will be subjected to a host of 'entities' seeking to influence them through marketing and advertising at one end and coercion and loyalty at

---

6   The idea of Black Swans was developed by American author Nassim Nicholas Taleb; see *The Black Swan: The Impact of the Highly Improbable* (Random House, 2007). For many years it was presumed that swans were only white, that is until Black Swans were discovered. Taleb used the analogy to describe the disproportionate role of high-impact, hard to predict and rare events that are beyond the realm of normal expectations in the fields of history, science, finance and technology.

7   Malcolm Gladwell, *Outliers: The Story of Success* (Little, Brown and Company, 2008).

the other. In fact, if we link together these three core commonalities we can derive a single certainty: changing individual and group behaviour before, during and after conflict is likely to become a pre-eminent factor in securing future success in an unpredictable world. In such a world 'we' will need far less established process and centralised bureaucracy and far greater adaptation and innovation, with people, 'our' people, educated and empowered to understand the motivations for certain behaviour, and subsequently to manage and channel that behaviour in specific directions.

We do know some interesting facts about 'our' people – those that don uniforms and serve their countries. For example, we know that the average age of a British soldier killed on operations in Helmand is twenty-two, which interestingly is the age of the largest single group of personnel in the UK Armed Forces.[8] In fact, by 2011, 200 British soldiers, all aged in their twenties, had been killed, and a further thirty-one teenagers killed. Since the UK Armed Forces will not deploy men or women aged under eighteen on front-line operations this means that those thirty-one people were aged between eighteen and just under twenty. Let's think about that a moment longer. Most people join the UK's Armed Forces as soldiers, sailors or airmen within a year or so of leaving school – let's say nineteen to twenty years old depending on whether they have been to college. We know that most officers join the Armed Forces within a year or so of leaving university – let's say twenty-one to twenty-two. So the vast bulk of 'our' people in harm's way are aged under twenty-five. Now, the Armed Forces typically allow you to serve for around twenty-two to twenty-five years. There are exceptions, of course, and there are people as old as sixty-two still serving but this is not the norm. And, since almost everyone has to undergo yearly fitness tests and pass gruelling physical tests to deploy on operations, it would seem that us old folks (and the cap fits both authors) are very much in the minority. What else do we know? Well we know that only 6.6 per cent of 'our' people come from an 'ethnic' background. We also know that whilst Britain's Armed Forces are home to very many well-educated people, with GCSEs, A levels and degrees, it is also happy to offer a career to a great many people with few, if any, qualifications. We also know that the Armed Forces attract people from every possible socio-economic background and that, whilst many will have global outlooks, there are many more who will have never left the country, perhaps even their city or town of birth, before joining up.[9]

These people, 'our' people, are the PlayStation generation, the couch potatoes, the 'youth of today'. They very often will have come from some of the most deprived areas of the country, seeking and finding escape and opportunity in the service of the Crown like countless generations before them. Some may be graduates, so many more will have not one single qualification. But they are most certainly the generation that will be doing all the fighting. We choose to refer to them as the

---

8   In the US the average age of a soldier killed on operations in Afghanistan is now 25, having fallen from a 2008 'high' of 28.

9   All statistics have been taken from the UK MoD's Defence Analytical Services Agency website at http://www.dasa.mod.uk

'Strategic Corporal', and in their hands lie tough but possibly mission-winning decisions.

Why all the detail? Well it allows us to say with some confidence that often very junior men (and increasingly women) with, perhaps, previously very limited views of 'foreign' cultures and customs, will be placed at the very sharpest end of the battle. They will be afforded positions of incredible responsibility, where their decisions ('fire', 'don't fire', 'advance', 'retreat'), made in the very heat of the moment, perhaps with bullets flying around them, can have a potentially disproportionate strategic effect on the battle and, perhaps, even the whole campaign. Look at the (bad) choices that young US National Guardsmen made in Abu Ghraib prison in Iraq, when they humiliated and abused prisoners for fun, taking photographs that subsequently had a devastating effect when they made their way onto the Internet and the front pages of newspapers across the globe. By way of contrast, look at the choices made on numerous occasions by other men and women of the West's Armed Forces under the most arduous of circumstances. The tales of single-handed bravery are many and numerous but all involved individuals making what they thought was the right choice, no matter how irrational their chances of survival might have seemed at the time. To that end, why would British Royal Marine Matthew Croucher dive on top of a hand grenade to defend his mates, and who subsequently lived to tell the tale, describe the whole act as: 'It was a case of either having four of us as fatalities or badly wounded or one. I thought I've set this bloody thing off and I'm going to do whatever it takes to protect the others.'[10]

Why do 'our' people do that? Why place their lives at risk? To run towards the enemy to deliver first aid to a British soldier, to throw yourself on a grenade, these are not 'rational' acts – are they? Well they were to the individuals, and indeed to 'us', because 'we' gave them medals and lauded them for their actions. The British media referred to them as heroes, as the 'bravest of the brave'. 'We' all therefore apparently understand why 'our' people would do things like this. 'We' might even understand, but not condone, why the Abu Ghraib abuses took place – the 9/11 attacks, a sense of great injustice amongst Americans, poor training and the rabid portrayal of Muslims and Arabs as enemies – not least in the dangerous cauldron of violence and inhumanity that was the Iraq War. Yet we often see reference to the irrationality of others' actions – of suicide bombers in Helmand, the occupied West Bank and Sri Lanka. And 'we' look at that behaviour and struggle to understand it; why would anyone blow themselves up for their beliefs? For their religion? For their friends? Scott Atran, in his seminal work *Talking to the Enemy*,[11] strips away much of what a Western audience might consider an irrational act by identifying that most suicide bombers do so because of familial and friendship relationships. They do it for them as much as Matthew Croucher did it for his team in Sangin. Surely the only irrationality here is the inability of 'us' to

---

10   'Marine who threw himself on exploding grenade to protect comrades awarded George Cross' (*Daily Mail*, 24 July 2008).

11   Scott Atran, *Talking to the Enemy* (Allen Lane, 2010, p. 477).

understand and differentiate between the two. 'We' don't understand a Taliban suicide bomber but 'we' do understand a Royal Marine prepared to be blown up for his mates.

In 1910 US President Theodore Roosevelt made a speech, at the Sorbonne in Paris, which was to become known as the 'man in the arena speech'. A key excerpt is worth repeating. He told the audience:

> It is not the critic who counts: not the man who points out how the strong man stumbles or where the doer of deeds could have done better. The credit belongs to the man who is actually in the arena, whose face is marred by dust and sweat and blood, who strives valiantly, who errs and comes up short again and again, because there is no effort without error or shortcoming, but who knows the great enthusiasms, the great devotions, who spends himself for a worthy cause; who, at the best, knows, in the end, the triumph of high achievement, and who, at the worst, if he fails, at least he fails while daring greatly, so that his place shall never be with those cold and timid souls who knew neither victory nor defeat.

As Roosevelt says, the credit belongs to the individual at the sharp end, not those who make policy from the comfort of Whitehall in London or the Capitol Building in Washington DC, and whose forays into the battlefield, invariably swamped by an army of press, provide them with an often illusionary impression of what is actually happening. This was to prove an issue of significant concern to the former British Ambassador to Afghanistan, Sir Sherard Cowper-Coles. In his book *Cables from Kabul*,[12] he mentions, repeatedly, his concern that visiting officials were often presented with over-optimistic assessments of progress by enthusiastic military officers. There was no dishonesty suggested or implied; it was simply the case of the British military's optimistic 'can do' mentality overshadowing caution and pragmatism. Indeed, so often was this noted that it even featured in a formal report produced by the UK's Land Command which noted that: 'The overriding impression from the reports is that they are unfailingly optimistic. Every commander reports that he has made progress and must claim to have achieved their aim.'[13]

But there are other people in this conflict ecosystem and strangely, with all of the West's undoubted military intelligence capability, they are the people 'we' may actually know the least about. They are the people 'we' will have come to protect or defend. 'We' expend inordinate amounts of time analysing and profiling our enemy, its leaders and their actions, yet what do 'we' really know about the population? This is invariably the population who has yet to make a choice between

---

12   See Sherard Cowper-Coles, *Cables from Kabul* (Harper Press, 2011).
13   Land Command, *Recurring Themes from Operation Herrick* (2009).

'our' enemy or 'us' – a choice that might just prove seminal to the success or failure of the mission. Humans are complex beasts and it would be unrealistic to expect to know everything about them – although this has not stopped previous attempts in the past. In the late 1990s the US pioneered the so-called 'effect-based approach' to operations, spending billions of dollars on new technology to attempt to figure out how to create the right effect at the right time to the right audience. With hindsight such action seems almost ludicrous: to presume that human behaviour can be predicted. As former US Marine Lieutenant General Paul Van Riper demonstrated, this was no answer to dealing with the level of complexity 'we' encounter on the battlefield.

Van Riper used the game of chess as an analogy. On the chessboard there are sixty-four black and white squares and, manoeuvring across them, thirty-two pieces. The movements of every piece are heavily prescribed by the rules of the game. In fact half of the pieces on a chessboard have very restricted mobility and are often sacrificed in order to gain a strategic advantage. With a little bit of mathematics Van Riper demonstrated that there were 10^{128} permutations of possible chess moves. By way of comparison it is estimated that within the known universe there are 10^{80} atoms. Effects-based operations came unstuck because they were trying to predict moves not in a bounded rules-based environment (and patently could not do so), but instead in a complex human system where there are contradictions, improbabilities and, let's name them, apparent irrationalities – where formal rules do not exist and a sort of fuzzy logic[14] prevails. If the possibilities for chess appeared endless then the possibilities for the human system must be a magnitude greater. Effects-based operations were doomed regardless of how much computer power was thrown at the problem. But understanding how to affect particular people's actions and behaviour is not. This may appear to be a contradiction and is worthy of a moment's consideration.

Think of an army of ants, winding their way across a pavement or lawn. Predicting what that group of ants will do next is quite impossible. Yet, if we placed a few cubes of sugar close enough to the ants we might very reasonably expect to now be able to predict their next moves – it we have placed the sugar in the right place they will eventually get wind of it and, in time, swarm all over it. This is the difference – effects-based operations tried to predict human behaviour. Period. What we are suggesting is that 'we' might be able to more clearly understand how human behaviour will change if 'we' know where, how and when to intervene. In the game of chess 'we' do not know or control all the variables, but in the example of the ants and the sugar, through 'our' intervention (which is based

14   Formal logic and fuzzy logic are technical terms in science. Chess follows formal rules and logic – in other words they can be stated precisely and there is no improbability. Human environments are fuzzy; there is a degree of probability associated with how rules are enacted. For example, a knight on the chessboard can move in a number of ways, but they are all perfectly specifiable, whereas a knight of yore on horseback might have rules from the king to follow, but whether he will or not, and how he'll actually carry them out and whether he has achieved the aim are always somewhat debatable, hence fuzzy.

upon 'our' knowledge of the ants' behaviour) 'we' have attempted to exercise some control. Can this be applied to people?

Perhaps we ought to start by asking who are the people? Since 2000 some of these people have been Mendes, Kissis and Konos (and the thirteen other tribes of Sierra Leone); they have been Serbo-Croats, Bosnians, Kosovars, Albanians, Unizzahs, al-Ribads, al-Zobaids, Kurds, al-Montifig (and the other tribal groups of the nearly forty that make up Iraq); Pashtuns, Hazaras, Uzbeks (and the other six major ethnic groupings that make up Afghanistan's rich tapestry of population); they have been Sunni, Shia, Orthodox, Agnostic, Christian, Catholic; they have been farmers, police, administrators, beggars, businessmen, men, drug traffickers, war lords, women and children. In fact you can divide them in any one of a hundred or so different ways and the only certainty is that they are the components of the population that 'we' are working within, for and sometimes against. And they will exhibit behaviour in ways which will have profound effects upon the manner in which military missions are conducted.

Finally there is the enemy. They are almost invariably, but not exclusively, drawn from the population 'we' will be situated within, and in the world of the insurgent will easily melt back into that population when the moment demands. As Chinese guerrilla leader, later the first Chairman of the Chinese Communist Party, Mao Zedong famously noted, the insurgent swims amongst the people as the fish swims in the sea. 'We' often ascribe collective names to these groups. In Northern Ireland they were the 'Provos', in Bosnia they were Serbs and Croats and in Sierra Leone they were the 'rebels'. In Iraq they were the insurgents and in Afghanistan they are the Taliban. But look beneath the surface and 'we' quickly see that such homogeneous groups are largely fictional. In Afghanistan the Taliban are not one unified, homogeneous group of ideologically driven fighters but disparate groups of individuals motivated to fight by a host of different reasons – ideology, poverty, anger at the presence of foreign troops, etc. In Iraq insurgents were former Ba'athists, former Iraqi army members, criminals, Al-Qaeda and warring tribes. They were Sunni and Shia. In Sierra Leone the rebels were the RUF,[15] the West Side Boys, Kamajors and civil defence forces; and in Northern Ireland they were the Red Hand Defenders, the Loyalist Volunteer Force, the INLA,[16] the IRA,[17] et al. In Afghanistan 'we' now group Afghans with Pakistanis and call the problem 'AfPak'. 'We' unite them into groups of 'our' making at 'our' considerable peril.

Together these different groups form a complex ecosystem where all react to each other and where each other's actions can have profound effects upon the other. When Andrew found he was to lead a Brigade to Afghanistan, old staff college books and papers were dusted off and read earnestly, searching for advice and guidance. This practice is military doctrine and it is supposed to be evolved to meet not current conflict but help with future battles. Yet in preparing 52 Brigade

---

15   Revolutionary United Front.
16   Irish National Liberation Army.
17   Irish Republican Army.

in 2006 Andrew found that the UK's latest doctrine for counterinsurgency had been released just days before the 9/11 attacks in 2001; the UK had been fighting in Iraq for 3 years by then. In fact as Andrew toured the MoD[18] he grew more and more despondent for nowhere did he find the capability, the interest or the innovation to help him with his deployment. For Andrew had looked back at the Brigades which had preceded him in Helmand and decided that none presented him with a viable model for what his deployment should look like. In fact none of the available documentation was fit to help him plan a mission where winning the consent of the organic population would be the primary aim. Instead of military doctrine he had to look in the *New York Times* best-seller lists for books such as Paul Collier's *The Bottom Billion*,[19] and, perhaps of most importance, the works of behavioural economists such as Daniel Kahneman and Amos Tversky.

In 2003, Steve was maritime spokesman for the invasion of Iraq, and every day he was deluged with the latest 'lines to take' and 'key messages' – generated by legions of press officers in the MoD and the FCO.[20] By the end of his time he could have piled them into a column as high as himself. Through all the paperwork he was directed to deploy three key messages: liberation, democracy and freedom. And at every press conference and in every piece of analysis he saw that such messages simply failed to resonate. As Her Majesty's Ambassador to Damascus noted at the time, Iraqis to do not want to be liberated at the end of the barrel of a gun by invading Western forces. As we will see in later chapters, both Steve and Andrew's experiences characterised the manner in which the West has conducted its operations since that tragic September morning in 2001: with well-meaning but nevertheless misplaced confidence and often without proper consideration for the most important component of warfare – understanding people and their behaviour. In writing this book we have sought to challenge this thinking.

---

18   Ministry of Defence.

19   Paul Collier, *The Bottom Billion: Why the Poorest Countries are Failing and What can be Done about it* (Oxford University Press, 2007).

20   Foreign and Commonwealth Office.

2
The changing nature of our society

In writing this book both of us have made copious use of previous material. Steve from his doctoral research, Andrew from his post-operational tour interviews and presentations. We have written pieces in other documents and papers which have some relevance to this book and, for ease, we have lifted them – just a couple of clicks of the mouse and they are in the master manuscript. Easy. And as we have both written our respective sections and chapters we have occasionally felt the need to check something out – maybe a reference or a quote, perhaps to identify a particular date or event. This too has proved easy and it takes just a few seconds to bounce from the word processor to the Internet search engine, find and check the data we are after and, maybe, cut and paste that into the manuscript as well. What could be simpler? Indeed for anyone born after 1980 rapid access to information via computers and the Internet has really been the norm, something that they have grown up with and used at school and in the home. To coin another's phrase, these are 'Digital Natives'. For those of us who were born and brought up before then – 'Digital Immigrants'[21] – who perhaps typed up their college dissertations with two fingers on ancient typewriters and who had to visit libraries to find things out, this has been a godsend. Yet 'we' tend to forget that 'we' live in the privileged global West, where access to information is pretty much now routine.

In many areas of the world, and in particular those areas where 'we' see current and future conflicts occurring, this is not quite the case. But it soon will be and we think understanding the 'information effect' needs to become a much bigger part of the Western Armed Forces' training and education. Indeed, given that the Armed Forces work more closely today, and in the future, with many of the other arms of government than ever before, we would venture that it probably needs to be afforded prominence in all government departments with a stake in conflict – in the UK this means the Foreign and Commonwealth Office (FCO), the Department for International Development (DFID), and perhaps even in the corridors of the intelligence services, SIS[22] and MI5. We believe this because we have seen throughout our operational deployments how public perception (and perhaps more importantly public misperception) can and does have a long-term and decisive effect upon the conduct of foreign policy and military operations. We have seen how conveying information and messages to specific audiences in order to effect behavioural change, for specific political and military objectives,

---

21   The terms 'Digital Natives, Digital Immigrants' is attributed to Mark Prensky and was first used in his article 'On the Horizon' (*MCB University Press*, vol. 9 no. 5, October 2001).

22   The Secret Intelligence Service or, as it is more colloquially referred to, MI6.

will, we believe, prove as decisive – perhaps even more so – in future battles as the placement of missiles and bombs upon a target.

Now let's be clear here. What we are not saying is that the Armed Forces should lose their ability to wage kinetic war. Far from it. Nations will always seek to ensure that their Armed Forces can unleash controlled and, if necessary, prolonged violence against their enemies. But, like never before, we believe that an iron fist of the future must have a more visible and tailored velvet glove. Neither civilian nor military leaders can afford to take a passive view of public opinion, for in foreign policy in particular it can constrain and limit action, and all too quickly public opinion can be swayed and public support lost with an ill-placed bomb.

The sheer volume of information and data available today is utterly astounding. Facebook has now surpassed 800 million signed-up users; if it were a country it would be the world's third largest, after China and India and significantly in front of the United States. The Web-based video-sharing site, YouTube, receives around one billion views per day. When it's written down, 'one billion' doesn't seem that much but let's just stop for a minute and think what a billion actually is. A useful indicator of relative size between million and billion is seconds, with a million seconds being about 11.5 days, and a billion seconds being nearly thirty-two years. In terms of YouTube it means that almost every man, woman and child in India looks at a video online – every day. The Google search engine produces similar results, facilitating over thirty-one billion searches each month. Or put another way, nearly five times the world's population run a Google search each month. And what are they all looking for? The amount of data online is, we think, mind-blowing. In 2009 it is estimated that 4 EB (4 exabytes: 4×10^{18}) of unique data was generated: that's more than all the information that was ever produced in the preceding 5,000 years. Critically, much of this is unstructured data – audio, video, social media messages – and is largely responsible for the explosion of data being utilised across the Internet. Some of the estimates of the amount of data being generated are barely comprehensible. Estimates for 2010 were that the total amount of electronically stored data was 1.2 million petabytes ($1.2m \times 10^{15}$) – a 62 per cent increase from a mere 806,000 petabytes in 2009. It is estimated that by 2020 the amount of data will have grown forty-four-fold from that of 2009 to about thirty-five trillion gigabytes.[23]

Effectively managing this amount of data will be impossible, yet we are confident that attempts will be made as it will contain no doubt 'valuable intelligence'. Look at it differently and from another angle – one of influence – and other figures are more compelling. To reach an audience of 50 million people took radio thirty-eight years; television took thirteen years to reach the same number; whilst the Internet took four; Facebook took just two.[24]

---

23   1 petabyte is 1,048,576 gigabytes, and a single gigabyte can store around 250 songs, so a petabyte can store over 262 million songs.

24   See the video *An Ever Changing World* at http://www.youtube.com/watch?v=yuKu6PZXCIY

Interesting as this may be, does any of it have meaning for the nature of future conflict, and, if it does, how does the military work within it? Can this environment be managed? It's big, it has untold inputs, and it is a complicated system. Can 'we' even hope to exercise any degree of control upon it? We think probably not. So if 'we' can't control it, we think 'we' may need to utilise the environment as best 'we' can to 'our' advantage. Beginning at the simplest end of the spectrum 'we' could start with an unbelievably quick win. Despite the world in which 'we' operate, the UK's Armed Forces do not currently train their soldiers and officers to type, despite all three services being frenetic users of keyboards, not just in offices in the UK but on the battlefield as well. By way of comparison, it is rare to encounter an American military officer who does not touch-type. However, if we were being momentarily cynical we might suggest that such a talent may be lost on one of the UK military's computer systems. If there is one certainty about UK government IT systems it is that they are uniformly awful compared to large commercial systems. For example, the UK MoD's most advanced computer system, Dii, is a rather unfortunate example. Designed to replace the multitude of single service systems, its origin was laudable, but like so many government IT systems it has never quite matched expectations. Based upon the now aged Windows NT system, it offers users only the most basic functionality, its performance is slow, erratic and unreliable and, as both Steve and Andrew witnessed in Afghanistan, was unable to accept the modern file structures and templates used by US forces on their substantially better SIPRNet[25] system. Although SIPRNet gained infamy during the Wikileaks saga, the system itself was unscathed; the issue was less to do with the system's abilities than the sheer number of individuals who had untrammelled access to it.

Dii also came to public notoriety when the entire system fell over as British soldiers based in Afghanistan tried to send a spoof 52 MB video file of 'The Road to Amarillo' back to the UK.[26] However, its ability to let its users down at the most inconvenient moments and its legendary reluctance to let you view some of the key social networking websites, such as Twitter, Google, LinkedIn and Facebook, means that, touch typist or not, the Armed Forces often communicate despite Dii and not because of it. What is perhaps most astounding about the system is its cost. To install a new PC in an office costs thousands; to move one to another desk only marginally less. In having to procure the cheapest up-front system, the MoD had to agree to a lifelong support package that made all but the most basic changes largely unaffordable to individual users' budgets. It is not a promising start with which to engage in an increasingly online and connected world.

More recently the UK MoD has issued Blackberry mobile phones to some of its more senior ranks. This is an incredibly useful and, for the ever-cautious MoD, revolutionary step forward, but one arguably lessened by the removal of some of the phone's most useful features (for example Internet access and the camera, but not, strangely, the games), and the imposition of a complex twelve-digit

---

25   SIPRNet is the Secret Internet Protocol Router Network.

26   'Squaddies' Amarillo video causes MoD meltdown' (*The Times*, 17 May 2005).

password, which changes monthly and comprises upper- and lower-case letters, numbers and characters. After five failed log-in attempts the phone's contents are wiped. Such security is perfectly understandable, and to do any less would rightly attract criticism as well as being a real security risk, but it does present users with real problems: an average senior British military officer will need access to Dii Restricted (one complex password), Dii Secret (a second complex password), a Blackberry (a third complex password), a Top Secret computer (a fourth complex password) and his or her laptop will be encrypted (with two complex passwords). In addition, the officer will need to access his or her pay and personnel system (JPA), which also has a regularly changing password. Little surprise, then, at the number of officers embarrassed by having passwords on post-it notes stuck on computers or 'hidden' in desk drawers.

Given the daily trials that military IT causes, it is perhaps strange that in preparing the military Command Estimate – the formalised military process whereby issues such as environment, logistics, people, intelligence, etc. are considered in advance of operations – the information environment has traditionally been largely absent or, if present, given only secondary attention, with primacy invariably afforded to hard power. Yet the information environment, and information effect, certainly features in the thinking of our adversaries. The problem is that 'our' formalised Command Estimate process, and the thinking that goes into it, has just not adapted to the demands of the information environment. In preparing his troops for deployment to Afghanistan, Andrew developed a non-kinetic lexicon (prominently featuring ideas such as persuade, inform, advise) to supplement the more common and widely known kinetic lexicon (which focused upon ideas of destroy, attack, disrupt), the logic being that establishing a common underpinning 'language' would help reinforce the primacy of influence-led operations. The estimate process often talks of 'effects' but only rarely do those effects include ideas such as persuasion, coercion and information. As we will see in the later case studies, the Afghan Taliban (for all their seeming rejection of the modern world) have become adept at using information to their strategic and operational advantage. And they are joining a long list of adversaries who are unafraid to innovate and persistently adapt to the circumstances they find themselves in, rather than those that they would wish for.

Research shows that apparently weaker 'asymmetric' actors seem to be performing increasingly well in their conflicts. What is 'asymmetric'? It's a term bandied around all too easily but do 'we' really understand it? An analogy may be helpful. In days of old the outcomes of battles were often decided by the number and range of archers. Volley after volley of sharpened steel raining down from the sky was often the defining feature of medieval conflict. Conventional warfare would seek to develop armour to protect and more powerful bows with greater range to effect the first attack. Asymmetric warfare may be thought of, in the case of the archers for example, as denying the enemy military advantage by cutting down and burning the ash forests from which their bows were honed. Asymmetry, then, is about finding advantage in unusual ways – like flying jets into the tower blocks of an enemy with the world's largest and most powerful military utterly unaware and unable to react in time.

There have been some groundbreaking, but largely ignored, academic studies on this subject that married acute historical analysis with hard and substantial amounts of data. One in particular was undertaken by an academic at the University of Cambridge, Ivan Arreguin-Toft, who found that, since 1800, stronger actors have defeated their weaker foes by a factor of 2:1.[27] So the stronger army has beaten the weaker army? No surprise, perhaps. Yet, between 1950 and 2001, weaker actors have significantly improved their performance. They have gradually achieved better and better results such that by the end of the twentieth century the stronger actor was actually in trouble in quite a few conflicts (and Afghanistan is perhaps the best example). This raises an obvious question: Why?

There are a host of reasons we could point to, but here are just a few. First, over the course of the last 100 years 'we' have seen huge improvements in weaponry. In 1911 many rifles were still single-shot. The horse was still the pre-eminent manner of moving men and equipment to and from war, and 'our' people still had to close within rifle bullet range of the enemy – seeing the whites of the enemy's eyes. It hardly seems credible, but cavalry charges still occurred in the First World War against an enemy with machine-guns, and so too in Poland, in the Second World War. Slowly, that weaponry has increased in sophistication and decreased in cost. Take, for example, the infamous AK-47 machine-gun. There are conservatively estimated to be around 100 million AK-47s on the planet – which, incidentally, is the same as the total number of sales of Michael Jackson's *Thriller* album. The weapons are manufactured in nearly thirty different places and they are increasingly easy and cheap to produce and distribute. In 1986, in a town in Kenya called Kolowa, you could trade an AK-47 for fifteen cows; ten years later an AK-47 would trade for only four. More recently it could be purchased for just a few dollars,[28] but with regional variations. The Yemeni coastguard, for instance, sells an AK-47 for $1,000 to security guards accompanying shipping through the Red Sea to the Suez Canal. Supply and demand sets the rate. Indeed, of all the AK-47s ever made less than 3 per cent are believed to rest in the hands of governments and their armies. In Lebanon, a 'Circle 11' AK-47 (so-called because of the unusual manufacturing stamps on the weapon's metalwork) costs as little as $500; the far more sophisticated US-made M-16 rifle costs just $1,250, whilst an Energa single-shot grenade launcher costs just $80.[29] Inevitably, weaker actors have been able to capitalise upon this and use it to their advantage and, as we

27 The Cambridge academic Ivan Arreguin-Toft has undertaken a particularly compelling study of conflict since 1900 and has noted who won and how the battle was concluded – be it the weaker or the stronger actor.

28 Moisés Naím, *Illicit: How Smugglers, Traffickers, and Copycats Are Hijacking the Global Economy* (Doubleday, 2005) Further information at http://www.carnegiecouncil.org/resources/transcripts/5279.html

29 Figures taken from Lebanonwire.blog, accessed May 2011.

have both seen at first hand for many homes in rural Afghanistan, the three key technologies to be found in a home are a radio, a mobile phone and an AK-47.

A second explanation is the acceleration of learning, and from that learning the willingness to take risk, to adapt and to innovate. Command of the skies has long given stronger actors, with their jet planes and helicopters, a clear advantage. Yet we have seen how in 2007 the Tamil Tigers launched an aerial attack on the Sri Lankan Navy's Palaly naval base from tiny light aircraft, whilst Al-Qaeda, unable to attain military jets, simply took over civilian ones for their own purposes. There are other explanations, but one in particular is of interest – the use of information as a weapon. When we examine the first few conflicts of the twenty-first century we see how information has become a key component. For example, in Lebanon in 2006 the vastly superior forces of the well-trained and well-equipped Israeli Defence Force (IDF) suffered a humiliating defeat – not in hard combat engagement but in the information space – by the irregular and untrained fighters of Hezbollah. Whilst we don't know what kind of victory was envisaged when, in 2008, Operation Cast Lead was instigated against Hamas in Gaza, if it was a victory it appeared a hollow one, for missiles still fly and in the court of public opinion the IDF's actions are often portrayed as being disproportionate and at times even barbaric. The ability to harness the information environment has empowered and emboldened weaker actors, who with increasingly regularity seem able to beat or force concessions from apparently much stronger forces.

In this security environment governments in general and defence forces in particular find themselves increasingly called upon to undertake a wider variety of tasks than ever before. In the aftermath of the 2003 Iraq invasion, the UK's Armed Forces looked over their shoulders to see what post-conflict reconstruction would occur. The landscape was barren and as a result the UK has now created the Military Security and Stabilisation Group (MSSG) to fill the vacuum of governance and stability that conflict brings. Yet, with more to do, the overall reduction in defence spending and a corresponding increase in capital costs present governments with hard choices. As we have seen, some countries, such as New Zealand (which deleted fighter jets from its air inventory and which refocused its Navy to a mainly coastguard rather than expeditionary blue water capability), simply cannot afford the Armed Forces they either desire or need. The UK's 2010 Strategic Defence and Security Review found it could fund only limited numbers of fast jet types, and the Harrier jet aircraft was deleted from its air inventory, as was the aircraft carrier HMS Ark Royal, from which they flew. It seems, therefore, that Western Armed Forces will need increasingly to search for other mechanisms to reduce the requirement for 'hard power' – by which we mean conventional warfare, using kinetics to destroy and disable one's adversaries – to deter and to defend.

Somewhere between the Falklands War in 1982 and the crisis in Bosnia in 1992, military commanders began to realise that their freedom of manoeuvre was being eroded, not by supply lines or the absence of intelligence – indeed just the opposite, for never before have Western military forces had the technological capability to conduct offensive operations as they do today – but by the presence and scrutiny of the world's media. Academics and doctrinaires contemplated the issue and ascribed to it a name – 'The CNN effect'. Twenty-four hour news coverage, it was argued, was impacting the conduct of nation-states' policies, and in particular their military interventions. In his paper 'Clarifying the CNN Effect: An examination of Media Effects According to Type of Military Intervention',[30] Professor Steven Livingston postulated how the media influenced agendas, how it could prove an impediment to the achievement of desired policy goals and, perhaps most crucially, how it acted as an accelerant to policy decision-making. Never has that been more self-evident than in the post-9/11 military response, where the campaigns in Iraq and Afghanistan have both been fought on a global media landscape. However, both Livingston and his contemporaries considered the word 'media' to mean the established, organised, news-gathering media of TV, radio and the press. They did not consider the utility of today's 'new media', which we might classify in three parts: first, the 'new' journalists – sometimes called 'citizen journalists'; second, new news-gathering technology (such as mobile phones and cheap video cameras); and third, a new distribution conduit – the Internet. Arguably these present government with a far greater management challenge than the established mainstream media, although the emergence of so many new and increasingly influential international channels is already causing Western governments, traditionally attuned to domestic media handling, significant problems. The impact of citizen journalists has been all too apparent: today, the public have the potential to no longer be just peripheral observers of news but also influential reporters, even makers, of news and, as such, key components in the battle for ideas.

When the British Government's COBR(A)[31] committee sat to consider its response to the dreadful events of the London Underground bombings, now referred to as '7/7', another British institution also struggled to manage the situation. During the course of that day the BBC received one thousand images, twenty videos – mainly from mobile phones – more than four thousand text messages and nearly twenty thousand emails. The 'iconic' photograph of the red London bus lying in pieces in Tavistock Square was received from a member of the public 45 minutes after the bombs went off, and became the lead image for the world's TV and newspapers. The 'new journalists' and their new news-gathering technology had deployed in force – citizen journalists, unpaid, untrained and occasionally with highly biased views and opinions, supplementing paid and trained BBC staff. For the BBC this presented colossal challenges. Whilst allowing it to build a comprehensive picture of what was actually happening – one that would eventually far exceed the limited resources of the government's COBR(A) organisation – it re-

---

30   Research Paper R-18, June 1997, John F. Kennedy School of Government, Harvard University.

31   This actually refers to Cabinet Office Briefing Room A, but is more commonly used to refer to the committee that meets there.

quired the validation and authentication of a huge barrage of information, some of which was wrong and some of which was deliberately mischievous. Similar dilemmas have been faced in other parts of the world: in the US the catalyst was 9/11; in Spain it was the Madrid train bombs. Even military dictatorships such as Myanmar/Burma's ruling junta have been unable to cope with the appetite and drive of citizen journalism. More recently the uprisings in Tunisia, Egypt, Libya and Syria have all had citizen-led media dominating the print and media output. Indeed, many news agencies have been reliant on citizen-led output to gain any images from states where the 'official' media is very carefully controlled. Scott Atran, in his book *Talking to the Enemy*, quotes from an email he received from an Iranian friend who expressed how helpless he had felt to stop the merciless beating of a young woman by government thugs, but went on to say: 'We will win this thing if the West does nothing but keep the lines of communication open with satellite Internet.'[32]

The November 2008 terrorist attacks in Mumbai, India, have been called by some observers 'Twitter's moment', in which more than one message (a tweet) every second was posted for the duration of the attack. That may be the case for Twitter, but new media more generally has been busy. During the Iranian presidential election crisis the Google Internet search engine very rapidly added a Farsi language tool to its translation facility, whilst Facebook quickly set up a similar Farsi portal for users. 'We hope that this tool will improve access to information for people inside and outside the country,' a Google spokesman told *The Times* newspaper. In turn, the Iranian government attempted to shut down or block the two new media sites, as well as SMS text messaging and more established and conventional media such as the BBC's Persian television news service. The regime's enemies retaliated in kind, *The Times* reporting that 'hackers ... have taken down President Ahmadinejad's website in an act of cyber sabotage'.

The utility of another new media tool, Wikipedia, as a source of information was demonstrated by the crash of the US Airways Flight 1549 into the Hudson River in January 2009, when 176 edits were made to the Wikipedia page in the first ninety minutes after the aircraft had crashed. It's worth pausing to think about that number. It suggests that whilst people were still onboard the aircraft, awaiting rescue from the Hudson, others were looking out of their apartment windows and reporting, on Wikipedia, what they were seeing, as it was happening. Still more were learning of the incident not from conventional news media but from online sources. All served to demonstrate that a thinking and active audience exists, and that twenty-four-hour news was actually no longer the problem Livingston had articulated. What potentially was of much greater concern was the sheer proliferation of news, the immediacy and urge to respond to it and the criticality of the two- to four-hour window that now follows major events – in essence that period of time in which the world's media expect answers to rapidly emerging issues and the period in which audiences' initial views and thoughts potentially coalesce into opinion and, perhaps, trigger behaviour.

32   Scott Atran, *Talking to the Enemy* (Allen Lane, 2010, p. 477).

'Our' post-9/11 adversaries have proved adept at fusing information with new media; $100 cameras and remote Internet connections can shape global perceptions: they can demoralise and intimidate. Critically, they also act fast and are very responsive to events. The old adage that 'a lie can travel around the world before the truth gets out of bed in the morning' has been demonstrably true. Information appears to move around the world in an instant, time and space seemingly collapsed by the speed of the Internet. Today's insurgents and terrorists seem intuitively to understand that opinions can be manipulated – and quickly. Such knowledge empowers and enables them, despite often facing militarily superior adversaries. It is a lesson that the West might usefully learn. Information – its utility, effect and management – should, we think, be considered at the very core of future campaigns and operational planning, and not in isolation but as a coupled contribution to the whole plan of operation. The BBC political correspondent Andrew Marr once noted that 'journalism is the industrialisation of gossip'. It would be enormously helpful if the West were able to ensure that its gossip – which it might instead choose to call 'narrative' – is as widely available and easily digestible as that of 'our' adversaries.

We mentioned the phenomenal growth of the video-sharing site YouTube earlier in this chapter. If there is one video, perhaps more than any other, that illustrates the phenomena of the site it is 'Dear Mr Obama', posted on 27 August 2008 by a former US Marine.[33] The young US Iraqi veteran speaks directly to camera and articulates why he will not vote for Obama in the, then forthcoming, US election. The video lasts for 1 minute and 56 seconds; a non-descript guy stands in front of a US flag, and to camera speaks of his political inclinations. Pretty boring surely? Yet not, it seems, to a vast number of people – indeed at the time of writing over fourteen million people had chosen to watch the video. Fourteen million? That is the same as the population of Cambodia.

So it seems to us that this video poses three interesting questions. First, how did fourteen million people even know that the video existed on YouTube? What social and communication networks funnelled and directed people to but one video amongst millions on the YouTube site? Very often commentators will talk about something going viral. How does that happen? In fact, how does a 'Mexican wave' start at a football ground? The mechanics seem similar but surely it would be all but impossible to predict. Second, what prompted fourteen million people to actually watch the video? It doesn't look very exciting from the outset and the subject matter would seem to have rather limited appeal. Of perhaps most importance is the third question: What effect, if any, did the video have on their voting intentions – particularly if we presume for convenience only that all fourteen million viewers were US citizens eligible to vote in the US election? Did fourteen million fewer people vote for Obama? Possibly, but that would seem unlikely. Did it have no effect at all? Equally possible and, we judge, equally unlikely. The answer to all three questions is that we simply do not know – we do not really understand how people use new media and what effect it has on them, if any at all.

33   See http://www.youtube.com/watch?v=TG4fe9GlWS8

This, then, is the dilemma that increasingly faces 'us'. How fast should governments respond to the new and immediate revelations supplied by the citizen journalist – revelations that are now not just in the mainstream news media but which are uploaded to the new and alternative distribution conduit of the Web. Or perhaps, should governments respond at all? Or, should governments even consider using these new media to their own advantage? People will argue that the British Armed Forces, for example, already do this. Each military service has its own YouTube channel, the MoD website provides Facebook and Twitter connections, and individual units can upload video to the Web provided that it falls within the guidelines of decency, security and morality. And yet, in 2008, Steve had to have a difficult conversation with the Head of Army Recruiting after a new army video (in which a female army clerk compared her twin day jobs of office work and accompanying soldiers on front-line operations to search female detainees) was found embedded in jihadist literature as 'proof' of the British Army's hatred of Islam and how it was used to positively recruit 'crusaders' to its ranks.

Paradoxically, people are today saturated by raw data. Understanding who is the right audience, and gaining and holding its attention are difficulties 'we' actually share with 'our' adversary. Recent military operations have shown that some of the most influential opinion-forming outlets fall at either end of a technology spectrum. In Iraq and Afghanistan centuries-old mechanisms for discussion and discourse – *shuras, loya jirgas*, honour codes such as *Pashtunwali*,[34] and traditions of story-telling – can carry great effect, whilst at the other end of the spectrum new and emerging media outlets such as blogs and social networking sites can also prove highly effective. In some societies they are complementary, in others less so. Yet opinion is formed not just by words but also by perceptions. These are highly complex, conditioned as much by the environment as by the deeds and conduct of the West, of the UK and of its representatives. Thus, when conveying information, there is a growing need to consider not just the technological needs of its transfer – indeed the 'Did you know' questions we posed earlier in this chapter were interesting, but not as relevant as the effect that all of this has on people's behaviour – but of greater importance is the culture, history and traditions of its intended audiences, for it is these that will determine if the message will succeed or fail. The West must recognise that in a globalised communication society, audience perceptions are based not just upon the conduct of Armed Forces but upon the conduct, attitudes and policies of the countries and organisations from which they emanate, and from the manner in which these are represented in the global information environment. In short, perception – or misperception – may very often equal reality and stimulate behaviours dangerous or counter to 'our' wishes.

---

34   *Pashtunwali* literally means 'the way of the Pashtuns'. It is best understood as the rules, regulations and laws of the Pashtun tribes. These rules are responsible for the survival of the Pashtun tribes for over 2,000 years.

3
The evolving character of conflict I

Throughout our respective military careers we have experienced conflict at first hand and witnessed its attendant uncertainties, confusions and friction. What is striking is how the nature of conflict has evolved faster than the militaries of the West, who are pulled, and sometimes pushed, into it. Perhaps this has always been the nature of conflict but in a networked world with a globalised media and the speed of the Internet there are causes and effects which can balloon unexpectedly in their importance yet deflate just as rapidly as attention is turned elsewhere. Conflict is invariably complex, not necessarily because of the trauma of casualties or the logistical challenges, but because of the conundrum of too much or too little information at any one time ensuring that our understanding is consistently incomplete and inconsistently reliable.

Gradually – probably – through trial and error we both came to understand that a better means of judging a situation was to dwell on likely human behaviour in both its rational and irrational forms. Andrew served in the Army and participated in operations in Northern Ireland, Bosnia, Kosovo, Lebanon, Iraq and Afghanistan. Steve, a Naval Officer, served in Sierra Leone, Iraq and Afghanistan. Although from two different services and with very different ranks our conclusions on the role of influence and the need to consider how behaviour is conditioned and manipulated are remarkably similar.[35]

It has been observed, many times over, that few, if any, nations and certainly no non-state groups have the resources, sophistication and military power of the US. How could they when the US spends as much on defence as the next twenty nations combined? The outgoing US Secretary of State for Defense, Robert Gates, recently noted that the entire EU spent less than half on defence than the US. The UK is close to the top of that list, but needs must and it has readily adopted the role of unequal partnership with the US, which, for their differing reasons, suits both parties. Yet that combined political and military power seems curiously ill prepared to deal with the manner in which the enemy has sought to fight its battles.

Who is the enemy? The UK's Development Concept Doctrine Centre (DCDC) based at the UK's Defence Academy runs a Strategic Trends programme which attempts to look forwards to the challenges, and risks, that the UK and its allies may face. The executive summary of its predictions to 2040 makes sober reading:

---

35   Like the term 'strategic communication', we talk at length about influence in later chapters, but for now we mean using all possible means to predispose the attitudes and behaviours of targeted groups of people.

The era out to 2040 will be a time of transition; this is likely to be characterised by instability, both in the relations between states, and in the relations between groups within states. During this timeframe the world is likely to face the reality of a changing climate, rapid population growth, resource scarcity, resurgence in ideology, and shifts in global power from West to East. No state, group or individual can meet these challenges in isolation, only collective responses will be sufficient. Hence, the struggle to establish an effective system of global governance, capable of responding to these challenges, will be a central theme of the era. Globalisation, global inequality, climate change and technological innovation will affect the lives of everyone on the planet. There will be constant tension between greater interdependence between states, groups and individuals and intensifying competition between them. Dependence on complex global systems, such as global supply chains for resources, is likely to increase the risk of systemic failures.[36]

Even at the time of writing, and as the multifaceted nature of the conflicts in the Middle East and North Africa play out on our television screens, it is apparent that violence and conflict in the twenty-first century are set to differ widely in their characteristics from those of the twentieth. The waves of protest in Tunisia, Egypt, Libya and Syria in the first half of 2011 were all different, and all require differing responses, although all have their roots in the dispossessed and disenfranchised deciding to behave differently from how their respective regimes were anticipating and expecting. All will have different outcomes and can be expected to have messy and inconclusive futures.

The nature of this type of dilemma – to be fair no one could have been expected to forecast the uprisings in the Middle East and North Africa – was recognised by the publication of the UK's 2010 National Security Strategy (NSS). Rather unfortunately, the Strategic Defence and Security Review (SDSR) which was announced the next day rather eclipsed the NSS. In their haste to write about the abolition of the Harrier aircraft, of the Royal Navy's aircraft carrier HMS Ark Royal and of cuts to manpower and budgets, the newspapers almost failed to notice one singularly important issue – Britain's Armed Forces were unprepared for future threats.

The NSS identified three tiers of threats to the UK. Tier 1 embraced cyber attack, terrorism, a major accident or pandemic and a state-on-state conflict into which the UK is unwittingly drawn. Tier 2 threats were serious organised crime, attacks on satellite and communication systems, a civil war abroad and a chemical, biological, radiological or nuclear (CBRN) attack at home. And Tier 3 were conven-

---

36   DCDC Strategic Trends Programme, available to download at http://www.mod.uk/NR/rdonlyres/38651ACB-D9A9-4494-98AA-1C86433BB673/0/gst4_update9_Feb10.pdf

tional attacks on the UK, attacks on other NATO members and attacks on a British overseas territory. Despite their tanks, aircraft and ships, the UK's Armed Forces would be largely impotent to deal with the majority of Tier 1 and Tier 2 threats. Much thought and study had clearly gone into the NSS – that it was overshadowed by the Defence Review is unfortunate but it does not take away the central issue – the UK's Armed Forces had not evolved to meet current trends and, as the much-respected defence commentator Michael Clarke has publicly noted:

> The malaise begins with strategy. We have recognised that we are not very good at it … none of our various national strategy documents, and certainly not last October's Strategic Defence and Security Review, have done this. They list a set of objectives with no clarity about the hard resources that will have to be devoted to achieve them.[37]

How do we approach such challenges? As we noted in the Preface, we believe a key component will be much greater understanding of human behaviour and the information environment in which it is exhibited and influenced. And so whilst our book looks at conflicts in which we have been intimately involved, we have also chosen to look at the Israeli attack on Gaza in 2009 – not because either of us were present, but because of the incredible effort that the Israeli government made to mitigate its experiences of Lebanon just three short years earlier. Our Armed Forces need the ability to dynamically and swiftly innovate to meet new threats and trends – just as the Israeli Defence Force (IDF) demonstrated. These are our experiences:

The Balkans: Bosnia

Few modern-day conflicts come as complicated as the Bosnian civil war, which ran from 1992 to 1995. Indeed, a BBC report marking the tenth anniversary of the start of the war was forced to concede: 'To this day there remains debate even over the origins of the conflict.'[38] A view, it seems, that the British Prime Minister at the time, John Major, shared: 'The conflict in Bosnia crept up on us while our attention was on the turmoil of the Soviet Union, and took us almost unawares … its roots are bewildering.'[39] Yet despite its bewildering roots, the reality is that the Bosnian conflict was the most destructive war in Europe since the Second World War, leaving close to 100,000 people dead, displacing millions more and causing untold misery, the effects of which, as we have seen with the 2011 arrest of former Serbian military commander Ratko Mladić, are still being felt today. Yet as these atrocities occurred, the pictures were beamed onto Western televi-

---

37   http://www.rusi.org/analysis/commentary/ref:C4E10D753A41ED/
38   'Bosnia Marks War Anniversary' (BBC News, 6 April 2002).
39   John Major, *The Autobiography* (HarperCollins, 1999, p. 111).

sion screens and dominated the front pages of newspapers. It was by no means a 'secret' war: more journalists covered the Bosnian conflict – and more were killed in it – than, at the time, any other conflict in history. The question, then, is: Why? Why – whilst the world was watching – was this hideous behaviour, supposedly banished from Europe by the 1945 Nuremburg Trials of leading Nazis, allowed to happen and what could 'we' have done to stop it?

The answers to such questions are not simple. Trying to understand the characteristics of what exactly was going on – even today – is difficult, and space doesn't allow for a comprehensive dissection of the conflict, but a certain amount of culpability must lie at the feet of ineffective communication along with a chronic inability to understand the motivations of local populations. Determining what, precisely, drove the three warring parties – the Bosnian Muslims, the Croats and the Serbs – and for the latter two their proxy supporters, Croatia and Serbia, to engage in genocide, ethnic cleansing, mass rape and the destruction of the infrastructure may well never be truly determined or agreed upon. Yet the behavioural aspects of the conflict were barely considered amidst the disintegration of the Former Republic of Yugoslavia as the UN, NATO and diplomats in Western capitol cities struggled to understand the geopolitical context. This was due in part to a lack of personnel on the ground who understood the human environment. As former head of the British diplomatic service John Coles points out, the Foreign and Commonwealth Office (FCO) were ill-prepared to provide intelligence relating to local human terrain at the start of the Bosnian conflict:

> Geographical departments in the Foreign Office which often handle situations of considerable significance for British interests, such as the Gulf War, the Arab-Israeli dispute and Bosnia are very much smaller than they were twenty years ago and command much less genuine regional expertise.[40]

The European peacekeeping forces that were deployed in Bosnia struggled to understand the nature of the conflict, accustomed as they were in the early 1990s to doctrine and training that was a product of Cold War thinking. Indeed, there was much debate as to whether or not the forces deployed were peacekeeping (therefore acting as a 'neutral' force) or peacemaking (and therefore, by default, choosing sides). Nation-building was a word that dare not speak its name, such was the aversion to the notion that this might be a consequence of any engagement. This attitude severely inhibited political and military progress once the multinational forces were deployed in Bosnia at the end of 1995, following the NATO bombing campaign and the Serb capitulation. To be blunt, the military found any notion of nation-building to be 'mission creep' and the politicians saw nation-building as a long-term commitment and thus to be avoided. Andrew recalls the

---

40   John Coles, *Making Foreign Policy* (John Murray Publishers, 2000, p. 147).

fevered debate at SHAPE[41] and in Sarajevo on the ethical dilemmas surrou
the military insistence on no 'mission creep', even as Serb homes in Sarajev. .. ___
ransacked and burnt to the ground. As for ineffective communication, one of the
key elements was the confusion surrounding the UN mandate and what it could
and couldn't do. Many on the ground were distinctly unsure of what they were
hoping to achieve, a sentiment perfectly summed up by the first British Commander of UN forces in Bosnia, Lieutenant Colonel Bob Stewart, who reckoned:
'I didn't know how we were going to deal with it and, quite honestly, we didn't
have much of a plan either.'[42] According to Field Marshal Sir Richard Vincent,
British Chairman of NATO's Military Committee in 1993, the first principle of
war is: 'for God's sake decide what you're trying to achieve before you go out
there and start doing it.'[43] Indeed. General Sir Rupert Smith, in his seminal work
The Utility of Force,[44] which considers Bosnia at length, states: 'that the starting
point to understanding all operations in the Balkans in the 1990s … was that they
were without strategies.' He goes on to add that: 'whatever political purposes the
forces deployed in to the Balkans served they were not supporting goals directly
related to a resolution of the conflict or confrontation in question.'

Seen from the coalface, one military officer summoned up the mood at the time
by stating: 'We did what we could but were continually hampered by the mandate and the lack of a clear statement of exactly what we were there to do. We did
not have the backing, or teeth, to peacekeep and the locals knew this.'[45] The locals,
it would seem, understood the foreign UN troops far better than the UN understood them. Indeed, we would suggest that it was this absence of understanding, coupled with a seeming inability to deliver a safe and secure environment,
that weighed down the Troop Contributing Nations' (TCN) strategy and morale
throughout that wretched war.

In an error we have seen repeated again and again since, TCNs over-promised
and under-delivered. Yet the actions of the TCNs – responding to the fevered
and chaotic reactions of policy-makers, predominantly within the UN and NATO
– continually raised expectations and failed to meet them. For example, in 1993
the UN Security Council set to establish safe havens for Bosnian Muslims with
a mandate to supply 35,000 troops on the ground, a number regarded as just
about the minimum if 'safe' havens were indeed to live up to their name. This
figure of 35,000 was later reduced to 10,000 and ultimately to just 3,500 – a tenth
of the original 'minimum' figure – when the actual funds were made available.
Not only do such actions have *direct* consequences – the atrocity at Srebrenica in
August 1995 that saw the massacre of around 8,000 Bosnian Muslim men and
boys who believed they were in a UN safe area being one such direct consequence

41   Supreme Headquarters, Allied Powers Europe, the NATO headquarters in Mons, Belgium.
42   *The Road to Bosnia*, Rumir Films.
43   Peter Almond, 'The First Principle of War' (*Daily Telegraph*, 29 April 1993).
44   Rupert Smith, *The Utility of Force: The Art of War in the Modern World* (Penguin, 2006).
45   Vaughan Kent-Payne, *Bosnia Warriors: Living on the Front Line* (Robert Hale Publishers, 1998, p. 352).

– they also send out entirely the wrong message. And such messages can resonate for some time. George Shultz, former US Secretary of State, recognised in 1994 the impact that not dealing effectively with the situation would have, describing the West's position as being: 'pathetic, shameful … the way you behave in one situation is transmitted all around the world and people take a lesson from your behaviour.'[46] Field Marshall Lord Vincent, chairman of NATO's Military Committee at the time, once described meetings within NATO as a 'hotbed of cold feet', such was the level of indecision and inability to develop a coherent strategy.

Whilst the nature of the war was somewhat fitful – long periods of superficial peace and relative inactivity, punctuated by bursts of savage conflict – the media war that occurred was far more fluid and continued long after the Dayton Agreement (signalling peace) was signed in December 1995. The post-Dayton period, considering the bloodshed and complexities which had preceded it, passed surprisingly without incident. Yet the landscape that greeted Andrew on his deployment to Bosnia in March 1996 – where he reported directly to NATO military commander General George Joulwan, ahead of elections scheduled for later in the year – was one where uncertain and weak NATO mandates, accompanied by power struggles amongst the ruling elites of Bosnia, created significant vacuums in governance and security. Into these vacuums stepped enterprising criminals who, through enlightened self-interest, managed to operate with near impunity, untroubled by governance or the rule of law. These criminal elements very adroitly drew in the support of quasi-militia forces, private security entourages and local politicians, all inspired by the opportunity to generate large amounts of illicit cash through any number of different criminal enterprises. Within this chaotic 'conflict ecosystem' each side was quick to realise that the media was a force that had to be influenced and, if possible, controlled through either pressure or persuasion. Both the local and international media were seen as key, provided there was the ability to approach each differently and shape the output accordingly. Therefore, the ongoing media war raged, with various sides jostling to be heard and seeking to influence the messaging that was directed at the respective ethnic entities within Bosnia and the international media.

There are a number of ways in which 'we' can influence behaviour, yet perhaps the most resounding – not to say complex – method is through the use of information, something that those on all sides of the conflict began to understand all too readily. US Army Lieutenant Colonel Steve Collins neatly sums up the situation during the war – a situation that continued long after:

> For most of its duration, the Bosnian War is best explained as a struggle for perception, with the ground war a supporting effort. Some have pointed to Bosnia, and the central role of the media, as providing a glimpse of conflicts in the future. The manipulation of the media by po-

---

46   William Shawcross, 'Around the World in Eighty Briefings' (*Spectator*, 9 July 1994).

litical leaders in the region was central to igniting and exploiting latent ethnic hatred.[47]

In terms of influence *within* the country, the Serbs wielded the power. Indeed, up until 1997 there was very little print media and the newspapers and magazines that did run were expensive and unavailable to most. Their main weapon was television, and it was a weapon used with alarming impunity. For many – for most – it was the only way to get news, and unsurprisingly Serbian national television (RTS) took a distinctly partisan viewpoint. During broadcasts, state television would routinely refer to the Bosnian leader as 'Alija Izetbegovic, Muslim murderer'.[48] A typical example of brazen Serbian bias is demonstrated in a 'news' feature broadcast on RTS:

REPORTER: Do you have an example where they [Croats] killed someone, cut his throat, or similar examples of such crimes?

INTERVIEWEE: I left earlier, I didn't see such things, but I heard from others that there was torturing.

REPORTER: Like what?

INTERVIEWEE: Well, slaughtering, they were cutting off fingers, pulling fingernails off children ... we have found children in pots ready to be baked. We discovered beheaded soldiers ...

REPORTER: They have no mercy for anyone, do they?[49]

Such reporting resonated, and continued to resonate, long after the Dayton Agreement. In the summer of 1997 the NATO Psychological Operations Task Force found itself constantly responding to disinformation coming from the Republic of Srpska radio and television outlets regarding both the war crimes operation and the internal power struggle. The Task Force was never able to reverse the negative spin created by the Bosnian-Serb media.[50] Yet although the Serbs effectively and resolutely communicated with the people of the Former Republic of Yugoslavia, their efforts directed towards the international media were both half-hearted and clumsy – due in no small part to wanting to keep the conflict a purely 'regional' affair and thus avoid outside intervention. The Bosnian Muslims, however, took an entirely different approach and realised that the key to

---

47   Steven Collins, 'Army PSYOP [Psychological Operations] in Bosnia: Capabilities and Constraints' (*Parameters*, Summer 1999, pp. 57-53).

48   Tracy Wilkinson, 'Trying to Extract War from Journalism' (*Los Angeles Times*, 26 April 1997).

49   Anes Alic, 'Balkans: Media and War Crimes' (*ISN Security Watch*, 24 June 2009).

50   Steven Collins, 'Army PSYOP in Bosnia: Capabilities and Constraints' (*Parameters*, Summer 1999, pp. 57-73).

gaining international assistance and intervention was that their predicament be viewed as one of fighting for their survival, and that the main opportunity lay in the way they portrayed themselves to Western media outlets. They fast became skilled in perception management and were aided by the vast majority of Western journalists who were holed up in Sarajevo, which, despite repeated and heavy bombardment throughout the war, remained a Bosnian stronghold.

As for Western involvement in managing both strategic communications and influence campaigns in Bosnia, 'we' faced a number of problems. First, there was a glaring lack of reconnaissance: little in the way of a local media assessment existed prior to early 1996. Nor, despite widespread media coverage about the overall situation, did 'we' understand much about the population on a *deeper* level. A lack of analysis meant that there was scant information regarding the triggers and drivers behind the local people's motivations, attitudes, beliefs and values. Second, at that time there were few people equipped to deal with ideas of influence, and even if there were the people, there was a distinct lack of facilities with which to conduct them. In short, the capability gap was a yawning one. This was a time when an increasingly media-savvy population was beginning to emerge and previous propaganda tools – loudspeakers and crudely constructed leaflets among them – became see-through and carried little weight or impact. Third, as we've touched upon, policy was often confused and mostly inadequate as a means for generating coherent implementation at the tactical and operational level.

Whilst influence operations are by no means a panacea, no matter how forcefully and credibly a message is conveyed, if the mechanics behind it are unsound it fails the credibility test and perceptions are permanently altered. Even if the message results in behavioural change, if the intent behind it is inconsequential, future message campaigns will, at best, be ignored. When the Secretary-General of NATO is forced to declare, 'I am the head of the most powerful military organisation in world history and I can do nothing',[51] then there is little chance of a strategic communication campaign being successful.

There is also the question of time. Influence campaigns can take up quite a bit of it, and by 1996 far too much damage had been done. And although it's very easy to dissect events with the benefit of hindsight, action should have been taken earlier. As former war correspondent Martin Bell writes: 'We in the Western democracies should look back at those terrible years of the war and blame not only the parties to it but also ourselves. We could have ended it much earlier; but chose not to.'[52] Whether we could have done that through military might or by sending out the right messages is painfully unknowable, but – perhaps unwittingly – David Owen seemed to hit the nail on the head when addressing the Commons Select Committee on Foreign Affairs in 1992 when he said: 'If we show enough determi-

---

51   Brendan Simms, *Unfinest Hour: Britain and the Destruction of Bosnia* (Allen Lane, 2001, p. 103).

52   Martin Bell, 'Radovan Karadzic and the Bosnian Conflict: "We could have ended it sooner"' (*Telegraph*, 24 August 2008).

nation that we are going to enforce [a no-fly zone] we won't need to enforce it.'[53] It should come as no surprise that David Owen found himself a keen advocate for a no-fly zone as part of NATO's operations against Colonel Gadaffi in Libya some nineteen years later.

The Balkans: Kosovo

On 24 March 1999, NATO began the largest air offensive in its history. Many, including leaders of NATO countries and Serbian President Slobodan Milosevic, thought the bombing campaign against Serbian forces would only last a few days – a few weeks at most.[54] In fact, bombs fell on Yugoslavia for the following seventy-seven days. On the day the first bombs fell, US President Bill Clinton explained that 'we' were acting, 'to prevent a wider war, to defuse a powder keg at the heart of Europe that has exploded twice before in this century with catastrophic results'.[55] In short, Clinton felt – or at least gave the impression that he felt – that the conflict in Kosovo had the potential to spill over into other parts of Europe and perhaps even spark a third world war.

In less woolly language, the NATO offensive began because Milosevic refused to accede to the terms of the Rambouillet Accords, which had been thrashed out in France some weeks earlier.[56] Essentially, it was agreed that Serbia should: (i) withdraw military and police forces from Kosovo; (ii) deploy a peacekeeping force to the province; and (iii) end the 'ethnic cleansing' of Kosovar Albanians. After eleven weeks of bombing, Milosevic agreed to the terms and the conflict was over. Except that it wasn't. Not really. Throughout the war – and beyond – a more insidious war was waged, one that Milosevic is widely considered to have won and, judging by the Kosovo post-mortem which lingers on even today, one that his legacy is still winning: the war of perceptions. Mirijana Markovic, Milosevic's wife, told a US journalist at the time that her husband was engaged in two wars: a bombing war and a media war. His efforts, she reckoned, would be best directed towards the latter.[57] And indeed they were. He acted quickly, decisively and with a fair degree of cunning to ensure that this was one war which wouldn't be lost. At the time, Britain's Prime Minister Tony Blair was led to grudgingly admit that it was 'frustrating' that Milosevic had 'to some extent, control of the media

53   Nicholas Timmins, 'UN may Have to Use Force in Bosnia, Owen Warns' (*Independent*, 11 December 1992). David Owen was then EU Co-chairman of the Conference for the Former Yugoslavia.

54   Tim Judah, *Kosovo: War and Revenge* (Yale University Press, 2000, p. 228).

55   Francis X. Clines, 'NATO Opens Broad Barrage Against Serbs as Clinton Denounces Yugoslav President' (*New York Times*, 25 March 1999).

56   Ibid.

57   Wayne A. Larsen, 'Serbian Information Operations During Operation Allied Force' (US Air Staff College, April 2000).

agenda'.[58] This control had begun well before the first bombs fell. Throughout the discussions at Rambouillet, NATO and the US were portrayed as being imperialistic, provocative and couching the situation in Kosovo as an opportunity to achieve a new strategic dominance in the area.

Milosevic had a well-entrenched propaganda machine that had been established for many years, and by March 1999 he had near total control over the media. The few areas that he didn't control were quickly and mercilessly bulldozed under the Public Information Law brought in months earlier. On 28 March the last remaining Yugoslav independent radio station in operation was raided. Two days later it was shut down. Print journalists were silenced. Within three weeks of the start of the NATO campaign any remaining forms of independent media were dismantled and replaced with state-controlled propaganda.[59] From then on, references to NATO during broadcasts were prefixed with the tag 'criminals'. The likes of the BBC and CNN were widely discredited, and referred to as supporters of the Kosovo Liberation Army (KLA) and 'tools of the aggressors'. Serbian state television news featured NATO planes bombing hospitals, showed footage of NATO planes being shot down, highlighted ecological disasters caused by the bombings and no doubt took delight in airing anti-NATO and anti-war demonstrations from across the world.

Television was brilliantly effective and convincing – especially as it was pretty much the only means by which those in the countryside received their news – yet there were some clever tricks involved in the print media, too. For example, the state-controlled Yugoslav news agency *Tanjug* used to send reports to the Chinese news agency *Xinhua*. When these reports were duly printed in newspapers in Asia, it was then reported *back* in Serbia that the Chinese were supporting the official party line.[60]

As well as control over the media, Milosevic had another vital tool in a message campaign: a receptive audience. He ruthlessly exploited centuries of ethnic tension (portraying the Croats as neo-Nazis and the Albanians as backward and illiterate), of old folk tales and stirring poetry where the central theme was that Kosovo would remain – and had always been – Serbian, even if no Serbs were to live there. As the first bombs fell and the missiles began to hit their targets, state television aired the feature film *Kozara*, which depicted the Second World War battle between the Germans and Yugoslav partisans (along with frequent showings of the film *Wag the Dog*, starring Dustin Hoffman, in which a Washington spin doctor hires a Hollywood producer to construct a fake war to divert attention from a sex scandal), and pumped out patriotic songs and slogans: 'All of us

---

58   Interview with Tony Blair in 'War in Europe: Episode 2', first broadcast on UK Channel 4, February 2000.

59   Joel Simon, 'Propaganda War in Serbia' (*Committee to Protect Journalists*, www.cpj.org, 5 May 1999).

60   Tim Judah, *Kosovo: War and Revenge* (Yale University Press, 2000).

are one party now – its name is freedom'[61] being one such slogan; 'No one shall beat you again' – a sound bite from a 1987 Milosevic speech – being another.

In some eyes, such tactics might seem overly heavy-handed and crude, yet Milosevic knew exactly the approach to take in order to motivate his audience, even those who were initially reluctant to adopt the party line. In short, he had an intimate understanding of those who he needed to influence. As one journalist reported from Belgrade at the time: 'Ordinary Serbs, stoked by the images on state television equating NATO with Nazism have found themselves rallying behind the master of half-truth, almost in spite of themselves.'[62] Rallying behind the master of half-truth? Almost in spite of themselves? Clearly, this master of half-truth knew what made the population tick. Although the Internet was very much nascent at the time of the Bosnia conflict, by 1999 its use was widespread. Again, Milosevic moved swiftly. Again, he employed no small degree of resourcefulness and cunning. It is interesting to note, when considering a more up-to-date conflict – Libya – that throughout the Yugoslav war years Colonel Gadaffi was staunchly loyal to Milosevic, even going to the trouble of aligning himself with the orthodox Serbs against Kosovo's Muslims. A closer examination of the propaganda war waged more recently in Libya bears some uncanny similarities.

In the first few weeks of the war several Internet sites sprang up. Ostensibly they were privately owned but they were in fact operated by officials in the Federal Information Ministry, the Yugoslav Army and Belgrade University. The messages were uniform and emotive: NATO were engaged in an illegal and morally corrupt bombing campaign; NATO's policies – and policy-makers – were fumbling; the Serbs were in Kosovo solely as a measure to deter terrorism. What is perhaps surprising is that Milosevic managed to put his stamp on what is essentially a fluid and almost uncontrollable technology. As one commentator pointed out: 'The promise that new information technologies – fax machines, the Internet, satellite telephones – would make it impossible for a dictator to ever again gain control of information has not been realised.'[63] Serbian ministers would regularly pop up in chat rooms to take part in discussions and would happily enter into email correspondence. After one such discussion in a chat room with paramilitary leader Arkan, a lady in Florida reportedly changed her opinion of the man: 'When I saw [Arkan] on TV I turned him off because he sounded a bit over the edge. But in the chat rooms when you're just reading his statements, I saw him in a totally different light. I became furious with our government for invading his territory.'[64]

But it may not have even been Arkan in that chat room; someone else may have been intellectually and emotionally seducing Florida housewives. This was a time when messages were becoming more blurry and sources were often unidenti-

---

61   Ibid., p. 238.
62   The Peace Pledge Union, 'Words at War Over Kosovo' (*Peace Matters Journal*, Summer 1999, available at http://www.ppu.org.uk/peacematters/peacematters/1999/pm_99sum_kosovo.html).
63   Ibid.
64   Amy Harmon, 'War Waged on Web: Killers without Context' (*New York Times*, 5 April 1999).

fiable. With a leaflet drop or a television broadcast the recipient can normally correctly ascribe the origin of (and the sentiment driving) the message. With the Internet, it's a little different. As the BBC reported:

> There is a problem with the personal accounts of the war – how do we know they are true? It is easy to spot the pointed propaganda of Websites [sic] such as those of NATO or the Serbia Ministry of Information, but emails are supposedly individual points of view rather than concerted campaigns. Yet they could be written en masse by government press officers or by hoaxers in California.[65]

Fast forward to today's conflicts and Twitter feeds fare no better.

Counteracting what amounted to slick, effective propaganda during 1999 wasn't easy. Initially, the bulk of the pictures reaching Western screens (and indeed, many of the words reaching newspapers) came directly from Serbian sources after Milosevic expelled, detained or refused visas to hundreds of foreign journalists.[66] As such, the images were distinctly partisan, and NATO spokesperson Jamie Shea recognised the power pictures wielded: '[we shouldn't] allow the adversary to have a monopoly of pictures. It's like science versus religion. What do we believe – the pictures or the words?'[67] Alistair Campbell, Tony Blair's Director of Communications and Strategy, summed this up rather more succinctly: 'No picture, no story.' There was, then, a feeling that 'we' were always on the back foot, that 'we' were always reacting to the Serbian point of view rather than establishing 'our' own and that, crucially, 'we' were determined not to have another Bosnia on 'our' hands. As Tim Judah points out: 'In the wake of Vukovar and Srebenica, the spectre of the past hung over Western policy-makers, and their constant fear was that sooner or later a truly enormous massacre could take place, leaving them exposed to criticism for having failed to act.'[68] As such, leaders in the West tended to up their rhetoric in an attempt to curb Milosevic's actions before it was too late. Unfortunately, this rhetoric often spilled over into exaggeration and, at times, falsehoods.

Today, controversy surrounds the West's role in fudging the number of casualties (NATO estimated over 100,000 dead; the real figure it seems is closer to 10,000[69]), misleading the world to the extent that 'ethnic cleansing' was occurring to the

---

65   'The Internet War' (BBC News, 16 April 1999).

66   Wayne A. Larsen, 'Serbian Information Operations During Operation Allied Force' (US Air Staff College, April 2000).

67   'It Began with a Lie: How German Officials Lead their Country to Another Aggressive War' (ARD Public Television Network, first broadcast in Germany, 8 February 2001).

68   Tim Judah, *Kosovo: War and Revenge* (Yale University Press, 2000, pp. 180-181).

69   Wayne A. Larsen, 'Serbian Information Operations During Operation Allied Force' (US Air Staff College, April 2000).

Kosovo Albanian population (an OSCE[70] report found little evidence of ethnic cleansing prior to the NATO bombing), massaging the truth with regard to how far the involvement of NATO in Kosovo was due to 'humanitarianism', and manufacturing evidence. For example, pictures beamed into living rooms in the UK of Kosovans fleeing their homes because of 'ethnic cleansing' have since been reckoned to be no such thing; that they were, in fact, fleeing because of the NATO air strikes. Other embarrassing mistakes were made, too, including pushing out a report claiming that the Serbs had murdered Baton Haxhiu, the editor of Kosovo's highest circulation newspaper. When Haxhiu was found fit and perfectly well the following day in London, NATO was forced to issue an apology.[71] Such apologies and misinformation were commonplace throughout the campaign, and NATO's reputation was therefore severely compromised; although perhaps not as compromised as many commentators have felt compelled to point out: 'The Western media, eagerly listened to in the past as the voice of truth is [now] merely another source of propaganda. A reputation lost is not easy to regain.'[72] This reputation was further compromised with the bombing of the RTS building in Belgrade,[73] which killed sixteen people and was considered in a Human Rights Watch report to be 'part of a psychological warfare strategy undertaken without regard to the greater risk to the civilian population'.[74] The burgeoning thirst for 24-hour news and the need at the time to counter Serbian propaganda led to many of these mistakes. Although Western forces should be commended for acting with speed and curbing a potential humanitarian disaster, there were a number of fundamental errors made in the information sphere which blighted the campaign. It was in essence preoccupied with headlines, concentrated as it was on the media battle, rather than with the more opaque area of dealing with perception, and nudging or seeking to influence behaviour (most of Milosevic's forces were conscripts and susceptible to pressure from home).

Could 'we' have countered Milosevic's propaganda efforts earlier? It appears that perhaps 'we' could. It's since come to light that the infrastructure behind one of Serbia's most effective information tools – the Internet – was rickety: Serbia had only four ISPs, and relied on three landlines and a single satellite link for international communications.[75] Yet, like Bosnia, it would seem that the greatest asset would have been to understand the underlying attitudes and motivations of the competing audiences.

---

70   Organisation for Security and Co-operation in Europe.

71   Craig Whitney, 'Facts at Briefings are Scarce, but Polemics are Abundant' (*New York Times*, 3 April 1999).

72   Andrew Fear, 'Looking Neither Forward nor Back: NATO's Balkan Adventure', from *Kosovo: The Politics of Delusion*, Michael Waller, Kyril Drezov and Bulent Gokay (eds) (Frank Cass, 2001, p. 92).

73   'NATO Challenged over Belgrade Bombing' (BBC News, 24 October 2001).

74   'Civilian Deaths in the NATO Air Campaign' (Human Rights Watch, February 2000).

75   Wayne A. Larsen, 'Serbian Information Operations During Operation Allied Force' (US Air Staff College, April 2000).

Sierra Leone

In May 2000, the Royal Navy Fleet Flagship, HMS Illustrious, was nearing the end of a seven-month deployment to the Mediterranean and Gulf. With just a few days of the exercise left the ship's company were looking forward to returning home – not least the 100 or so members of the Royal Air Force's GR7 Harrier Squadron which had embarked for the exercise that would end the ship's deployment. In support of that exercise large numbers of Reserve personnel had embarked; so too a number of family members taking the opportunity of the Royal Navy's 'sons at sea' programme which allowed children to see what 'Dad' (and sometimes 'Mum') really did when away from home. All was progressing well until Steve took the opportunity to log onto the ship's sole Internet terminal in the main communications office and found a BBC report about the capture of UN peacekeeping personnel in Sierra Leone, West Africa. Classified signals were already flying between the ship and London; the deployment was not about to end anytime soon.

Early the next morning the ship's broadcast system clicked on. The Captain – Captain Mark Stanhope – told the ship's company that all visitors to the ship (although not the embarked RAF squadron) were to be ready to leave in 30 minutes for transfer to other units of the task group. He would address the ship's company again once they had all left. The ship was off to Sierra Leone and, as Stanhope later told the rather surprised ship's company, his objective was to put Harriers 'over the beach' in Sierra Leone on Thursday morning – little more than 72 hours away. The ship quickly picked up speed and in the rapid transit to West Africa a planning team was established to determine what the mission was and what Illustrious could do.

The mission was, initially, simple. Illustrious and her ship's company of 1,200 men and women would undertake, in military parlance, an NEO – a non-combative evacuation operation – of the many British, European and Commonwealth citizens who were living or working in Sierra Leone. The UK's Joint Force Headquarters had already deployed under Brigadier David Richards, and the strategically vital Lungi airfield, a short distance out of the country's capital Freetown, had been secured. However, by the time the ship reached Freetown the situation on the ground had shifted and the capital was no longer in imminent danger of falling to the Liberian-backed rebel army, the RUF, of former government minister Foday Sankoh. The NEO was cancelled and the issue then became how the UK forces in the country could support the fledgling democratic government of President Kabbah.

With a number of other West African nations publicly claiming that this was an example of the recolonisation of Africa by Britain, and some Sierra Leoneans themselves openly calling for the UK to return as the colonial administrator, the mission became politically tricky; British Prime Minister Tony Blair was unwilling to see the UK depart but needed to play down its role. The solution was to step back and attempt to support the UN peacekeepers under their Indian commander Major General V. K. Jetley – and support would not be kinetic (unless in self-defence). On this issue the government was clear, and in the days that followed this was strictly adhered to.

It very quickly became apparent that the UK would need to heavily influence the RUF rebels, dissuading them from an attack upon Freetown and, importantly, to kick-start the peace process for a lasting solution. To that end the deployed Harriers of the RN and RAF flew regular missions across the country – flying low and loud to frighten the rebels in their jungle positions. Despite requests being made to drop ordinance – specifically onto unoccupied mud flats to demonstrate effect – permission was never granted and the aircraft flew armed only with the pilots' 9 mm pistols for personal protection should they have to bail out. President Kabbah, embarked on Illustrious, commented that the sound of the jets was 'the sound of freedom'. So low were the jets flying that on more than one occasion they took bird strikes, but the missions, which were often followed some hours later by photo-reconnaissance aircraft, revealed that the noise had had a significant coercive effect on the rebels, who in many instances fled when the 'gods from the sky descended'.

Concurrently, the maintenance of two rather ancient Soviet-built Hind helicopter gunships, flown by South African and Fijian mercenaries, became an issue of almost strategic importance. The cannibalised aircraft, all that remained of the disparate Sierra Leone Air Force, were well past their sell-by dates. But their influence extended far further than their actual capabilities, and whilst they were unafraid to engage the rebels – and did so frequently – their true value was probably psychological. The remains of the Sierra Leone Army fought with far more enthusiasm and competency if the Hinds were in the air – regardless of the state of the pilots (who invariably enjoyed a glass or two for Dutch courage before each mission) or the helicopters' weapons! Neall Ellis, the helicopters' hired South African pilot, told the British media that: 'The gunship strikes the fear of God into the rebels. They run into the bush as soon as they see it. In Africa the man who makes the loudest noise wins the battle. The helicopter, with all its weapons and engine, sure fits that bill.'[76] Meanwhile, outside Lungi, elements of the British Parachute Regiment were sending their own psychological messages to the Rebels, harassing and ambushing them as they moved towards the airfield.

Afloat, the Sierra Leone media were invited on board Illustrious for a firepower demonstration – an event that did not go entirely as planned. The UK's PJHQ[77] had directed that the small organic media team be shown the 'might' of the UK Armed Forces and various weapons and equipment had been prepared for demonstration. Yet when they arrived on board they showed no interest in the pre-

---

76   Anton la Guardia, 'Airborne Adventurer Keeps Freetown Free' (*Daily Telegraph*, 18 June 2000).

77   Permanent Joint Headquarters, the operational headquarters of the UK Armed Forces in Northwood, Middlesex.

pared stances, explaining that their lives had been dominated by weapons of war and they wanted to see no more of them. Instead they noted that women served alongside men and asked if they could do a number of interviews with the female sailors. This, they argued, was a more tangible demonstration of liberty and freedom for their audiences (and a visible sign of what the British presence represented) than weapons being fired. Such a request, coming as it did directly from the very people that 'we' sought to influence, could not be refused and the gunners and Royal Marines were stood down, and in their place female members of the ship's company were quickly found. Ashore, the UK military information operations effort had begun with a series of leaflets being dropped across Sierra Leone, whilst the Harrier jets photographed every inch of the country to provide the UN with badly needed intelligence on rebel positions.

In November 2000 the rebels again threatened the government, and the decision was taken to run a further information operation – one that would unequivocally demonstrate the UK's military capability and resolve. The HMS Ocean Amphibious ready group was diverted south from exercises in the Atlantic to land troops on Lunghi beach (in 'Operation Silkman') with the Sierra Leone and world media watching and reporting. After dramatic demonstrations of capability inland, the forces were returned to the Ocean, which then immediately departed and returned to its home port of Plymouth some days later. However, the pretence of its presence, just over the horizon, was maintained and Sierra Leone's fragile peace endured.

In just a few short weeks the British presence had turned the tables on the RUF rebels and it had been done almost entirely using influence and persuasion to make a substantive change to the population's behaviour. It also demonstrated how, despite the massive firepower of the UK's flagship and the troops deployed ashore, non-kinetic activity was actually to prove decisive. Although the directive to not use weapons had been enforced upon the military, and at the time had caused some consternation amongst seasoned war fighters, the use of information had quickly been substituted for bombs and bullets and a very effective information campaign launched. However, it also clearly demonstrated how the 'man on the ground' was in a far better position to make decisions on effects than planners and analysts some 3,000 miles away in London. The decision to run a media facility based on women's service in the RN was a difficult one to justify to military planners deep underground in PJHQ but, at the coalface, it was quite clearly the right decision to take and, importantly, came as a result of listening to the intended audience. The whole operation was, of course, not without incident and sadly British troops were killed in later incidents but, as the US Ambassador to Sierra Leone told the officers of HMS Illustrious when he visited the ship, 'the US' military might could have rolled over the country quite easily but it could not have achieved, in the same time frame, what the British had'.

The Levant: Lebanon 2006

The northern part of the former Ottoman Empire province of Syria, Lebanon finally gained its independence from its imperial master, France, in 1943. Its early history was troubled; its recent history has been traumatic. With eighteen different confessions (six different Muslim sects and twelve different Christian ones[78]) in this most volatile part of the world, internal strife has come to seem inevitable and the civil war, fought on ethnic and religious divides, which lasted from 1975 to 1990 perhaps came as no surprise to those who had observed the country's fortunes. The war left the country physically, politically and financially devastated. The process of rebuilding has not been easy, not least because of the presence within its national borders of the Iranian-backed Shi'ite Hezbollah organisation, now part political party (with seats in the Cabinet), part militia, part social force whose visceral hatred of its southern neighbour Israel has further polarised the various confessions. In turn, this ensures that the international perception of Lebanon is one of volatility and of being one spark away from further violence. The short war that occurred in 2006 was not state on state. It was Israel attacking Hezbollah within its strongholds of southern Beirut and southern Lebanon, but for all intents and purposes it was the state of Lebanon that suffered extensive infrastructure damage and the attendant consequences on its trade and economy. Perhaps more importantly, it was also the point at which a non-state actor – Hezbollah – demonstrated that it had its 'own Principles of War' but these reflected its own heightened awareness of what 'war' now encompasses.[79]

It was to here, in April 2006, that Andrew travelled to conduct an assessment of the Lebanese Armed Forces (LAF). The US were keen that a review of the LAF was conducted in order that it could align its policy and desire to provide equipment to the LAF that reflected the reality that Lebanon's threats were internal and not external. Clearly it would not have been appropriate for the US to conduct such a review and so it was decided between the US, France and the UK (and in conjunction with the Lebanese) that the UK would provide a tri-service team to conduct the review, the conclusions of which would be handed to all parties for consideration. Those conclusions, particularly about the army, made for difficult reading. In essence, after years of neglect and underfunding, the LAF was now hopelessly ill-equipped to deal with potential problems from within its *own* country, let alone able to cope with threats from elsewhere. As an entity it had managed to steer an adroit and careful path through the many years of conflict and there was no doubting that it was an multi-ethnic organisation that served Lebanon and its government rather than any particular ethnic grouping. However, it was also apparent that a very delicate balance of capabilities was required (so no Apache helicopters but far more armoured vehicles and ISTAR[80] capabilities) to

---

78   See CIA World Factbook online at https://www.cia.gov/library/publications/the-world-factbook/geos/le.html

79   Observation made by Lieutenant General Paul Newton in discussion with Andrew Mackay.

80   Intelligence, Surveillance, Target Acquisition and Reconnaissance.

ensure that it was equipped for internal but not external security. Unfortunately the war of 2006 ensured that the LAF has remained unbalanced in its capabilities and it is consistently dwarfed by the military capabilities of Hezbollah.

Three months after conducting his initial assessment Andrew was back in Lebanon heading up a team consisting of FCO, DfID and his own Bde HQ in order to reassess his original recommendations in the light of the war that had broken out in July 2006. Hezbollah fighters had captured and held hostage Ehud Golwasser and Eldad Regev, two Israeli army reservists who had been patrolling the Lebanese–Israeli border.[81] Tensions between the two countries had been building for some time and if this *particular* incident hadn't sparked conflict, then something else surely would have. As a consequence of the kidnappings, Israel's Defence Forces (IDF) began to bombard both Hezbollah military targets and the wider Lebanese infrastructure – a 'completely disproportionate' response, in Jacques Chirac's (and others') view. In response, Hezbollah launched a series of rockets into northern Israel and the fighting continued for thirty-four days, leaving 1,100 Lebanese and 156 Israelis dead.[82]

In the early stages of the conflict, the then International Development Secretary Hilary Benn visited Lebanon and his first task – within hours of arriving – was to attend a briefing of the situation provided by the British Embassy team and then an update by Andrew and his team on the LAF's ability to play a role. It was early morning. Coffee and croissants sat on the table. 'So,' said Benn, picking up a croissant, 'before we get down to business *what's the media play for today?'* In truth, it wasn't a bad question. In fact, it may even have been an excellent one for it cut right to the heart of the problem. Throughout the conflict the Hezbollah public relations operation consistently and comprehensively overshadowed Israel's and the West's attempts to wrestle control of the media – they were able to respond with agility and with simple core messages. They also had in Sayyed Hassan Nasrallah, the Secretary-General of Hezbollah, an astute media operator who was all too willing to use all the means at his disposal to convey the Hezbollah message. Arab media is also much more willing to display graphic images of injured civilians and so there was a constant stream of gravely wounded children and women being shown after every Israeli bombing raid. In the south of the country, Hezbollah's fighters had fought the IDF to a standstill. The IDF had the wrong equipment, the wrong doctrine and the wrong approach, a fact that has since been recognised in the many reviews that have subsequently taken place as to how they performed as badly as they did. So successful was Hezbollah's operation that even today that 2006 war is one that many commentators believe Hezbollah to have won – the first time in history that Israel's forces have been defeated. How did they manage it? Or, rather, how did an irregular group of

81   Conal Urquhart, 'Israel Planned for Lebanon War Months in Advance, PM Says' (*Guardian*, 9 March 2007).

82   Jenny Booth, 'Ceasefire Holds as Lebanon Awaits Peacekeepers' (*The Times Online*, 14 August 2006).

Iranian-funded terrorists so successfully convince not just the people of Lebanon but also the wider global audience that they had managed it?

Military historians may study that conflict and offer views on Hezbollah's military preparedness, on their flat command and control structure, on their starfish-like ability to regenerate after military attack. Others will suggest that it had more to do with the 'clear, realistic' goals they set their forces.[83] All may be true, but from the bird's-eye view of the conflict from within the country itself it was blatantly obvious that, for all the IDF's military advantage, it was the global information campaign, so effectively executed by Hezbollah, that ultimately 'won' the battle. As Al-Qaeda's master strategist Ayman al-Zawahiri once observed: 'We are in a battle, and more than half of this battle is taking place in the media.'[84] Hezbollah needed no lectures. That Hezbollah was able to dominate the media war, against the sophistication and resources of a nation-state, is extraordinary. That they were able to provoke sympathy for their cause throughout the wider world is perhaps more extraordinary still. Such effective influence operations warrant closer examination.

Hezbollah – otherwise known as 'The Party of God' – was formed in 1982 under the direction of the Iranian Revolutionary Guard and has worked hard since then to be seen as a force for good, both domestically and further afield. Various community projects in Lebanon have helped to establish and maintain a strong, loyal following within the country – from the rebuilding of homes after the civil war to providing free education and medical facilities. More recently they have even opened up a museum in southern Lebanon – detailing past exploits and boasting a battered Israeli tank and toy rocket launcher. A measure of its and, perhaps more importantly, of their, popularity is that only four months after opening, in May 2010, the museum had attracted over half a million visitors.[85] The ability of Hezbollah to influence those not just in Lebanon and the Levant but in the wider Western world is, perhaps, of particular interest. The murderous, bloodthirsty – cowardly, even – image associated with Hezbollah has largely receded over the last few years. Throughout the 2006 war they were portrayed (or rather, they portrayed themselves) as defenders of Lebanon and the Lebanese people, and not as an aggressor. Andrew remembers driving through Beirut after hostilities ceased and a ceasefire had been agreed – Hezbollah flags were everywhere and they had already started clearing rubble in southern Beirut and funding families affected by the war.

In support of this they had a few simple narratives which they steadfastly promoted and regularly repeated. Such an approach may, at first glance, seem facile, but to effectively convey a simple message that garners an emotional response

---

83   Ralph Peters, 'Lessons from Lebanon: The New Model Terrorist Army' (*Armed Forces Journal*, October 2006).

84   Hanna Rogan, 'Abu Reuter and the E-Jihad: Virtual Battlefronts from Iraq to the Horn of Africa' (*Georgetown Journal of International Affairs*, Summer/Fall 2007).

85   Alistair Lyon, 'Hezbollah Theme Park Draws the Crowds' (*Independent*, 15 August 2010).

along with a change in attitude and, more importantly, a change in behaviour, is, as we will see in later chapters, far more complicated than it seems. One such narrative was centred around Lebanon – not just Hezbollah – being overrun by outside forces. As the political leader and legal representative of the organisation, Sheikh Adib Haydar, was keen to point out: 'To eliminate the weapons of resistance is to eliminate the Shi'ites, and to eliminate the Shi'ites is to eliminate Lebanon.'[86] Other messages focused on the 'pure and noble' spirit of Hezbollah.[87] Perhaps what most resonated with Western audiences, however, were the images of injured or dead children, images that were guaranteed to both engender sympathy and focus rage on those responsible. Civilian casualties were virtually assured during the conflict (indeed, around four-fifths of Lebanese casualties were civilian), not least because many of the sites which Hezbollah used to launch their Katyusha rockets from were non-military locations, including holy sites and schools. Similarly mosques, day-care centres and other civilian buildings were employed as hideouts or places to store weapons. Hence, when the inevitable IDF counter-attacks occurred they were seen as being 'egregious and disproportionate when portrayed in the media'.[88] Very quickly Israel was portrayed to the wider world as being bullies and as using excessive force against the people of Lebanon, without really getting the chance to put across their own 'party line'.

Hezbollah had successfully built up a formidable communications machine, one that included TV and radio stations, newspapers and magazines, Internet sites, the liberal use of billboards and a publishing wing. However, it was the power of moving images – and the strict control that it exercised over them – that led to the world witnessing these 'egregious and disproportionate' IDF attacks. Step forward Al-Manar TV. By 2006, Al-Manar ('The Beacon') had become firmly established in Lebanon and throughout the Middle East and was even broadcast in parts of Europe. From humble beginnings it has transformed itself into a professional, effective and popular public relations machine that, at one time, could count Coca-Cola and other Western products among its advertisers and, despite its headquarters being bombed in southern Beirut, it spent only a few minutes off-air throughout the entire campaign. Al-Manar's greatest talent (it is a creative talent) is to cleverly blend factual reporting with heavily stylised propaganda and, according to a former policy advisor at the Israeli Treasury Department, Avi Jorisch, 'every aspect of Al-Manar's content from news to filler is fine-tuned to present a single point of view'.[89] During the 2006 conflict, that single point of view was that children were being bombed and killed by Israeli Defence Forces. Foreign journalists were encouraged to report from bombed hospitals and schools and more or less prohibited from filming Hezbollah's various defence facilities, depots and bases. Nick Robinson, of the BBC, was forced to acquiesce to such

---

86   *Hizbollah and the Lebanese Crisis* (International Crisis Group Middle East Report no. 69, October 2007).

87   Ibid.

88   Sarah E. Kreps, 'The 2006 Lebanon War: Lessons Learned' (*Parameters*, Spring 2007).

89   Avi Jorisch, 'Al-Manar: Hizbullah TV, 24/7' (*Middle East Quarterly*, Winter 2004).

tactics, and later found himself on CNN's 'Reliable Sources' programme where he was accused of anti-Israeli propaganda. His defence? That agreeing to be supervised by a Hezbollah 'press official' was the only way to get the story and covering it would have been impossible without assistance. He conceded that their media operation was 'very, very sophisticated and slick'.[90]

 According to scholar Abdallah Schleifer, 'by its astute use of the video camera, Hezbollah demonstrated how it was possible, with only a few simple pieces of equipment and creative thinking, to net huge military and psychological dividends'.[91] And what dividends. As images were broadcast throughout the world, over 700 Somali Islamic militants travelled to Lebanon to fight the Israelis. The leaders of Jordan, Egypt and, perhaps most surprisingly, the staunchly Sunni Saudi Arabia, all shifted their opinions on the conflict and, even if they didn't actively support, they certainly sympathised with Hezbollah. It helped that Hezbollah had such a prominent and inspirational figurehead. That they managed to so overwhelmingly dominate and control the media landscape owes much to their leader, Sayyed Hassan Nasrallah. During the 2006 conflict he succeeded in taking over screens not only in Lebanon but in Israel too. At one point he invited the bureau chief of Al-Jazeera into his hideout in order to conduct an interview:

> I can confirm at this moment, this is not an exaggeration and not part of psychological warfare, but facts, that the command structure of Hezbollah has not been harmed. Certainly, I would like to tell you and the viewers that when a martyr falls, we inform his family and we then announce this. We do not hide our martyrs until the end of battle. We have never done this. On the contrary, we always take pride in our martyrs.[92]

A good talker with bags of charisma and a subtle sense of humour, he comes across as engaging, honest, trustworthy and reliable. And when he talks, the public listens. 'Every time there is a speech by him the entire town becomes quiet and everyone is listening either to the radio or television',[93] says a forty-year-old farmer from Baalbek, a town in northeast Lebanon. His messages resonate with youth, too, 'One day when I grow up I want to become like Sayyed Hassan Nasrallah',[94] being one such sentiment from a twelve-year-old boy, also recorded from Baalbeck.

One of the most effective ways of communicating with younger audiences is through the Internet, and Hezbollah run websites in Arabic, English and French

90   'Blogging the Conflict in Lebanon' (BBC News, 9 August 2006).

91   Gabriel Weiman, 'Hezbollah Dot Com: Hezbollah's Online Campaign' (New Media and Innovative Technologies).

92   Ibid.

93   Strategic Communications Laboratory's report on Lebanon, 2009.

94   Ibid.

– and even Hebrew. Accordingly, the Internet has been seen as a boon for Hezbollah and has helped to boost its publicity and communication both domestically and outside its constituency. Again, the movement has been very shrewd. Such shrewdness is evident in its promotion of a game aimed at children and adolescents called 'Special Force'. Based on actual Hezbollah battles of the past, the game allows the player to take on the role of the guerrilla forces and even practise their shooting skills on former Israeli Prime Minister Ariel Sharon. The game took years to develop, according to Lebanon's *Daily Star*, and, in the words of Mahmoud Rayya, an official from the Hezbollah bureau, it offers 'mental and personal training for those who play it, allowing them to feel that they are in the shoes of the resistance fighters'.[95] Its unimaginatively titled sequel, 'Special Force 2', was released in 2007 and focused on the 2006 conflict. Although it is worth noting whilst there are plenty of computer games available in the US and the West that involve shooting Arabs, the likes of 'Special Force' and its sequel neatly illustrate the lengths that certain factions will go to in order to become influential with selected audiences, and also demonstrate that there is no age barrier to propaganda. In essence, Hezbollah have proven to be singularly adaptive, which, allied to a deep understanding of the environment they exist in and seek to influence, is no mean feat. As Joshua Cooper Ramo observed of Hezbollah, 'they paid scant regard to success but obsessed over failures'.[96] Contrast this with the coalition forces in Iraq and Afghanistan, where the 'obsession' became that of promoting successes, minimizing failures and ignoring some of the harsh realities of the environment they were living in.

The Levant: The Israeli Defence Force in Gaza 2009

Although neither Andrew nor Steve were directly involved in the events in Gaza in 2009, these merit inclusion, if only because they identify how quickly the Israeli Defence Force had sought to learn the lessons of Lebanon. In January 2009, the IDF launched Operation Cast Lead, a mission to end the ability of the Palestinian group Hamas ('Enthusiasm') to launch rocket attacks from the Gaza Strip into southern Israeli settlements. As well as its hard kinetic effect operation, the IDF also began a concerted soft power information war with an emphasis on new media and 'close co-ordination and unified messages between agencies'. The Israeli National Information Directorate (NID), established as a result of media co-ordination failures highlighted in the 2006 Winograd Report,[97] which in particular had criticised the Israeli government for a failure to engage with international audiences, sought to develop a cross-governmental information strategy that would 'synchronise the content and tone of Israel's message', primarily among the Foreign Ministry, the IDF Spokesperson's Unit, the military co-ordinator in the Oc-

95   'Hezbollah's New Computer Game' (WorldNetDaily.com, 3 March 2003).

96   John Cooper Ramo, *The Age of the Unthinkable* (Little Brown, 2009).

97   Submitted to the Office of the Prime Minister of Israel, 30 January 2008; see http://www.ynetnews.com/articles/0,7340,L-3500764,00.html

cupied Territories and the Prime Minister's Office. Key elements of that strategy were to be the exclusion of most domestic and foreign journalists from the Gaza area, a proactive focus upon online media and the deployment of fluent Arabic and English speakers as spokespeople. But it was its willingness to engage with new media outlets that is perhaps most noteworthy.

The IDF YouTube channel 'idfnadesk', set up on 29 December 2008, allowed viewers to watch videos, posted on an almost daily basis, of the IDF in action. The channel provided videos in three languages – English, Hebrew and Arabic – and was a mixture of briefing, fronted by IDF personnel, and video footage of operations in Gaza, much of it from the air. Table 3.1 provides a broad summary of the content.

Total number of videos (at 3 April 2009)	47
Total number of views (at 3 April 2009)	7,539,455
Average number of views per video	160,000
Number of videos in Arabic	2
Number of videos in English	45
Number of videos with the word 'terrorist' in their title	9
Number of videos on humanitarian aid	3
Number of videos receiving a 4* rating or above	47

Table 3.1 Summary of output of the IDF YouTube channel 'idfnadesk' during Operation Cast Lead.

Of particular note is the inability of viewers to leave a comment on the video – a feature that is usual for YouTube. Much of the YouTube videos reappear in a parallel blog at http://idfspokesperson.com, which at the time of writing has had nearly 200,000 hits. Like the YouTube site, it also prevents commentary from users. Concurrently the IDF English language website carried longer articles covering both military and human-interest stories about the conflict – such as soldiers injured, the reservist call-up, military successes and places/people targeted. The Israeli Consulate General in New York established a blog, administrated by David Saranga, the Consul for Public and Media Aşffairs, who also ran the first governmental press conference ever held on Twitter, in text-speak – attracting over 2,500 participants – on 30 December 2008. Any member of the micro-blogging site was able to take part and some of the questions and answers from the conference were published on Israel Politik. For example:

EXPLORE4CORNERS: How many attacks have there been against IS in the last 6 months? How many casualties? The MSM doesn't report that here.

ISRAELCONSULATE: ovr 500 rockts Hit IL in the 6 mts of CF. per the last 72 hrs mre thn 300 hit IL. kiling 4 ppl & injuring hndrds.[98]

Saranga claims that 'since the definition of war has changed, the definition of public diplomacy has to change as well'.[99] The event certainly gave Israeli government officials direct exposure to the concerns and questions of the (predominantly) Western public, and an opportunity to promote the Israeli message. Twitter was not the Consulate's only foray into cyberspace. They also created a Facebook page, allowing Facebook members to join. This complemented the long-running Israeli Ministry for Foreign Affairs website – tri-lingual (Arabic, English and Hebrew) and was copied by Israeli Embassies around the globe, who used their own hosted sites to spread the Israeli message in a multiplicity of languages. Indeed, Facebook, with its approximately 160 million users, appears to have become an influential forum for Israel. According to the Israel News Agency, within two hours of the start of the conflict, Israel had created a Facebook group entitled 'I Support the Israel Defense Forces In Preventing Terror Attacks From Gaza', which quickly racked up users. According to its mission statement, its aim was to provide support to the IDF involved in Operation Cast Lead and also to provide an open forum '24/7 as public opinion directly affects life on the ground'.[100]

Occasionally the gap between official and unofficial efforts seemed to blur. The Israel Project, whose website describes itself as 'an international non-profit organisation devoted to educating the press and the public about Israel while promoting security, freedom and peace', issued a language guide advising supporters of how best to describe Hamas's 'Iran-backed war on Israel'. Other sites scoured international opinion polls and urged supporters to vote in Israel's favour. HonestReporting.com proclaims that: 'Israel is in the midst of a battle for public opinion – waged primarily via the media. To ensure Israel is represented fairly and accurately "HonestReporting" monitors the media, exposes cases of bias, promotes balance, and effects change through education and action.'[101] It and its weblog Backspin watched for perceived anti-Israeli media bias and sought to correct specific false claims made against Israel. According to its website, HonestReporting has 130,000 subscribers worldwide. Similar 'citizen-journalism' is visible on video-sharing sites such as Liveleak.com, which claims to be 'redefining the media'. Here can be found pro-Israeli footage which receives thousands of hits within hours. A particularly prolific contributor of Gaza conflict material is 'barnesy' who has 1,161 subscribers.

---

98   See http://twitter.com/intent/user?screen_name=israelconsulate
99   See http://www.liveleak.com/view?i=8a6_1231367421
100   See http://www.facebook.com/group.php?gid=69810300128
101   See http://honestreporting.com/about/

Hamas, too, has utilised the power of information but in a much less structured manner than their adversary. Surprised Israelis started to receive text messages and emails warning of imminent rocket attacks on their homes. At the same time, Hamas's willingness to allow Arab TV channels such as Al-Jazeera and Al-Arabiya to film the effect of the Israeli bombardment seriously undermined the Israeli war effort. Even Palestine civilians found the media to be an important conduit. The deaths of three daughters of a Palestinian doctor who practises extensively in Israel have given a human face to the conflict for Israelis. Izzadin Abu Alaish, a gynaecologist, had broadcast daily on Israeli radio, and when his house was hit he called a friend at an Israeli TV station, which put him live on Israeli TV. His pitiful pleadings coupled with his educated and Western-leaning background may well have been very difficult for moderate Israelis to deal with.

It is clear that the 'new media' campaign had been the subject of careful preparation. Strong criticism that during the second Lebanon war the IDF public relations campaign was run by incompetent and inexperienced junior reserve officers forced change. Brigadier-General Avi Benayahu, the IDF's spokesman, was quoted as saying that 'in terms of communicating our message, new media is the future'.[102] He has overseen the change at the IDF Spokesperson's Unit resulting from 'an intensive new media workshop at the Interdisciplinary Centre, Herzliya, in mid-2008'.

At the beginning of the conflict, the overall view, both in Israel and abroad, was that the new media strategy had allowed Israel to gain the upper hand in consensus-building and forming a positive narrative. Former UN Ambassador Dan Gillerman (brought into the PR campaign shortly before the start of the offensive) is quoted, in an article published on 30 December 2008, as suggesting that 'Israel has no small measure of understanding and support', and that there were no 'dramatic condemnations, only the expected and generic calls for calm and cease-fire'. Similarly, a survey by *Le Figaro* revealed that 55 per cent of respondents were 'understanding towards the Israeli operation' versus 45 per cent against it.[103]

However, declarations of success may be unduly optimistic. The conflict followed the Christmas holiday period when people were either away or not inclined to follow contemporary news events as assiduously as they do at other times of the year. The IDF's ban on foreign journalists entering Gaza despite an Israeli Supreme Court decision to the contrary did, however, force Western news presenters to focus on the rocket attacks on towns in southern Israel. While these stories focused international attention on Israel's plight, the low casualty figures did little to balance the pictures of suffering and misery coming out of Hamas-controlled Gaza. As the Government Press Office Director Danny Seaman admits: 'Television is inherently a medium that likes drama, blood and tears',[104] and in

102   See http://www.jpost.com/LandedPages/PrintArticle.aspx?id=127397
103   *Le Figaro*, 29 December 2008.
104   Jan Thomas Otte, 'Cyberspace and Propaganda: Israel and the War in Gaza' (February 2009, available at http://www.princeton.edu/~lisd/archived/commentary_february2009.pdf).

denying Western media access to this directly, they are forced either to make do with long shots of Gaza or rely on Al-Jazeera and Hamas footage.

The Israeli government faced an uphill struggle once the ground offensive started on 3 January 2009, and it appeared to be able to do little about the damaging claims that hundreds of civilians, including children, had been killed by IDF forces. The images of dead Palestinian children, reinforced by IDF strikes on a UN school and later claims that the IDF were committing war crimes by using white phosphorus against civilian targets created a storm of global public protest against Israel in the second and third weeks of the offensive. The violence and virulence of these anti-Israel and frequently anti-Semitic protests, as well as the deep sympathy for Hamas, shocked Israeli public opinion. However, the policy of a media black-out over Gaza might have paid dividends once the active conflict was over, with the implementation of Israel's unilateral cease-fire on 18 January 2009. It was justified by Seaman at the beginning of the offensive as denying Hamas direct access to Western journalists hungry for stories because 'foreign journalists don't have the backbone and courage to speak against Hamas in Hamas-controlled territory'.[105] Frustrated by recycled images and curtailed budgets, foreign reporters have been recalled, as a worsening global economic outlook has pushed Gaza from the top headlines. And as BBC reporter Mark Urban acknowledges on his blog: 'With each week that passes, the newsworthiness of this material will diminish.'

Dominique Wolton, a media specialist at France's National Centre for Scientific Research (CNRS) in Paris noted that: 'Israel are the ones who have a grip on communications, but Israel will not win the communications battle because, whatever Israel's legitimate rights are, the unbalanced use of force and the unleashing of violence by Israel is acting against it.'[106] Charles Tripp, professor of Middle East Politics at the School of Oriental and African Studies (SOAS) in London took a similar view when he stated that: 'the very powerful images of what's happening to civilians in Gaza must be having a greater impact than seeing Israeli spokesmen talking about the war on terror. In many ways, one of the main targets of the Israeli propaganda is Europe and the US, and I would have thought they're not doing too well there.'[107]

And yet undeniably Israel's 'new media' strategy has made their public relations message during wartime much more cohesive, far quicker to react to allegations and more focused, through the public's easy access to its material online. However, the difficulty of balancing pictures of Palestinian suffering and destruction in Gaza with a message of self-defence means that Israel arguably again lost the PR war. Politically, Israel also appears to have gained less than they may have hoped, for not only the Arab 'street' but also various Western governments have condemned the offensive in the face of such high casualty rates among civilians. Israel now lies under the pressure of hostile global public opinion, which argua-

105   Ibid.

106   See http://www.liveleak.com/view?i=8a6_1231367421

107   Ibid.

bly contributed to its ceasefire and partial withdrawal from Gaza. Did Israel win? This is not a discussion of the conflict per se but one cannot help but notice that rockets are still being fired into southern Israel and that the IDF are being accused of war crimes; peace and stability, on which their campaign was very publicly fought, seem a long way off. What is undeniable, however, is that the IDF chose to conduct at least part of their operation in the information environment – and to invest in new technology and new conduits, to engage new, perhaps younger, audiences without any guarantee of success. Crucially they did so in a co-ordinated manner across the government. Whilst we debate their success, we might also question how their position would have looked to the international community if they had not engaged in an information war. Concurrently, we also consider whether their broad-brush approach, in which information was not specifically targeted to groups or opinion-formers, would have been improved with the benefit of more robust Target Audience Analysis.

4
The evolving character of conflict II

Iraq – a backwards notion of influence

Many words have flowed to describe the nature of the Iraq conflict. There is little point, in this account, in trying to capture its rights or wrongs, its legality, its poor execution or, indeed, whether or not that war made Iraq and the surrounding region more or less susceptible to future conflict. Tom Ricks sums up the first few years in one word in his book *Fiasco* and how the US 'occupied the country negligently' and 'assembled an agonizingly incompetent occupation'.[108] The absence of any real planning for the post-conflict aftermath (Exhibit 1 would be the hopelessness of thinking that a retired three-star General, Jay Garner, – and a motley collection of individuals within a hastily stitched together organisation – the Office for Reconstruction and Humanitarian Assistance (ORHA) – would be enough to co-ordinate the post-conflict route to governance and security) and the sheer dysfunctional nature of the Coalition Provisional Authority (CPA) that replaced ORHA can, in retrospect, at best be described as incompetent, at worst blatantly negligent. It is instructive that even in late 2005, when the insurgency in Iraq was in full swing, US Secretary of Defense Donald Rumsfeld refused to countenance using the word 'insurgent', preferring instead the term 'enemies of the legitimate Iraqi government'. Quite how any form of influence could be brought to bear on this broad description is hard to imagine, but clearly it was never intended to. Andrew recalls being corrected by a senior State Department official when he was providing an update on the Iraqi police and used the term 'insurgent'. He was told in no uncertain terms that the State Department preferred either 'Former Regime Elements' (FRE) or 'Former Regime Loyalists' (FRL).

Capturing the essence of what a behaviourally based influence campaign might have looked like in Iraq is, by necessity, a rearward look. Andrew was there for nearly a year in 2004 and saw at first hand the chaotic conditions that prevailed. In fact much of what he learnt in Iraq was absorbed into how he approached and adapted counterinsurgency later, in Afghanistan. In essence, however, the behavioural component was very much tied up in personalities and their place in organisations. In fact it seemed almost as if the kinetic battle was of secondary importance.

---

108   Thomas E. Ricks, *Fiasco: The American Military Adventure in Iraq* (Penguin, 2007).

The key relationship he established with General David Petraeus[109] was also influential in how his approach to the role of the UK's Task Force Commander in Helmand was undertaken. In considering Iraq, therefore, we thought it more interesting to start from the point at which the campaign began to turn in the favour of the Coalition and the nascent Iraqi government, a time that has now passed into history as 'the Surge'. To understand the role of influence it is worth starting with a discussion that Andrew had a with a senior US Army General who, when asked to describe the turning point, did not do so in terms of additional manpower, greater diplomatic effort, improved security sector reform, better institutions or a rejection of the Baker/Hamilton Report.[110] Instead he described it thus:

> In 2005, as debate raged on what to do with Iraq and we peered over the precipice of Strategic failure, we essentially asked ourselves two questions. The first was 'How on earth did we get ourselves into this mess?' And although we found that question hard to ask (in a formal open sense) we discovered the answers were rather easy to arrive at. In fact the list was lengthy but it proved easy to reach consensus as to what should be on that list. It included, in no order of importance: the disbandment of the Iraqi Army, over-vigorous de-Baathification, having the wrong equipment, doctrine, training and force structures, a lack of understanding of the people and the environment. Self-inflicted trauma such as the disaster of Abu Ghraib also play into the sense that in the initial years the Coalition in Iraq struggled and reeled from one self-inflicted agony to the next with each playing a role in re-energizing the various layers of opposition that gathered momentum throughout those years.

Readers will, no doubt, be able to add to such a list. However, the General went on to explain that the most important question that was asked was actually the second question:

> Why did it go wrong? And that again was agonizing in reaching an answer but easy to identify its component parts. The answer was about leadership and the politics and in particular too many of the wrong people, in the wrong place, doing the wrong thing at the wrong time and with the wrong ideology.

---

109   Commander, ISAF Afghanistan, until 2011.

110   James Baker and Lee Hamilton, *The Iraq Study Group Report: The Way Forward – a New Approach* (Vintage Books, 2007). The Iraq Study Group was facilitated by the United States Institute of Peace, which released the Iraq Study Group's final report on their website on 6 December 2006.

In being able to hold up such a mirror and answer those two questions the US was able to begin to turn the tide of what, to many, had become a hopeless, impossible cause. Furthermore, whatever is added to the list above it is pertinent to remind ourselves of the extraordinary levels of organisational dysfunction that existed within the Coalition Provisional Authority. Having worked for a year in Kosovo within the United Nations Mission in Kosovo (UNMIK), and thought it to be a rather poorly organised institution, Andrew came to view UNMIK as a model of efficiency and good governance compared to the CPA. In an interview that he gave to Anthony Cordesman in 2005, and which was subsequently published in the latter's book *Iraqi Security Forces: A Strategy for Success*,[111] he recalled:

> The vacuums created by CPA dysfunctionality were inevitably filled with bureaucracy, endless committees, the inept, the displaced, and those brought out of retirement. We should not underestimate how much further on we would be in Iraq if we had been organised from the beginning with a reasonably coherent organisation managing the post conflict phase and equipping it with the right people.

In the interview, he went on to state that:

> Some of the consequences I suspect, were that our engagement with the Iraqis suffered horribly, the information campaign was a near disaster and the political and military intent were never synced and then executed in any meaningful sense … but the one thing coherent, well-led organisations can do is retrieve, recover and stabilise the consequences of poor policy decisions. Poor organisations find this next to impossible and end up living with the legacy rather than addressing the outcome.

This is not to say, however, that within both the CPA and the Coalition HQ arguments were not raging about the nature of the insurgency (there were many who recognised it as such), about whether or not the operational tactics being utilised were appropriate, or about ideas to fix the fractured political/military/diplomatic balance. Those issues – and many more – were being endlessly discussed and contemplated at all levels. However, such was the dysfunction that there was an inability to recognise the nature of the problem. Symptoms rather than causes were continuously tackled, and with great vigour. The pressure for results was such that any notion of subtlety, of how influence might be applied, was completely lost in the chaotic conditions that prevailed.

---

111   Anthony H. Cordesman, *Iraqi Security Forces: A Strategy for Success* (Praeger, 2005, p. 55).

Politicians and diplomats rarely give much attention to the organisational design of an institution – it is normally considered fairly esoteric, boring stuff and far removed from the more interesting arena of strategy, geopolitics and policy. More often than not the initial struggle was to gain positions of influence within an organisation (and here the military are just as guilty in arguing over 'star counts' – in essence, which senior officer, of which nationality, will do what job and who will be their deputies) with little, if any, thought given to how the organisation might actually work, go about its business, and to the allocation of its authorities and responsibilities. Once set, and we are mindful that these organisations are often forged in the turmoil and confusion of a post-conflict vacuum, further change becomes virtually impossible as each nation hunkers down in support of the key appointments they have secured. They make the mistake, we believe, of imagining that this is how influence from their respective capital cities is exercised. We would argue that within this morass of dysfunctional organisation the ability to exercise influence in terms of how we describe it in this book becomes all but impossible.

We would argue – admittedly retrospectively – that a key component in the wholesale adaptation and change that the 'Surge' brought was the placing of influence into a more recognisable role and one that had a dramatic effect. Organisational rigour was established – and critically between the diplomatic (Crocker[112]) and the military (Petraeus). Soft power was employed to build working institutions, non-kinetic approaches were funded, kinetic operations were industrialised to destroy Al-Qaeda, the counterinsurgency policy emphasised contact with the population and placed them firmly in the centre of operations as 'the Prize'. Diplomacy and the roles and co-ordination of civil and military effort were given renewed attention and vigour. Considerable effort was made to understand the environment, culture, ethnicity and sectarian divides. We would not wish to view all of this through rose-tinted spectacles, but it is self-evident that when the necessary effort is made to place hard/soft power, kinetic/non-kinetic operations and civil/military effort into a more coherent whole the effects can be dramatic.

Afghanistan: the Taliban as a learning organisation

Both of us have direct experience of operations in Afghanistan. Andrew, as we will see in a moment, commanded his Brigade in the southern province of Helmand between 2007 and 2008, a tour in which Steve assisted with the formulation of the influence plan. Latterly, Steve has been working directly in tactical information operations in Helmand. So, in this section, rather than look at our own endeavours first, we have chosen to examine our adversaries' use of information and influence in their campaign. And what we found has come as a surprise.

---

112   Ryan Crocker, US Ambassador to Afghanistan.

The early years of the Taliban's[113] rule in Afghanistan were not known for their press freedom. Technology was unwelcome, images of human beings were considered apostate and world public opinion was largely irrelevant to an organisation that actively sought to return Afghan society to that of the Prophet Mohammed's time. Traditional Afghan pastimes such as kite-flying were banned, as was listening to music. Public executions were common. Yet the success of Al-Qaeda's use and manipulation of the media in its global insurgency, and more latterly in its operations in Iraq, had not gone unnoticed by the Taliban. A primary strategic objective for Al-Qaeda – probably an imperative – has been the need to mobilise Muslim populations. Analysis of jihadist communiqués between 2001 and 2005 shows a clear preference for Muslim audiences. Ninety-two per cent of their output targeted Muslim audiences, 6 per cent was designed for an undifferentiated audience, and only 2 per cent was directed specifically at non-Muslim audiences.[114] As one of the principle strategists of Al-Qaeda, Abu 'Ubeid al-Qurashi, wrote: 'They did not aspire to gain Western sympathy; rather, they sought to expose the American lie and deceit to the peoples of the world – and first and foremost to the Islamic peoples.'[115]

And yet, in more recent years jihadist groups have developed an increasing interest in 'Western' audiences. Many Iraqi Sunni insurgent groups created English mirrors of their Arabic websites, adapting their output to meet Western tastes. For example, they sought to glorify 'Juba', the sniper of the Islamic Army of Iraq – who may or may not have existed. A specialist Juba website honouring his achievements contained English commentary and claims of responsibility for the deaths of hundreds of Coalition soldiers. Another significant example is the Iraq insurgency's engagement in a 'black propaganda' operation called 'Lee's Life for Lies'. This operation involved fabricating a history of American soldier Lee Kendall, whose USB flash drive was found by insurgents.[116] They utilised the information contained in the USB to write a fake letter that described the 'desperate' situation of US soldiers in Iraq and the existence of widespread abuses and unpunished war crimes. This material could be obtained in a downloadable video which contained the reading of the false letter by an anonymous narrator using American-accented English. Between 2005 and 2007, Al-Qaeda's arch-strategist Ayman Zawahiri has quadrupled its video output,[117] seeking to confront both the *near* (the Islamic regimes) and *far* enemies (the US) that he defined in his Decem-

---

113   It is recognised that the term 'Taliban' is problematic, implying a homogeneous group with similar aims and objectives. The authors note that such characteristics do not define the insurgents of southern Afghanistan and of the Pakistan tribal areas but use it simply for convenience.

114   M. Torres, J. Jordan and N. Horsburgh, 'Analysis and Evolution of the Global Jihadist Movement Propaganda' (*Analysis and Evolution of the Global Jihadist Movement Propaganda*, vol. 18 no. 3, Fall, 2006, pp. 399–421).

115   'Al-Qa'ida Activist, Abu 'Ubeid Al Qurashi: Comparing Munich (Olympics) Attack 1972 to September 11' (*MEMRI*, 12 March 2002).

116   http://www.lee-flash.blogspot.com

117   Bruce Hoffman, 'Scarier than Bin Laden' (*Washington Post*, 9 September 2007).

ber 2001 treatise 'Knights under the Prophet's Banner' in the London based pan-Arab newspaper *Al-Sharq el-Awsat*.[118] The Taliban had much to learn.

This is not to suggest that such operations were unknown to Afghan fighters. During the Soviet occupation of Afghanistan, two Afghan Islamist insurgent organisations, Gulbuddin Hekmatyar's Hezb-e-Islami and Ahmad Shah Massoud's Jamiat-e-Islami, had both used media campaigns in their operations[119] – inexpensive magazines, local radio broadcasts, newsletters, video- and audiotapes, and posters – to promote their cause in Afghanistan and Pakistan. However, these were largely amateur in design and production and the targeting of their audience sporadic and ill-defined. In their jihad against the US much more sophisticated mechanisms were needed, and by mid-2002 the Taliban had taken the first steps in the construction of a widespread traditional propaganda campaign that would include 'the distribution of dictums, leaflets, cassettes and books that call for jihad and explain the punishment for those who cooperate with or work for the crusaders'.[120]

Over the next few years intermittent reports[121] suggested that a growing synergy existed between the insurgency in Iraq and that of Afghanistan. Whilst the increase in number and sophistication of IEDs[122] was the most obvious operational consequence of this synergy, another was clearly that of the media battle, and by late 2006 the Taliban had formed its own media organisation, modelled on Al-Qaeda's al-Sahab ('The clouds'). Between December 2006 and August 2007 the Taliban slowly, but steadily, developed the information environment into a key – and fully integrated – component of their military campaign. They may seek to regress their country by many hundreds of years but this does not mean they cannot apply an agility of mind and, perhaps more astonishing, a highly developed grasp of the role of information, to their heavily outgunned and outnumbered insurgency. Indeed, the words of Mullah Abdul Salaam Zaeef, a former Taliban ambassador to Pakistan, are particularly interesting. Holding his iPhone close by he provided an interview to Associated Press at his residence in Kabul, Afghanistan on 25 February 2009. Zaeef had spent almost four years in Guantánamo Bay prison. Wearing a black turban and resplendent in thick beard, he admitted to being a big fan of Apple's iPhone. 'It's easy and modern and I love it', he told journalists, while he pinched and pulled his fingers across the device's touch-screen to show off photos: 'I'm using the Internet with it. Sometimes I use it for the GPS to find locations.'[123]

---

118   Available at http://www.scribd.com/doc/6759609/Knights-Under-the-Prophet-Banner

119   *Terrorism Focus*, vol. IV issue 15, 22 May 2007. See also A. Borovik, *The Hidden War: A Russian Journalist's Account of the Soviet War in Afghanistan* (Grove Press, 1990).

120   *Jamestown Terrorism Focus*, vol. 4 issue 10, 17 April 2007.

121   Classified reporting unsuitable for specific reference or release.

122   Improvised Explosive Devices.

123   See http://seattletimes.nwsource.com/ABPub/zoom/html/2008809017.html

This new campaign began in earnest in April 2007 when the Taliban stumbled across, by accident, an Al-Jazeera TV journalist.[124] Initially unsure of what they should do with their captive, higher authorities directed that he be, to coin a Coalition term, 'embedded' with the Taliban. The result was a five-part news series for the channel's multimillion Arab and Islamic audience. One 'episode' was entitled 'The People's Movement', and it gave the first indication of a concerted Taliban 'hearts and minds' campaign. In that piece, a female Afghan (alleged) doctor declares her support for the Taliban, her burqa conspicuously absent. That she is a doctor is 'confirmed' by the presence of a stethoscope in front of her as she speaks. Later, in the same episode, tribal elders speak with approval of the 'peace and security' that the Taliban had brought to their region.[125] That same series of news features also spoke of the importance with which the Taliban treated the safety of civilians, noting that Coalition helicopters were never engaged over poppy fields, lest they fall from the air and destroy the livelihood of the poppy farmers.

Yet it was a June 2007 video release which really began to cause interest. The video was of a Taliban suicide graduation ceremony for would-be suicide bombers of Western targets.[126] The video, which purports to show a 'graduating class' of ready-to-travel bombers, their sights set on targets in the United States and western Europe. The video is notable for a number of reasons. First, it deviates from usual suicide bomber propaganda which is traditionally usually post-mortem and seeks to glorify the martyrdom of the bomber, celebrating his life and his sacrifice for Allah. Previous videos have also sought to focus on individuals or, as in the case of the 9/11 attackers, on very small and discrete groups. This video, however, shows a large number of individuals, lined up by nationality and apparently ready for suicide operations. It is self-evidently designed not for a Muslim audience but for a Western viewer. One young man stands up and states: 'let me tell you why I will be making a suicide bomb in Britain'. Others talk of taking attacks to Ottawa, Canada, and to Germany. Indeed, the Taliban's leader, Mullah Dadullah says: 'Listen, all you Westerners and Americans. You came from thousands of kilometres away to fight us. Now we will get back to you in your countries and attack you.'

The graduation ceremony, which has the appearance of a college graduation, has the 'students' organised in six national 'brigades' (British, American, Canadian, German, French and Afghan) who take turns in pledging future action. In Western military terminology the video is clearly part of an 'information operation', seeking to divide the NATO alliance and weaken its commitment to assisting and supporting President Hamid Karzai's Afghan government. And it had some effect. A Canadian official told the Canadian Television News channel that they

---

124   The author discussed this incident with Whadah Kanfar, the former Managing Director of the Al-Jazeera TV channel, during a visit to the station's headquarter in May 2008. Kanfar confirmed the genesis of the coverage.

125   We have placed this video online at http://www.youtube.com/watch?v=YuW4DukwnHk

126   The video can be viewed at http://www.youtube.com/watch?v=H8RERSoYzpg

took the Taliban threat 'very seriously',[127] stating that Canadian intelligence had known for some months that the Taliban leadership had directed its commanders to 'take the fight out of the country, to take it to us'. Celebrated Pakistani journalist Hamid Mir confirmed the report as 'absolutely true' – suicide bombers, it would appear, were heading to Canada, America and Europe.[128] Whilst the large Pakistani diaspora in the UK might well be a likely proving ground for such operations, the claims that the Taliban and their acolytes might have the capability and resources to cross the Atlantic does seem unlikely. And yet, whether they could or not was largely an academic point for, as with the female doctor in the earlier video, they are fine pieces of directed information operations, designed to intimidate and instil fear in Western audiences.

In June 2007, the new Taliban commander Mansor Dadullah provided a long and detailed interview with Al-Jazeera, and in July 2007 the Taliban announced to the world, again via the conduits of Al-Jazeera and the Web, that they had rebranded themselves as 'neo-Taliban'. It was this later proclamation that was perhaps of most interest, for accompanying the rebranding announcement was a feature on the Taliban's 'media centre'.[129] Although not the most sophisticated video-editing equipment, the news feature showed Windows-based software (along with the ubiquitous PowerPoint presentations), in English, being used to create videos and CDs immortalising the Taliban's fight. The piece caused one colleague from the security service's JTAC[130] to speculate that perhaps young radicalised British Muslims were now choosing to fight their personal jihads not with AK-47 assault weapons but with computers and video-editing equipment.

Perhaps conscious that up until now they had engaged only with Arabic-speaking audiences, in October 2007 the English-language outlet of Al-Jazeera was sent fourteen videos by the Taliban. Among the footage were attacks on Afghan police vehicles. One tape shows a person trying to escape, before being shot. The cars are then set alight. Another tape shows Taliban fighters proudly displaying what they discovered at an empty US military outpost. They appear particularly intrigued by the night-vision goggles.[131] As the Al-Jazeera correspondent notes: 'The desire to gain the psychological advantage has meant that armed groups here and across the Middle East have now embraced propaganda in a big way. On all sides of the Afghan conflict there is an awareness that while the battles are important, the message may help win the war.'

In September 2008 the Taliban courted the renowned French magazine *Paris Match*[132] posing for its photographers partially dressed in the uniforms of dead

127   http://www.ctv.ca/servlet/ArticleNews/story/CTVNews/20070618/taliban_
       bombers_070618/20070618

128   http://www.canadafreepress.com/2007/cover062107.htm

129   http://www.youtube.com/watch?v=E2IjuNYAF4Y

130   Joint Terrorism and Analysis Centre.

131   http://www.youtube.com/watch?v=5jCUeUNbnQE&feature=related

132   http://www.indepedent.co.uk/news/world/europe/paris-match-taliban-photoshoot-shocks-
       france-919109.html

French solders, killed only days beforehand. The French Defence Minister Herve Morin asked: 'Should we really be doing promotion for people who understand the importance of communication in the modern world? This is a communications war that the Taliban are waging. They understand that public opinion is probably the Achilles heel of the international community.'[133]

The depth, quality and sophistication of this Al-Qaeda-inspired spin machine are noteworthy; it would appear from the vast numbers of Internet videos that not only does no attack on the Coalition go unrecorded but, as in the case of the Afghan doctor, no wider propaganda opportunity is missed. As a returning British Brigade Commander noted from his time in Helmand: 'There has been a lot of talk about asymmetry. The true asymmetry of the campaign is that the Taliban rely on 90 per cent psychology and 10 per cent force whereas we rely on 90 per cent force and 10 per cent psychology in an environment where perception is reality, memories are very long and enemies easily made.' As visiting researcher at the Defence Academy Dr Dave Sloggett notes: 'We are faced by a second generation asymmetric insurgency that is backed by a sophisticated media operation … that reinforces a number of key but simple messages. These include the need to do duty through Jihad, to fight Zionist and Christian aggression that are targeting Islam and setting this in some fourteenth-century period of world history.'[134]

So to what do we attribute this apparent change in communications priorities? Undoubtedly Al-Qaeda have been disappointed at the response of the Muslim *ummah*. In spite of Al-Qaeda's capability to mobilise significant activist support, the reality is that the dream of a global Islamic insurgency has yet to be achieved. Furthermore, Al-Qaeda have been conspicuously absent during the course of the Arab spring (although, no doubt, they will be seeking to fill the vacuums created in post-conflict societies). Polls in the Muslim world indicate that jihadist propaganda has not significantly increased the levels of popular support towards Al-Qaeda and its objectives. Yet this explanation would belittle the agility and intelligence of Al-Qaeda. Jihadists recognise that the determination of their 'crusader armies' to fight depends on the support of the Western general public, and it seems likely that this is the new target of our adversaries. Thus the Taliban has slowly learnt that placing information at the centre of their campaign can add significant value – and undeniably it is a lesson they have learnt from Al-Qaeda. As Hamir Mir, the biographer of Bin Laden, once noted: 'Al-Qaeda militants fleeing US bombs in November 2001 – every second member was carrying a laptop alongside his Kalashnikov.'[135] It is a campaign that has a marketplace, and it is difficult to see how the huge amounts of material available online and in more mainstream media can have done anything but help to support the radicalisation process. In short, there is a profound battle for hearts and minds – both Afghan

133 John Lichfield, '*Paris Match* Taliban Photoshoot Shocks France' (*Independent*, 4 September 2008).

134 David Sloggett, '*Information Operations: The Challenge of Second Generation Insurgencies*' (King's College London, unpublished).

135 Abdel Bari Atwan, *The Secret History of Al-Qa'ida* (Saqi Press, 2006, p. 122).

and Western audiences – and whilst the US-led Coalition may not be losing, it is difficult to assess if its message is prevailing.

Helmand: preparing 52 Brigade

'Do not believe what you want to believe until you know what it is you need to know.'

R V Jones[136]

The deployment, and the retaking of the strategically important town of Musa Qala by Andrew and 52 Brigade (around 7,750 personnel in total), has been well documented in other publications – most notably Stephen Grey's book *Operation Snakebite*[137]; perhaps less so has been the development of the command thought process that proceeded it – and why. Andrew led the fourth brigade-size deployment to Helmand Province. It deployed at the eighteenth-month point of the UK's commitment to Helmand and was conscious that the end of its tour would mark the two-year point. Each successive brigade had fought a differing campaign: 16 Air Assault Brigade's first tour, with limited resources, was highly kinetic; 3 Commando Brigade, because of force levels, went raiding and created manoeuvre outreach groups to disrupt and interdict; 12 Mechanised Brigade engaged in a more industrial scale of conflict which involved large clearances, but without the force levels to subsequently hold and build in those areas. Each of these deployments had a significant effect on the local population who were, inevitably, constrained in making appropriate choices through either lack of ISAF[138] presence or an inability to do so without fear of the Taliban returning. An early decision was therefore made in Andrew's planning process to place the population at the forefront of the operational design. It was determined that Andrew's troops would 'clear, hold and build' where it could, and concurrently 'disrupt, interdict and defeat' where it could not. Underpinning this would be a commitment to ensure a singular focus on influencing the population of Helmand in order that the brigade could gain and retain their consent. It was decided that the 'population is the Prize'.

This was an easy enough order to state, but what did it actually mean for the soldiers on the ground? How does it differ from the cultural familiarity training that they will have undertaken and how is it actually achieved? One of the problems lies in appreciating the heterogeneous nature of the term 'population'; it covers 'good', 'bad' and just plain 'indifferent' attitudes, ethnic grouping, tribal grouping, educated, uneducated, wealthy, poor, literate, illiterate, religious moderates,

---

136   R. V. Jones, *Most Secret War: British Scientific Intelligence 1939-1945* (London, 1978).
137   Stephen Grey, *Operation Snakebite: The Explosive True Story of an Afghan Desert Siege* (Penguin, 2010).
138   The International Security Assistance Force is the NATO-led security mission in Afghanistan, established by the United Nations Security Council Resolution 1386 on 20 December 2001 and comprising representatives from over forty nations.

religious zealots, government supporters, government enemies, et al. It is, in essence, a conflict ecosystem where the actions of one actor have an impact on the others – for good or for bad – and where each actor is seeking some degree or level of advantage over other actors. Critically, the military, the diplomat and the aid worker are all actors in that system, and each can impact positively and negatively on each other as much as on those they are directly or indirectly seeking to influence. Given the inherent complexity that exists in such conflict ecosystems, and the imprecise nature of considering second- and third-order consequences, it is the role of influence that can, we believe, provide the means that allows understanding and coherence to take root. Is it realistic to place such an apparently nebulous construct at the centre of the commander's thinking? We would argue that, in counterinsurgency, the commander actually has no choice but to place such ideas at the core of his thinking. To do otherwise would be to ignore the population who are the ultimate determinants in who wins or who loses a counterinsurgency campaign. However, we are also of the view that whilst placing the population at the centre of thinking is easy enough to say, it is not enough to then pursue a largely kinetic approach or to think that killing increasing number of insurgents guarantees success. Whilst this last point is now widely understood, and by and large commanders – at all levels – seek to avoid its consequences (predominantly civilian casualties and collateral damage), what has not been applied effectively is the means by which that same population will be cajoled, persuaded, informed, reassured and convinced. Or, to put it another way, the choices made by the population ultimately determine success or failure. The same argument might also be applied to the insurgent. Reconciliation, for instance, is only possible when the insurgent has decided it is the more pragmatic choice given the prevailing circumstances. We should be in no doubt, though, that if we do not shape the prevailing circumstances the enemy most surely will. Influence operations are therefore at the very core of 'shaping', but their role is too often relegated to the fringes of operational thinking. In the current operating environment this is akin to placing form before substance and quantity before quality. Neither will do.

In planning the deployment, the MoD's lack of corporate understanding of this challenge soon became an issue. The Staff Colleges could provide no corpus of texts or body of military experts to provide appropriate advice. The initial expectation that support could be sourced from the MoD's Directorate of Targeting and Information Operations (DTIO) was dashed when it became clear they saw themselves as providing generic strategic messaging, whereas what the brigade needed was dynamic influence at the tactical level. Dr Dave Sloggett, a visiting researcher at the Defence Academy, was finally able to assist with the development of the brigade's thinking, as were members of the Academy's small (now defunct) Advanced Research and Assessment Group, although both met with ardent resistance from the DTIO, who, despite being able to offer no substantive support themselves, were reluctant to see others working 'in their area'. Sloggett identified very clearly why the DTIO and cross-governmental products were of very little use at a tactical level:

Any relatively simplistic analysis of the audiences that one is trying to reach in Iraq would quickly realise that it would not be right to have a simple set of messages for the Sunni and Shia communities. The same point applies in some areas of Afghanistan. Whilst there may well be some aspects of the messages to these community based audiences, which try to resonate with the communities as a whole, there will be elements that will also need to be highly localised. These must attempt to recognise specific local issues and grievances on the ground. Such ideas of balanced messages into communities at the regional and local level are clearly an element of a way forward. They must also be set in context with what one may refer to as strategic attempts to communicate to much wider audiences on the international stage as to the intent and objectives of the ongoing operations.

It was clear to both of us that not only were Whitehall messages a diluted and distant memory by the time they reach the tactical level, but that they have little relevance at ground level anyway. This is not because they are unimportant (indeed, we recognise that for domestic and coalition audiences they may be vital) but because they have little or no relevance – to either a soldier or a local – during, for example, a patrol one kilometre outside a forward operating base. The art therefore becomes how to ensure that the message is tuned to local events and local perceptions whilst retaining awareness of the operational context. There must be primacy given to local dynamics, and this can only be achieved by striking a delicate balance between consistency and flexibility to fit local circumstances. So, for instance, what 52 Brigade could not allow was two patrols, one in the Upper Gereshk Valley and one in the Upper Sangin Valley, to say something different about narcotics – saying in the one case 'don't worry, we won't eradicate because we don't want the insurgency to grow as a result', and then in the other 'we are going to eradicate'. There has to be a degree of consistency across the board whilst allowing for local variation – and this is a very challenging area in which to operate. 52 Brigade referred to this as applying 'dynamic influence'.

In essence it involved delegating to the lowest levels the ability to apply influence and to take account of local events, incidents and personalities. To enable a dynamic approach to influence, an organisational architecture was created at brigade, battalion and company level (NKETS – Non-Kinetic Effects Teams), for, just as we organise for the management of say ISTAR[139] processes, we must organise for those processes related to influence. Such granular understanding, we argue, allows COIN[140] situational awareness and thus understanding to prosper. Each compound, street, village, district or town contains a mass of ever-evolving contradictions, dichotomies, hopes and fears. Tapping into and turning this to

139   Intelligence, Surveillance, Target Acquisition and Reconnaissance.
140   Military abbreviation for counterinsurgency.

our advantage is, by necessity, local in nature and cannot be achieved by generic messaging from afar. An integral part of this is trust and we must empower our people, particularly the strategic corporals and privates, and our observation is that this empowerment in any meaningful manner is rarely forthcoming.

Influence operations have been described in various British military doctrine books as 'information operations plus targeted kinetic operations'. This is, we believe, too narrow a description. In fact it is inherently misleading. It seems to endorse a raiding approach to counterinsurgency. A raiding approach cedes the initiative and battleground of perception to the enemy. As a consequence, actions associated with a raiding approach tend to reinforce rather than counter the enemy's propaganda. Similarly, clearing without holding cedes advantages to an enemy that can quickly exploit such a limited approach. But with the experience of 52 Brigade's deployment, we believe that a broader definition is required. One of the earliest conclusions 52 Brigade reached was that the MoD was unhelpfully 'stove-piped' into not only information operations, but also psychological operations, media operations, consent-winning activities, and profile and posture activities. Yet all of these are actually subsets of what 52 Brigade wished to call 'influence'. They are all key enablers of what is effectively one and the same thing. This may be a symptom of information operations concepts not having evolved as quickly as our other concepts of operations. During the Cold War, responsibility for information operations could not be decentralised. Sensitivities about whether you were in the realms of propaganda, black ops and deception led to retaining control at the highest level because the consequences of getting it wrong were so severe. But in counterinsurgency, we argue that decentralisation is absolutely essential. Indeed, it should be taken to the point of discomfort. In their book The Starfish and the Spider,[141] Ori Brafman and Rod Beckstrom identify the requirement for hybrid organisations where hierarchy and central control sit comfortably with autonomy and delegation. More authority and responsibility has to be devolved to platoon and company commanders – they know the population, local life, its tempo and what influences it. They know how strong, or not, the insurgent may be in a specific area. They understand the context in which a local population views its circumstances, and can therefore empathise – or should at least try to, no matter how hard it is in reality. And taking responsibility for local influence includes living with the consequences. Brafman and Beckstrom also identified the requirement for identifying the 'decentralised sweet spot' where, dependent on the organisation being considered, the point along the centralised-decentralised continuum was just about right. To achieve this, individuals at the sweet spot of decentralisation need to be enabled, and to be given responsibility. For the Armed Forces to achieve this we need to formalise what is corporately understood by the term 'influence'.

---

141   Ori Brafman and Rod Beckstrom, *The Starfish and the Spider: The Unstoppable Power of Leaderless Organizations* (Portfolio, 2008).

Academics and theorists: shaping command thinking

Quite aside from the normal preparation that a commander routinely makes before taking men into battle, be it logistics, personnel, politics, legal, personal, et al., we found that in preparing for Andrew's Afghan deployment a surprising amount of time had to be devoted to the self-study of key texts, not just on the well-trodden path of counterinsurgency theory – which is relatively well understood within staff colleges – but on the considerably less-well-known military arenas of behavioural psychology, economics and, as this thinking broadened, some philosophy. This learning path lasted throughout the deployment, and indeed has continued post-deployment to inform our thinking on this subject. None share any time on military staff courses or in pre-deployment training packages. Yet it is here, amongst dusty textbooks, that we believe the key lies to formalising influence within organisations and to delegating it to as low a level as possible. 52 Brigade's command team carefully considered a number of conceptual ideas in their preparation (we might, perhaps, call this pre-deployment education), and much of that work was later incorporated into the operational design. In essence the command team sought to set aside conventional thinking – to unlearn – and to rethink the nature of the problems that the deployment would face. The starting point, perhaps unusually, was to conceptualise what motivated people and the first model that was considered was *Homo economicus* ('economic man').

Homo economicus is a caricature of what, for some time, economists generally assume people to be. The model suggests that humans are rational and broadly self-interested – although what constitutes or defines the notion of 'acting rationally' is debatable, What really attracted 52 Brigade's interest was that *Homo economicus* had proved hugely influential in public policy circles because it suggested that influencing human behaviour was actually rather simple. To fight crime, for example, politicians need only make punishments tougher: 'When the potential costs of crime outweigh the potential benefits, would-be criminals would calculate that the crime no longer advanced their interests and so they would not commit it.'[142] A derivative of *Homo economicus* is rational choice theory, which at its simplest level contended that a person reasons before taking rational action. As Matthew Taylor noted:

> For some time the model of *Homo economicus* seemed to serve well enough: offer people choice and they will act in their own interest and in so doing will make the system work better for everyone. It is not a complete view of human action but it was a useful shortcut, and it had become the prevailing view of most policymakers in the US and Britain.[143]

---

142   Dan Gardner, *Risk: The Science and Politics of Fear* (Virgin, 2009, p. 46).
143   See http://www.prospectmagazine.co.uk/tag/brain-and-behaviour-research/#

Would this help the brigade form a workable basis for its influence strategy? As 52 Brigade progressed its planning it seemed so – although it was keenly recognised that all these theorists had both supporters and detractors. Much later, and with the benefit of hindsight, we are not so sure: 'Over the past two decades, economists have been rediscovering human behaviour—real, irrational, confusing human behaviour, that is, rather than the predictable actions of the "economic man" who used to be pressed into service whenever modeling was to be done.'[144] But preparation needed to start somewhere, and in the absence of wider support it became a journey of discovery for Andrew and his command team. That journey next led to the work of Kahneman and Tversky, whom we have already mentioned in an earlier chapter. In particular, Andrew was attracted to their paper 'Judgment Under Uncertainty: Heuristics and Biases' which initiated a debate between economists, philosophers and psychologists alike and laid the foundation stones for the conceptual thinking that has subsequently developed into behavioural economics. The critical issue in their debate was the acceptance of human fallibility in making judgements and decisions. Heuristics are nothing more than common-sense 'rules of thumb', shortcuts or 'intuitive judgements' that are utilised by individuals to arrive at a choice – or a decision. Kahneman and Tversky's paper made the point 'that people rely on a limited number of heuristic principles which reduce the complex tasks of assessing probabilities and predicting values to simpler judgemental operations. In general these heuristics are quite useful, but sometimes they lead to severe and systematic errors.'[145] In other words, heuristics lead to bias and bias can be exploited in the manner in which choices are framed or presented. For example, consider the following problem: a bat and a ball cost £1.10. The bat costs £1 more than the ball. How much does the ball cost? Most people, at least for a few moments, decide incorrectly that the ball costs 10p. Kahneman and Tversky argue that the reason for this is that we use two systems for judgement and decision-making. One is intuitive and fast – the 'gut' – and often provides the right answer, but it can lead to errors (for the ball in this example actually costs 5p). The second system for judgement and decision-making is a slower and more deliberate set of thought processes – the 'head'. Whilst more likely to come up with the correct response they are also more demanding on our cognitive resources, hence the bias towards intuitive guesswork – and the wrong answer. Decisions of this nature – particularly in a conflict environment – also require continuous reassessment.

But what relevance is this to our view that understanding behaviour deserves greater resonance and involvement in the contemporary operating environment? Our contention is that in the realm of both strategic communication and information operations we have for several decades applied the equivalent of 'Economic man' to our information operations policy rather than genuinely applying psychology to the behavioural aspects and then drawing different conclusions as to

---

144   Tom Chatfield, 'The bestselling persuaders' (*Prospect*, 2009, issue 164).

145   'Judgment under Uncertainty: Heuristics and Biases' (1982, p. 3).

how our messaging and framing of choices can be applied. If we seek to influence behaviour in order to determine more appropriate choices then we will have to radically change both our approach and our methodologies. The recent book *Superfreakonomics*[146] states boldly that: 'People aren't "good" or "bad." People are people, and they respond to incentives. They can nearly always be manipulated — for good or ill— if only you find the right levers.' Influence is all about learning what the right levers are and how to apply them. For 52 Brigade that meant investigating further concepts – notably ideas about choice.

The final chapter of this book is written by Dr Lee Rowland, an expert on the science of influence. It is not our intention to pre-empt his words in this chapter, but five key ideas and concepts from the world of behavioural economics provide a particularly rich vein of research for considering how operations in Afghanistan might look if kinetics (bombs and bullets) were placed on the periphery and influence given primacy.

Prospect theory

Prospect Theory deals with risk and choice. Of particular interest in planning the deployment were findings about what economists call our 'discount rate' – the fact that we value owning something today much more than a larger quantity of the same thing in the future. This theory assumes that people are more motivated by losses than by gains and as a result will devote more energy to avoiding loss than to achieving gain. There are clear and obvious implications here for how we might communicate with a population that has suffered several decades of conflict. We would argue that the here and the now becomes critical with the 'discount rate' amplified by a perfectly understandable reluctance to consider 'next week' when getting through 'today' is the value attached to and the prism through which any messaging is viewed. An example of how Prospect Theory can be distorted in conflict is a tendency by both the military and development specialists to over-promise but to subsequently under-deliver. Hopes are raised and subsequently dashed, causing individuals to mistrust longer-term development plans with the consequence that they seek to avoid further loss rather than buy into overstated 'gains'. Another example are claims made on behalf of the benefits to be accrued if the Kajaki Dam in Helmand is made fully operational and power generation efficiency dramatically improved. For most Afghans the perceived benefits – or 'prospect' – of a more efficient dam are so far away that they cannot possibly consider it to be a factor that might alter their behaviour or seek to limit insurgent activity around the dam. The lesson here for influence is that it must relate to something that is tangible and apparent and not fuzzy and indistinct, regardless of how strategically important a project such as the Kajaki Dam really is. Influence must address context.

---

146   Steve Levitt and Stephen Dubner, *Superfreakonomics: Global Cooling, Patriotic Prostitutes and Why Suicide Bombers Should Buy Life Insurance* (Penguin, 2010).

Anchoring

Kahneman and Tversky's work demonstrated that individuals, when conflicted between 'gut' and 'head' can be easily manipulated by 'anchoring' their choice to a predetermined value. They demonstrated that people make estimates starting from an initial value which is adjusted to yield the final answer. The initial value can be suggested in the formulation of the problem or it could be the result of a partial computation. It was this phenomenon that they called 'anchoring'. It is best illustrated by quoting directly from their paper:

> In a demonstration of the anchoring effect, subjects were asked to esti-mate various quantities, stated in percentages (e.g., the percentage of African countries in the UN). For each question a starting value between 0 and 100 was determined by spinning a wheel of fortune in the subjects' presence. The subjects were instructed to indicate whether the given (ar-bitrary) starting value was too high or too low, and then to reach their estimate by moving upwards or downwards from that value. Different groups were given different starting values for each problem. These ar-bitrary values had a marked effect on the estimates. For example, the median estimates of the African countries in the UN were 25% and 45%, respectively, for groups which received 10% and 65% starting points.[147]

In other words, the arbitrarily chosen figure had a profound effect on the deci-sions that an individual subsequently made. We believe this principle offers con-siderable utility in how the military can influence behaviour in conflict, and that it may have profound implications for the way the military's actions can be shaped and influenced by an opponent. For example, does a leaflet drop depicting brutal images of the Taliban inflicting casualties on innocent civilians lead individuals to make a choice not to support the Taliban or does it, in fact, 'anchor' their belief that support to the Taliban is a better choice in order to avoid the outcome de-picted on the leaflet?

The wisdom of crowds

The wisdom of crowds considers how important the opinion of individuals in influencing the activity of a crowd can be. The theory holds that members of a crowd are too conscious of the opinions of others, indeed they may even begin to emulate each other and conform, rather than to think differently. Afghan society tends not to arrive at individual but at collective decision-making. Consider a roomful of people in Afghanistan, a *shura*, considering a number of difficult is-

---

147   'Judgment under Uncertainty: Heuristics and Biases' (1982, p. 14).

sues related to a key question: How do we reject the Taliban in our area? If they do it badly, the Taliban will come back and kill them. If they speak out too loudly as an individual, they run the risk of being murdered. So how do you influence those individuals? How does the wisdom of that crowd come through into that decision? How can we assist in the right choice being made? Sometimes in an Afghan context it can be that a single individual has so much charisma, weight and such power that everybody does what he wants anyway, and it is not so much collective decision-making as a polite way of endorsing his decision. So in this case, the influence effort is subtly different: How do you empower the individuals in that *shura* who have the right ideas but the least amount of authority?

The framing of choices

Kahneman and Tversky also conducted in-depth research into how choices can be 'framed'. In terms of applying influence this is of significant importance as it relates specifically to how messaging might be framed. An example is instructive. Two groups of subjects were told that the US was preparing for an outbreak of a disease that would kill 600 people. Two alternative programmes to combat it are then suggested: Which one should be chosen? Group One is offered Programme A, which, if adopted, will guarantee 200 people will be saved or Programme B which will offer a 1:3 probability that all 600 would be saved and a 2:3 probability that no one would be saved. They then asked the group which option they favoured. The second group of subjects were given the same preamble but offered these choices: Programme C would, if adopted, see 400 people perish and Programme D a 1:3 probability that no one will die and a 2:3 probability that 600 people will die. Again they were asked which of the two programmes – C or D – they would choose. Clearly the choice between A and B is exactly the same as the choices presented in C and D, and yet the subjects provided different answers depending upon the manner in which their choices were framed. At the heart of this is the fact that the questions in A and B are framed positively – lives saved – and in C and D the questions are framed as lives lost. What Kahneman and Tversky discovered is that most subjects preferred Programme A (save one-third for certain) to B (gamble on saving everyone) but when the framing of the question was changed they preferred Programme D (accept a two-thirds risk of killing everyone) to Programme C (certain that two-thirds would die). What Kahneman and Tversky showed in this and many other similar experiments was that although the apparent cost and benefits of the two scenarios did not change, individual choice did.

In Afghanistan we believe that the Coalition has struggled to frame the choices we are asking a war-torn nation to consider, and in a manner that would make sense culturally and that is sympathetic to the environment. To be sure, caution is required when taking experiments such as that above from laboratory conditions to the arena of real life but, as we will demonstrate later, we do sense that an influence-orientated approach might have paid substantial dividends had it taken into account how choices for Afghans (for instance) were presented. The simplest example would be the offer of democracy. Whilst well understood in liberal Western countries, it requires far greater explanation and framing in low-income, conflict-ridden countries where the decision to vote or who to vote for is largely irrelevant when compared with choices presented by the Taliban, or just by social circumstances, of life and death. We would contend that, to date in Afghanistan, we have paid little attention to how choices might be appropriately framed to change individual and collective behaviour. Many of the choices that are currently presented are too stark: poppy is bad/wheat is good; Taliban is evil/ISAF is good. The reality is that we have consistently failed to understand that what seems to us to be irrational behaviour is entirely rational to the individual facing tough choices.

Libertarian paternalism

This idea uses behavioural nudges to influence choices in positive ways, while still leaving individuals options. Cass Sunstein and Richard Thaler, in their book *Nudge*,[148] write: 'In the past three decades, psychologists and behavioural economists have learnt that people's choices can be dramatically affected by subtle features of social situations.' Findings of this kind suggest that even when people have freedom of choice they are influenced, or nudged, by the context in which their decisions are made. Much like the previous example, this idea considers the 'architecture of choice', altering the way choices are presented in order to 'nudge' people towards a beneficial action, without actually banning anything or creating incentives. Again it is worth asking whether there is room in a field of conflict for such high-minded ideas. Is it possible to introduce such concepts as 'nudging' the population of a village to resist Taliban influence? What would the 'choice' architecture look like? One early example of 'choice' architecture being utilised in Afghanistan was the National Solidarity Programme, which in 2004 sought to nudge thousands of village communities into managing their own reconstruction process. Critically, the programme sought to decentralise decision-making and to localise authority and responsibility. Block grants were allocated provided that three simple criteria were met: the village was required to elect its leadership by secret ballot, to hold communal meetings to design its reconstruction plan and to post its accounts in a public place. The rest was left to the community. Simple nudges were applied that were not explicit in determining specific outcomes or targets, and which in order to work were very local in nature.

---

148   Richard Thaler and Cass Sunstein *Nudge: Improving Decisions About Health, Wealth and Happiness* (Penguin, 2009).

Reflexivity

In a speech that he gave to an MIT conference in Washington DC in 1994,[149] George Soros, the legendary financier, explained that his theory of reflexivity, one that had guided him in both making and giving away money, had received very little serious consideration. He found it curious that the theory he has utilised to brilliant effect, and which he relied upon for his decision-making, had, by and large, been completely ignored. What intrigued Andrew when he stumbled upon Soros's book *The Alchemy of Finance*[150] (in which Soros expounds his theory in detail) was the notion that there is a tendency to assume that financial markets correct themselves as they tend towards equilibrium, when in fact there is almost continuous disequilibrium present. This was a light-bulb moment for Andrew. As anyone with any experience of counterinsurgency will know, such is the lack of information (and what information we do have is more often poorly managed and unexploited) that there is rarely a moment when true understanding of the environment is achieved. Soros goes on to explain how:

> The connection between the participants' thinking and the situation in which they participate can be broken up into two functional relationships. I call the participants' efforts to understand the situation the cognitive or passive function and the impact of their thinking on the real world the participating or active function. In the cognitive function, the participants' perceptions depend on the situation; in the participating function, the situation is influenced by the participants' perceptions. It can be seen that the two functions work in opposite directions: in the cognitive function the independent variable is the situation; in the participating function it is the participants' thinking.

Now this is difficult stuff – and it took a meeting with Soros for Andrew to understand it more fully – but it allowed, quoting Dr Matt Ridley's book *The Rational Optimist*, 'ideas to meet and mate, to have sex with each other'.[151] To that end the ideas were married with the ideas behind counterinsurgency existing within a 'conflict ecosystem' where cause and effect can only be understood if it is acknowledged that all of the participants in that conflict ecosystem understand that any action they take (positive, negative, rational and irrational) has an impact on all of the others (and the attendant second- and third-order consequences), and that the root of all this is behavioural. The means by which this could be simplified was to place the role of influence at the centre of that conflict ecosystem.

---

149   http://churchandstate.org.uk/2011/04/george-soros-theory-of-reflexivity-mit-speech/

150   George Soros, *The Alchemy of Finance: Reading the Mind of the Market* (John Wiley & Sons, new edition 2003).

151   Matt Ridley, *The Rational Optimist* (Fourth Estate, 2010)

Economics

In applying influence effectively to behavioural conflict there is little point in seeking to apply it solely to fixing security or a lessening of violence. Any political settlement – of the sort we seek in Afghanistan – requires governance (alongside its bedfellow of rule of law), security and economic development to be brought along in tandem, not sequentially. In his book *The Bottom Billion*,[152] Paul Collier outlines the four traps that ensure divergence and prevent development for the billion bottom people of the world's population: conflict, natural resources, land-locked countries and bad governance. He argues that the presence of one or more of those traps features in every country caught in the bottom billion. Afghanistan features all four traps. Conflict causes poverty, and low income contributes to tension. Low growth means high unemployment and thus plenty of angry young men ready to fight. Conflict destroys infrastructure and scares away investors, further reducing opportunity.

The discovery of untapped mineral wealth in Afghanistan (a US Geological Survey reported that Afghanistan is home to $1 trillion of mineral wealth) should provide a little comfort. However, such is the scale of devastation after so many years of conflict that none of it is today capable of being commercially exploited for the benefit of the country. And even if it was, Collier's work highlights that it is rare for natural resource wealth to come back to the people because of the consequence of poor security, formidable logistical problems and ruling elites plundering resources with impunity.

The issue of being landlocked poses a real problem for social development and it can be largely out of the control of the country itself. If your neighbours do not like you, there is no way you can export. Whilst Switzerland can export via Italy or Germany – neither presents a problem – Uganda must work with Kenya, Sudan, Somalia, Rwanda, Congo and Tanzania. For Afghanistan the choice is equally as troublesome, either Iran or Pakistan – the northern 'Stans' are ruled out for their own remoteness – and without dependable ways to export, landlocked countries are unable to participate in the global economy. In this instance the application of soft power and influence – on a regional basis – is the only means of realising the value of mineral wealth or seeking out food export markets. Mangetout being packed, frozen, flown out and arriving in supermarkets in the UK from Kenya is viable. Seeking to achieve the same in Afghanistan is not, which is why its food markets will be local (in a regional sense), provided it can wield the right levels of influence to make this so.

Finally, bad governance: three-quarters of the bottom billion live in countries that either are failing, or recently were failed states. Most current conflicts are occurring in that bottom billion. The recent Afghan election in the autumn of 2010 has damagingly illustrated the limitations of Afghan governance and capacity. Col-

---

152   Paul Collier, *The Bottom Billion: Why the Poorest Countries are Failing and What can be Done about it* (Oxford University Press, 2007).

lier also provides a convincing analysis of how low-income countries struggle to absorb democracy and how it is only in middle-income countries that democracy can take root. Afghanistan is set to remain low-income for many years ahead.

Such considerations, and we accept that there are many more, should, we believe, form part of the pre-deployment educational process for both current and future operations. Many of 52 Brigade's soldiers had experience of Iraq and, whilst there were some areas of read-across, there could have been a real danger that the two arenas would be conflated in thinking. Indeed, if we accept Collier's argument then we may conclude that Iraq is not a good model for the insurgency in Afghanistan. Iraq, we might argue, is predisposed to succeed; conceptually Afghanistan is predisposed to failure. Yet with different choices Afghanistan could choose to develop its infrastructure, to feed its own population and perhaps to grow as an economy. Conventional wisdom suggests that this is impossible whilst the insurgency continues, but experience suggests you cannot sustain a COIN campaign when it is being fought from the bottom up. A political settlement has to meet it from the top down at some point or the bar that can measure success is set too low.

Why is all of this relevant to the British military presence in Afghanistan, and to future conflicts? We argue that such understanding is absolutely seminal to how we might conduct influence operations in an era of hybrid conflict. All of the examples above seek to influence behaviour and the choices that are made, but within the context that they find themselves in, not the circumstances that we wish might prevail. But we also recognise that such ideas do not exist in a vacuum and that they must be set in the relevant social, cultural and economic environment. This is vital to success – applying these ideas through the prism of Western liberal democracy will end in failure, and a commander's appreciation needs to extend into other areas of expertise. In the case of Afghanistan, 52 Brigade's command realised that grasping some of the straightforward economic considerations for a country listed as 181 out of 182 in the United Nations Human Development Index would also affect the success of the influence mission.

International Security Assistance Force HQ – KABUL 2011

In Spring 2011, Steve was asked to visit the Communications Directorate in ISAF headquarters in Kabul. Just a few miles from the city's heavily fortified airport, ISAF HQ is a surprisingly large compound of some fifty assorted buildings, and at their centre lay the offices of ISAF Commander General David Petraeus (formally known as COMISAF and informally as P4 – Petraeus 4 Star). The whole complex is ringed by 10-metre-high walls, the inner perimeter guarded by Macedonian troops and the 'green zone' around it ringed by Afghan army and police checkpoints. Within the HQ, and beneath the General's elevated level, are a series of separate divisions: Stability (headed by a German General), Operations (commanded by a US General), Resources (the preserve of a Polish General), Intelligence (headed by a US General), Communications (commanded by a US Navy Admiral), Re-integration (headed by a UK General) and Transparency (headed by a US General). Between them, and under the guidance of COMISAF, resides the conduct of operations across the country and, with the various Afghan ministries, the future of the country. The Communications Directorate (in NATO terminology DCOS COMM) includes not just the NATO spokesman and media and public affairs officers but, crucially, the Directorate of Influence and Outreach, commanded by a British Brigadier. Here a small NATO staff determine the policy for information operations, traditional Afghan communications and the broader issue of influence.

In a series of meetings, Steve proposed that ISAF move to a concerted behavioural approach, one that would be initiated across the country. Four specific examples were provided. First, the dreadful retention figures of the Afghan National Security Forces (ANSF) needed to be addressed. Whilst recruiting has been largely successful, the retention rates have caused considerable concern. Indeed, no lesser figure than US Army Lieutenant General William Caldwell observed that 'based on current attrition rates, to expand the security forces by 56,000 [ISAF] will need to recruit 133,000 personnel'.[153] What is perhaps most surprising is that ISAF has no concrete idea why so many are leaving the service. In the West we might consider a whole host of reasons for leaving a job. Finding a better-paid one is an obvious reason, but in the case of Afghanistan this does not seem intuitively to be the case. The World Bank estimates the average Afghan salary to be in the region of $800 per annum. The most junior rank of Afghan National Police (2nd Patrolman) earns approximately $120 per month, whilst a senior NCO earns around twice that. For those joining the Afghan Gendarmerie (ANCOP), the figure for service in a dangerous district is $350 per month, whilst the most senior figures in the Afghan National Army can expect nearly $8,000 per year. These figures are significantly in excess of most Afghans' pay. So if it is not pay, why do people leave? There are any one of a hundred possibilities, but the truth is that ISAF simply does not know, and until it definitively understands the problem, the solution is likely to evade it as well. The proposal, then, was simple. Undertake a thorough and systematic analysis of why men leave the ANSF (not a survey but a series of qualitative and quantitative interviews and focus meetings with the police, their families and the communities in which they live). With this knowledge, a behavioural intervention campaign can be crafted that will address the issues over a period of perhaps 18 to 24 months.

A second proposal was to divert young males of fighting age away from the attractions of the insurgency to alternative livelihoods, in particular to agriculture. Superficially this may not seem a particularly attractive alternative. The insurgency may well appear incredibly glamorous for young and uneducated men whose far horizons extend no further than the next valley or mountain range.

---

153   'Towards Transition' *Defence Management Journal*, issue 51.

But a deeper inspection of Afghan culture will reveal the honour of providing for one's family; countless Afghan fables and stories refer to the obligations of young men to marry, to procreate and to provide. Fighting an insurgency would appear to seriously limit all three options. The issue is: How do you make the alternative livelihoods more attractive such that young men of fighting age will substantially alter their behaviour? Once again ISAF has a serious understanding deficit. We guess that many young men are attracted by the glamour of the fight, many more dissatisfied by their own opportunities and many more still who simply do not understand the nature of the fight and their role within it. This is the ideal project for a deeply rooted behavioural study, and with the huge amounts of money being invested in the country by Western Provincial Reconstruction Teams there are increasing opportunities for young men to embrace. ISAF simply has to find the leverage.

Third, there are yet more; only 3 per cent of the Afghan army is southern Pashto. It would be disastrous for Afghanistan's future if the army became or was perceived to be one of northern ethnic groups only. Why do southern Pahsto feel disinclined to join? What motivations can be applied to them to change that behaviour? Finally, Afghanistan is the world's largest heroin exporter. The drugs trade, for which the poppy farmers receive comparatively little for their hard work, appears ripe for further analysis. Indeed ISAF has huge resources looking at the trade, the key players, the logistics, in fact almost every element of the organisation's infrastructure, and yet despite all this knowledge the problem persists. Knowledge is not necessarily power. The hard reality of the trade is that ISAF could very probably eradicate the product from the air but it could not fill the income void that would be left behind. A humanitarian crisis on top of Afghanistan's myriad other problems would not advance ISAF's course, and so it is relegated to attending only to the periphery, the symptoms of the problem, rather than its cause. But this is a hugely complex human system with many interlinked and inter-related parts. Is it really understood? Can NATO declare that it understands what motivates behaviours and can it use that knowledge to its advantage? We fear the answer to both is 'no'.

At the time of writing it is unclear if all or indeed any of these ideas will be taken up by ISAF. To run pilots for each would cost less, in total, than $2 million, a mere drop in the ocean in comparison to the total aid budget to the country. Unfortunately such ideas are still seen as being revolutionary and need a sponsor prepared to take risk and invest in alternative means of winning conflicts. Our fear is that both the opponents of today and those of tomorrow will not be so risk-averse.

5
The challenge of communication

> There is no more complete way to misunderstand a foreign civilisation than to see it in terms of one's own civilisation.
>
> Paul Bohannan[154]

In Chapter 2 we considered the effect of technology on contemporary societies and suggested that whilst it was clearly interesting (perhaps even a bit scary) it was not as important as the behaviours that it triggered, either deliberately or, more subtly, how it led to an undercurrent of opinion. In this chapter we want to think a little bit more about the manner in which governments and militaries communicate with groups. How 'we' inform 'them' (and 'we' need to ask: Who is 'them'?) of what 'we' are doing, or are about to do, and how 'we' seek to find understanding and agreement with those groups. But before we do, let's start with a couple of old, but nonetheless extremely entertaining, chestnuts.

An urban legend exists on the Internet that concerns the American car manufacturer Chevrolet. In the 1960s Chevrolet developed a model that it named the Nova. It was extremely popular and sold widely in the United States. Yet the urban legend has us believe that the car never sold in the Spanish-speaking world – the reason, supposedly, was because Nova in Spanish sounds just like *no va*, the term for 'does not go'. Ergo the 'Chevrolet Does not Go' model did not sell well in South America. All very entertaining but, sadly, untrue because the urban myth is just that – a myth. Indeed, the myth's storytellers display a key error in comprehension, for they presume that English words and phrases when translated *literally* carry the same meaning. Yet the Nova / *no va* story does not work, for whilst cars may well 'go' in the English language they do not do so in Spanish. Instead they may *functionar* ('function'), *marcher* ('march') or *caminar* ('walk') – terms that in English, when applied to a car, sound faintly ridiculous.

There are other, factual, examples which make the case equally well. The German aircraft manufacturer Grob was bemused at its failure to penetrate the Russian market in the 1990s, even when it was explained to them that the word *grob* is Russian for 'coffin'. The US *Parameters* journal tells the tale of 'a surprise multinational nuclear weapons inspection on a suspected nuclear facility in Iraq was fouled up because Americans counted the ground floor as the first floor whilst

---

154   Paul Bohannan, *Social Anthropology* (Holt, Rinehart & Winston, 1963).

Brits counted the first floor as the one above the ground floor'.[155] Words, their meaning and their context are clearly important.

Two further illustrative examples are worthy of consideration. The first is the syntax in which the post-9/11 'War on Terror' has been defined. A casual search on Google for the term 'Roman Catholic Terrorist' reveals 5,090 hits,[156] a surprisingly small number for the wholly accurate description of the religious beliefs of the Provisional IRA, an Irish Catholic terrorist organisation that fought a 30-year campaign against the British Army's 'occupation' of Northern Ireland. Yet a Google search for 'Islamic Terrorist' – a comparatively new idea that even for the most assiduous student of history will probably only date back to early 1990s – reveals over 29 million entries. Twenty-nine million? Wow!

The second example is the absence of a directly equivalent word for the English noun *reconciliation* – quite a key word – in the Afghan Pashto language. Interpreters have to make a choice from different words to establish context; that choice, of course, being based entirely on their own education and understanding. One of the words they may chose is 'surrender', which would be wholly unsuitable to both sides. British Ambassador to Kabul Sherard Cowper-Coles recalls a briefing note given to the Governor of Kandahar province in 2010. The first page of the note included a bullet point, in English, suggesting that the Governor should 'develop a plan for Kandahar', whereas in Pashto it read 'a development plan for Kandahar'. As Cowper-Coles noted, this was a 'rather different concept'.[157] As all the examples illustrate, failing to understand the importance of the right words in context for a particular situation can, in a benign environment, be embarrassing or just plain confusing. In less benign environments, and particularly in conflicts, such confusion can be dangerous and we believe 'our' people need to have a much more detailed understanding of why. We have therefore chosen to give this concept a term – we have called it the 'asymmetry of communication'.

One might perhaps be forgiven for believing that communication is easy. After all each and every one of us communicates in one way, shape or form, every day of our lives, and we largely achieve our intended objectives. Yet on those occasions when the communication process fails the consequences can be dramatic. Take, for example, the case of the next-door neighbours discussing one of Britain's most watched TV programmes, *Britain's Got Talent*. The programme searches out talented (or otherwise) members of the public and invites them to perform on TV. Singers vie with magicians, jugglers with dancers. Over the last few years it has become one of Britain's most popular Saturday night TV shows. So, the neighbours are discussing the previous night's show when one neighbour tells his wife that a particular act had only got through to the next stage of the competition because of the 'bored housewives' vote. But this was not what one of the neighbours heard. Instead he heard not 'bored' but 'bald' and, believing it was a reference to

---

155   Richard Halloran, 'Strategic Communication' (*Parameters*, Autumn 2007, pp. 4–14).
156   Google search conducted 10 June 2011 on search term "roman catholic terrorist".
157   Sherard Cowper-Coles, *Cables from Kabul* (Harper Press, 2011, p. 270).

his mother (who suffered with female hair loss), promptly assaulted the neighbour. Sadly, the story is absolutely true.

Of course mis-hearing a word is one thing, misunderstanding a word quite another. In tomorrow's conflicts, understanding our enemy, and understanding the community from which that enemy is drawn, will be vital. This is not new; since the days of the Empire, on which it was said the sun never set, the British Army has prided itself on understanding its environment – indeed, it has always been one of its greatest strengths. And yet, in the last conflicts of the twentieth century and the first ones of the twenty-first century, the Army has, seemingly, stumbled. The conflicts of the Former Republic of Yugoslavia, and the attendant massacres and atrocities, were shocking and, to an average soldier unversed in Balkan history, utterly inexplicable. How could one neighbour, who seemingly has peacefully coexisted with another for decades, suddenly turn upon the other? The same problems confronted those who witnessed the massacres in Rwanda, the Civil War in Sierra Leone, and the disintegration of Iraq after the invasion of 2003. As we have explained in previous chapters, the truth is that coalition forces will probably never really understand the human dynamics of Iraq and, sadly, we feel that is also the case in Afghanistan. Indeed, former ISAF Commander General Stanley McChrystal, who so kindly wrote the Foreword to this book, said just this in an October 2011 speech to the US Council on Foreign Relations: 'After ten years in Afghanistan, the US still lacks the knowledge to bring the conflict to a successful end. We didn't know enough and we still don't know enough.'

In the absence of a mechanism with which to embrace complexity, the West, we worry, has retreated to its 'home base' – exporting values and beliefs that it does understand to environments that it does not in the hope that clarity will ensue. Never was this more clearly visible than in the Coalition's attempts to communicate its mission in Iraq, and again in Afghanistan, to the outside world. Whilst in the UK the 'new' Labour party proved itself adept at political communication, its government appeared utterly unable to convince the British public of the need for the Iraq war, of its justness and of its legality, and even today in Afghanistan 'we' seem to struggle to explain, cogently, to 'our' soldiers and 'our' population what it is 'we' are doing there, let alone to the Afghans themselves. One of Steve's young officers, recently back from a six-month tour in Helmand, noted that whenever he asked an Afghan why he thought British soldiers were in the country, he would receive completely different answers. Some were bizarre: we were there for the organic minerals for mobile phone production, one Afghan elder was convinced; many more had no idea we were not Americans and could offer no explicable reason for our presence. When engaged in discussion there was general bewilderment at the turn of events that had led to our presence. Tall buildings in New York ('Where is New York – is it in the next valley?') had fallen down. Really? 'Well that happens all the time here because of shoddy building or earthquakes – what was the big deal?' Cynical? Maybe, but the observations are anchored in science. The November 2010 'Afghan Transition: Missing Variables

Survey', conducted by ICOS[158] asked 1,500 men why foreign forces were in Afghanistan: 31 per cent believed the answer was to make violence and destruction on Afghans; 25 per cent believed it was to help Afghans; and 17 per cent believed it was in their (the foreigners') own defence. When asked about 9/11, 92 per cent had never heard of it. Perhaps 'we' should not be surprised at this. The *CIA World Factbook* states that 42 per cent of the Afghan population are aged under fourteen and that the median age is eighteen.[159] Why would events of ten years earlier resonate with such people, who struggle daily to survive the present? What relevance has the past to them?

Part of the problem, we believe, has been an almost intuitive belief on the part of the West that the process of communication will be successful; that what is communicated will always be heard, without interference, and it will be understood. Except that we already know from the 'bald housewife' story that this is probably a step too far. All of our collective experience of conflict tells us this is wrong. The process of communication is actually far more complex than people believe. It is our view that on military operations communication success should actually be considered the exception, not the rule, and for it to have any chance of success, we think practitioners must understand the very basic principles of communication. To do that, we apologise, but we need to get a bit technical.

In the 1950s a model of communication was developed which latterly became known as the 'message influence model'. This model was based upon some work undertaken by two academics, Claude Shannon and Warren Weaver. In 1949 they published their *Mathematical Theory of Communication*,[160] which at its inception was designed to examine interference in telephone communication. It has subsequently – and perhaps erroneously (because it was never particularly bothered by the syntax of communication) – been used as a post-9/11 model for the failure of Western-led communication with global audiences. So, what does it look like and why is it relevant to us?

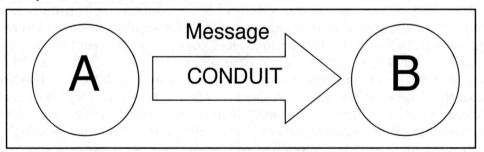

Figure 5.1 The message-influence model of communication. Adapted from Shannon & Weaver's 1949 study *The Mathematical Theory of Communication*.

---

158   International Council on Security and Development: see http://www.icosgroup.net/2010/report/afghanistan-transition-missing-variables/

159   https://www.cia.gov/library/publications/the-world-factbook/

160   Claude Shannon and Warren Weaver, *The Mathematical Theory of Communication* (University of Illinois Press, 1998).

For communication between two parties the model is represented quite simply as in Figure 5.1.

The source, (A), which has ideas, intentions and information, communicates them as a message, which is transmitted via a channel to a receiver – the audience, (B). The inferred purpose of the process is to influence the receiver (B) to understand the message in the same way as the source (A) transmits it and to subsequently behave in a specific manner. The problem with this model is that it is highly simplistic and assumes, first, that there is no outside interference to the message, and second, that the audience is passive, i.e. the audience applies no contextualisation to the message and accepts it at face value. A key underlying assumption of this model is that the process of communicating the message to the audience will be successful unless there is some interference in the transmission process, i.e. the message is presumed to be right; it is only the communication method, or the skill of the communicator, (A), that might interfere with its effectiveness.

Although simple enough to understand, the model has a number of flaws. First and foremost is that it simply does not reflect reality. Audiences do not sit passively and receive messages; instead they contextualise them according to a host of external factors. For example, in the case of Iraq, if we presume (A) was the US and (B) the Iraqi people, the message of liberation and democracy may be heavily contextualised by elements of (B) in the light of revelations of torture by (A) at Abu Ghraib prison. Second, the model suggests that communication only occurs when a message is actually being transmitted, whereas actions and deeds (which are not modelled) send messages just as effectively as words – actions, as every schoolboy learns, speak louder than words. Third, the message presumes success – a potentially perilous supposition. This is perhaps best illustrated by an article from the *Washington Post* which records the attempts of US soldiers to combat stone-throwing youths in Iraq. The article reported that Coalition forces in Sadr City, Baghdad, were facing a daily barrage of rocks thrown by young children. The problem for the Coalition was how to stop it. Patently violence, or even the threat of violence, against small children, was not an option, yet the stone throwing needed to end. An army psychological operations team believed that they had an answer and crafted a series of leaflets which demanded that the children stop throwing stones. Yet the leaflet campaign failed. Why? In this example the messages to stop were interpreted by the children not as a warning but as a sign of their success against the Coalition. The message source was self-evidently 'the enemy'. The communications channel (the leaflets) did not resonate with the young children who either could not read or were not minded to read 'adult' leaflets. Indeed, in this example, only the intended audience for the message was correctly identified by the US psychological operations team. Since the messages were received by the children without interference, the presumption, using the message influence model, was that the plan would be successful; clearly a more sophisticated model is needed.

The Arizona State University based Consortium for Strategic Communication (CSC) was established to examine just this kind of 'stuff', and they too have concluded that this overtly simple model has formed the backbone of post-9/11 US (and in our view, British) communication. CSC's Professor Steve Corman presents a series of contemporary arguments to support this assertion. For example, he notes the number of references to 'messaging' made by representatives of the Bush Administration post-9/11 and notes a 2004 RAND report[161] that comments that the failure of US communication strategy is a failure of message delivery and that:

> It is important to communicate the rationale motivating these [foreign] policies. In these instances U.S. policies reflected and furthered the values of democracy, tolerance, the rule of law and pluralism. The over arching message public diplomacy should convey is that the U.S. ... tries to further these values regardless of religion, ethnicity ... highlighting the instances in which the U.S. has benefited Muslim populations by acting on these values may make this point more salient.[162]

The CSC believes that this is a recipe for failure. The message influence model assumes, it is argued, that communication transfers meaning from person to person and that the message sent is the message received. Yet, as the report notes, a meaning cannot simply be transferred. Audiences create meanings from messages based on factors, Corman suggests, such as: 'Autobiography, history, culture, local context, language systems, power relations and immediate personal needs. We should assume that meanings listeners create in their minds will probably not be identical to those intended by the receiver.'[163]

An April 2006 video of the Iraqi insurgent leader Abu Zarqawi is an example of this over-simplistic approach to communication. The video, released by the insurgents, showed Zarqawi firing a machine gun in the Iraqi desert. However, a month later US forces found the complete and unedited video, in which Zarqawi is shown repeatedly jamming the machine gun and walking off in Adidas training shoes. In the ensuing press conference, organised by the US, Major General Rick Lynch sought to ridicule Zarqawi, pointing out his incompetence with a weapon and that 'real' soldiers did not wear training shoes to battle. The General did his best to reinforce this point, repeating again and again the accusations of incompetence – repetition being a key theme in the message influence model. Yet

---

161   Charles Wolf, Jr. and Brian Rosen, 'Public Diplomacy: How to Think About and Improve It' (RAND, 2004).

162   Steven R. Corman, Angela Trethewey and Bud Goodall, *A 21st Century Model for Communication in the Global War of Ideas: From Simplistic Influence to Pragmatic Complexity* (Consortium for Strategic Communication, Arizona State University, Report #0701, 3 April 2007).

163   Ibid.

this was not what the intended key audience – the Arab media – took with them from the conference. They contextualised it differently and told their viewers that this was simply US propaganda – after all, if he was that incompetent, why had the US not yet caught him?

As countless academic studies have shown, messages are heavily contextualised by outside events. So it seems 'we' might need a new model on which to base 'our' communication. One possible solution is something called the 'Pragmatic Complexity Model', which draws on research undertaken by Niklas Luhmann. Luhmann believed that communication was not the simple transmission of messages between two minds but rather a complex system between sender and receiver. In any communication between party (A) and party (B) Luhmann believes that 'The success of A's behaviour depends not only on external conditions but on what B thinks and does. And what B thinks and does is influenced by A's behaviour as well as B's expectations, interpretations and attributions with respect to A.' [164]

This model presumes that in any communication the success of (A)'s message depends not only on the message alone but upon what (B) thinks and does. And what (B) thinks and does is influenced by (A)'s behaviour and (B)'s expectations, interpretations and attributions with respect to (A). The model assumes that messages are always interpreted within a larger and ongoing communication system and that (A) and (B) are therefore locked into a relationship of simultaneous and mutual interdependence. This can be represented by Figure 5.2.

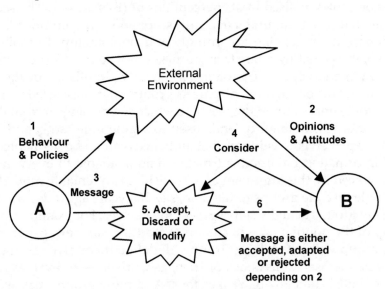

Figure 5.2 Author's representation of the pragmatic-complexity model of communication.

164   Niklas Luhmann, *Social Systems* (Stanford University Press, 1995).

Here the success of (A)'s messages are dependent upon the wider external environment and, in particular, on (B)'s perception of (A)'s role in that environment. It is against that role that (A)'s messages are processed; they may be dismissed out of hand or they may be accepted, but in a contextualised manner. This model, which we think presents a much more realistic interpretation of society, suggests that there is no independent audience (B) waiting to be impacted by (A). Instead, both parties are locked into a relationship of interdependence.

The following real-world example illustrates the point well. In April 2003 the UK Maritime Component Commander in Iraq, Admiral David Snelson, bemoaned the fact that the Arab media would not report the reopening of the Umm Qasr to Basra railway after the repair of the line in April 2003 by UK military engineers. Despite widespread Western media coverage the Arab media refused to attend the media facility. At the Commander's request their refusal to attend was analysed. It was found that the Arab media did not regard the repair of one rail line as newsworthy, when compared to the collateral damage and loss of Iraqi lives that the wider invasion had wrought. This example clearly illustrates that (A)'s message (which was 'the Coalition are rebuilding Iraq') was contextualised by the recipient (and intended conduit) against the backdrop of the wider invasion, and subsequently discarded.

Unfortunately, this model raises at least three further issues of complexity. The first is that the model presumes that (B) is passive. However, in reality (B) may itself be engaged in attempting to influence (A). Therefore (A)'s messages may themselves be contextualised by its perceptions of (B)'s actions. The second consideration is that if (A) can understand (B)'s opinions and attitudes in advance, (A) can prepare its messaging accordingly and thus attempt to mollify the effect of step 5, thus creating a far stronger message. The third issue is identifying exactly who (A) and (B) are. The names are overly simplistic, for they actually encompass many different, often disparate, groups, and these groups may themselves have some impact upon the message which may change it from that envisaged at sending. This ambiguity lends itself to segmenting target audiences at a time when the perceived wisdom is that audiences cannot be segmented because the global information environment makes data available to everyone. We are just not convinced by this argument and, whilst it is undeniably more difficult to message single discrete groups today than, say 100 years ago, it is not impossible because many groups actually self-segment themselves. For example, in the UK a large group of the population will choose to read the *Sun* newspaper every day, a different group will not. A large group will define themselves as English, others will define themselves as Scots, or Irish, as Christians, or even as Arsenal or Manchester United, Red Sox or Yankee fans. And these groups may well exhibit certain social characteristics, be it education, class, status or income. In conflict these are points of leverage, which can be exploited to 'our' advantage – but only if 'we' know how.

The communication moment

There is also an important fourth complexity when communicating, and that is time. Communication is highly time and condition sensitive. Messages that work one week may not work the next. For example, in late 2008 the West might have collectively criticised the Iranian theocracy for its apparent universal stand on the Iranian nuclear development process. And yet by July 2009 such blanket messages would have been inappropriate as it became clear that the theocracy was actually split between moderate and hard-line elements and the West would have needed to adjust its rhetoric, possibly even supporting some elements of the theocracy against others. All of this is summarised in Figure 5.3, which seeks to illustrate what we have chosen to refer to as the 'communication moment' and to address the shortcomings of other models.

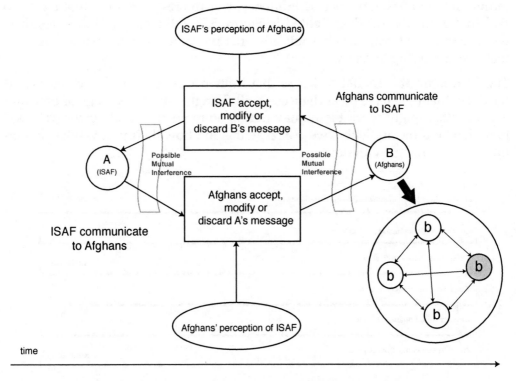

Figure 5.3 Author's representation of the 'Communications Moment'.

The model is a refinement of the Pragmatic Complexity Model shown in Figure 5.2. It shows a source (let's say this is ISAF headquarters in Kabul) and an audience (let's say these are Afghans). In the model we can see that ISAF (A) is messaging the Afghans (B). That message might be: 'Insurgent's destroy, ISAF and the Afghan government build.' But at the same time that (A) is talking to (B), the model illustrates that the Afghans are messaging ISAF. This messaging could be undertaken in a variety of ways – they may decide not to vote in the elections or to provide shelter to IED makers or express at village *shuras* that they are dissatisfied with the level of corruption and bribery that they experience in their everyday lives. The point is this. The messages ISAF (A) send are heavily contextualised by the audience and they may even be dismissed completely on the basis of what the audience experiences or sees: 'Afghan police are there to look after the community' will not resonate well with Afghans who have had bad experiences of the Afghan police.

Where this model does become more complex is in its appreciation of the audience (B). One of the mistakes that we have noted earlier is that Western militaries tend to think of a single homogenous group but in reality the audience is in fact lots and lots of very diverse groups – lots of (B)s, not one, single (B). And within that audience there will be, almost certainly, a group or perhaps even an individual who has very specific influence over the rest. We think that trying to find that particular (B) (highlighted in Figure 5.3) will be key in future conflicts because they are far more believable and credible than 'us' to the wider audience that 'we' are trying to reach.

The final point this model makes is that influence is temporal – messages and the effect that they have on audiences – will change with the passage of time and events. What might work today may not do so tomorrow, and again 'we' need to understand the audiences we are targeting and how their motivations and attitudes may change with time.

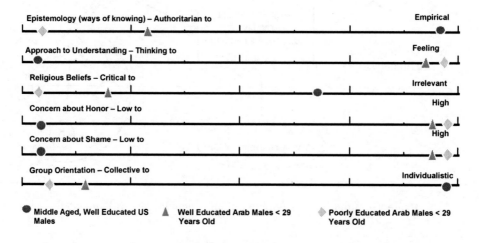

Figure 5.4 Cognitive attributes of Arab males. From a study by Christine McNulty, Applied Futures USA. Reproduced by kind permission.

A study undertaken in the US also helps the debate. The cognitive attributes of two groups of Arab males were mapped (Figure 5.4 is but a tiny subset of the much larger work presented to a NATO Conference by Christine MacNulty of

Applied Futures[165]) and compared against the cognitive attributes of educated, middle-aged Americans. Although only a subset of the research, the chart is illuminating, for it shows that at no point do the cognitive attributes of poorly educated Arab males – whom for convenience we may choose to refer to as the Arab street – match the attributes of educated Americans – whom for convenience we might refer to as policy-makers.

Thus, the study suggests, when policy-makers articulate what they consider to be a reasoned policy for a particular action, their audiences are likely to be swayed more by feeling and emotion than the 'irrefutable' reasoning that 'we' in the West might find so compelling. This in no way implies that Western culture is superior to that of Arab or Muslim culture; instead it recognises the concept of 'bounded rationality', irrespective of education. That is, an individual's actions are driven by a desire to rationalise and make logical decisions but the model recognises that individuals do not necessarily have all the necessary information to make a decision and that decision-making may very often be limited by time. Or, in other words, decisions may not be fully thought through and can be conceived as rational only within limits – those limits may be based upon time but just as equally upon cultural understanding.

For example, former SAS commander Brigadier Ed Butler noted during his command of British Forces in Afghanistan in 2006 that: 'There were days you thought you had it [understanding of Afghans] but then they, the Afghan people, the Taliban, President Karzai, would do something completely unpredictable and you wondered if you did know them at all.'[166] What might seem to Coalition forces as profoundly irrational behaviour may actually be entirely rational to an indigenous population. We touched on this in the opening chapter when we considered the actions of British military personnel who had risked their lives for their friends and colleagues. Such determinations are normally made with the benefit of hindsight. What it highlights is that a granular understanding of audiences is extremely important because it should directly affect the manner in which we communicate our message. For example, it is clear that in societies where there is no history or understanding of democracy, a message suggesting that terrorism is counter to democracy is unlikely to resonate. But, using the model above it can been seen that honour is of great importance, therefore a subtle readjustment of the message, to read that terrorism is dishonourable, may have more cognitive effect. We will use this word again, so, to be clear, by cognitive we mean the instinctive and intuitive thought processes of a particular individual or indeed group of similar individuals.

A further example, which we have already seen in outline, illustrates this point. Key UK MoD Iraqi information strategy messages included reference to the key trinity of democracy, liberation and freedom. Yet as a British Embassy telegram

---

165 'Using Strategic Communication and Public Diplomacy for Deterrence', NATO Centre of Excellence, Rome, 2008.

166 Interview with Steve Tatham, 10 December 2009.

from Damascus noted: 'Syrians say that the Iraqi people do not want to be liberated by foreign soldiers.'[167] Reviewing these messages after the war, a US-based *imam* noted that: 'the US should explain that they are the followers of Jesus Christ and that they are the Sons of Abraham, just like all Muslims. They should say that the US came to the Holy Land, from where Abraham came, to rid the world of Lucifer – Saddam Hussein.'[168]

Can you imagine Steve, as the Naval spokesman in Iraq, saying to his admiral that he wanted to talk not about freedom and liberation at the next press conference but instead about the devil and the Abrahamic tradition? Of course not – it would be ridiculous to do so, and in any case that was not what the *imam* was saying. He was simply trying to remind 'us' that 'our' messages have been developed and situated within a Western cognitive dimension; for them to work with the Arab audiences for whom they were intended they needed to be situated within a different cognitive dimension, one that understood the intended audience. We both worry that for all the sophistication of Western armed forces, this may be a step too far. Let's take an example to illustrate why such a big leap of faith is going to be needed. In 2008, academics at Harvard University mapped the Iranian blogosphere, determining that it was one of the largest in the world. Indeed, Iran has a very youthful and educated population, many of whom lean towards the values of the West. Their study identified some key areas of Web discourse. There were small centres of discussion over President Ahmadinejad but given the level of censorship that is endemic within the country this is comparatively, and understandably, small. There were slightly larger areas of discussion by secular and expatriate communities; there were religious sections and those, again small, devoted to reformist politics. But by far the greatest area of blog discussion centred on Persian poetry.

Ever since the Iranian hostage crisis of 1979 the conservative Shia theocracy in Iran has proved difficult to deal with. Their development of a nuclear capability has been the latest in a long line of diplomatic conundrums with which the West has had to grapple. We saw in 2010 how the nuclear plant at Bashir was mysteriously struck by the STUXNET computer virus, with both the US and Israel denying that they had been responsible. The virus, malevolently released or not, clearly did its job and nuclear production was significantly reduced. For many people this was a far more satisfactory manner of achieving the desired effect than launching missiles or air strikes. But there may well be other means of achieving the same effect.

If the West wished to influence a largely Western-leaning, educated and youthful population against its theocracy it might choose to do so not in a direct attack upon its leaders (which form only a very small part of the blogosphere) but instead perhaps in the section on Persian poetry. To even consider this as a possible means of attack requires a leap of faith; to conduct it requires much, much more.

---

167   Recorded in Steve Tatham's contemporaneous notebook, whilst spokesman for operations in Iraq, March 2003.

168   Imam Husham Al-Huseini, director of the US Karbala Center.

It may be that we are perhaps asking too much, for, as we have seen, communication is surprisingly difficult even amongst English speakers (think of the 'ground floor, first floor' example earlier), without the additional complication of translation and the contextualisation, in this case, of Persian poetry.

In their 2007 paper 'A 21st Century Model for Communication in the Global War of Ideas' the CSC noted that:

> The US and their allies in the West have a strikingly similar set of communication goals. They seek to spread a counter-ideology of Western values like democracy, legitimize their actions, gain public support and intimidate the terrorists and their supporters ... that message strategy is based on a conventional twentieth-century message influence model of communication which contributes significantly to recent poor performance in communication aspects of the Global War on Terror.[169]

President Bush's now infamous use of the word 'crusade' is another example. The US president used the word – perhaps innocently and without thinking – as a verb, but it was of course taken as a noun and summoned up images of Muslim heads on Christian spears on the road to Jerusalem. Neither is it helped when words so patently fail to match deeds.

When the US speaks of democracy, audiences question how that can be, when the US continues to support single-family Arab regimes; the US speaks of human rights yet maintains the Guantánamo detention facility, and of course the images of Abu Ghraib and of waterboarding only compound the dilemma. Indeed, the very notion of democracy is for many the antithesis of the strict monotheism of Islamic principles. In short, the US narrative may well be comprehensible and understandable to those in the West, but for the audience its message is easily susceptible to mass misinterpretation. In Steve's 2006 book, *Losing Arab Hearts & Minds*,[170] he explained how the preferred conduit for the Coalition's message was one that found almost no traction with the intended Arab audiences. Organic Arab channels such as Al-Jazeera have consistently been stigmatised by the US in favour of US-created outlets such as Al-Hurra TV. Criticism of the West's approach is widespread and perhaps best summed up by the words of Richard Holbrooke, former US Ambassador to the United Nations: 'How could a mass murderer who publicly praised the terrorists of September 11 be winning the

---

169   Steven R. Corman, Angela Trethewey and Bud Goodall, *A 21st Century Model for Communication in the Global War of Ideas: From Simplistic Influence to Pragmatic Complexity* (Consortium for Strategic Communication, Arizona State University, Report #0701, 3 April 2007).

170   Steve Tatham *Losing Arab Hearts and Minds: The Coalition, Al-Jazeera and Muslim Public Opinion* (Hurst & Co (UK), Front Street Press (US), 2006).

hearts and minds of anyone? How can a man in a cave out communicate the world's leading communications society?'[171]

There are two compelling answers to this question. The first is that 'our' adversary's narrative, for all its distortion, is quite compelling, and the second is that the West has not only failed to understand the nature of communicating across the asymmetric divide but it is utterly unprepared to even attempt to. Arguably this is a greater challenge, for it requires strategic innovation.

Understanding narrative

The word 'narrative' has become increasingly popular in discussions concerning post-9/11 events. But what is a narrative, and what importance does it have to contemporary military operations? The *Concise Oxford Dictionary* offers the following definition of the word: 'a spoken or written account of connected events in order of happening.' Communication scholar Dr Paul Cobley defines narrative as 'a story with an associated discourse'. In turn he defines discourse as a 'process of delivering the narrative to a target audience'.[172] Both are pertinent. In the former the key word is 'connected', for that word implies that a narrative is a story, one that has evolved and one that should be as compelling and understandable – and this author would argue, as simple – as, say, more traditional tales from the world of literature. Cobley's definition reiterates the issue of story but then points out that the process is aimed at a specific target audience – a key theme to which this book will return momentarily.

In the post-9/11 conflicts, the narrative (be it its presence or absence) is commonly and often discussed and yet paradoxically, for all their enthusiasm, Western governments appear to struggle to devise a meaningful narrative for such simplistic ideas as why their forces are even in Afghanistan. The narrative is important to contemporary conflict because it provides the bedrock upon which all activity should be built and upon which the participants and the audiences contextualise their views and opinions of events. As US scholar Wallace Martin notes: 'By changing the definition of what is being studied, we change what we see; and when different definitions are used to chart the same territory the results will differ, as do topographical, political and demographic maps, each revealing one aspect of reality by virtue of disregarding all others.'[173] For an example of a successful narrative, one has only to look at the rhetoric of Al-Qaeda.

Although one might presume that the liturgy of events in the Arab and Muslim world is enough to provide a self-sustaining demand – Palestine, Chechyna, Kashmir, Iraq, Afghanistan, Mindanao, et al. – our adversaries have been adept at reinforcing the message through the creation of a single narrative, a version of

---

171   Richard Holbrooke, 'Get the Message Out' (*Washington Post*, 28 October 2001, p. B07).
172   Paul Cobley, *Narrative: A Critical Linguistic Introduction* (Routledge, second edition, 2001).
173   Wallace Martin, *Recent Theories of Narrative* (Cornell University Press, 1986).

history that emphasises Islam's struggle against victimisation. It is highly selective and the extent to which it is accepted by its audience – like any communication – is largely dependent upon their circumstance – in particular their education and their existing view of the world. However, it is undeniably compelling, for it is around the single narrative that Al-Qaeda and its associates' actions reside. Their narrative is based on an interpretation of both historical events and theological references, but at its heart is the idea that Islam is the last revelation of God – for it post-dated Jesus Christ by over 600 years. Since it is the last revelation, so the narrative goes, it must therefore be the final and absolute word of God, and deviation from it is heretical.

The narrative's authors have long memories. They note, for example, that Pope Urban II (1042–1099) launched the Crusades in 1095, and the Crusaders besieged and slaughteredthe population of Jerusalem, which remained captive until Sala-ad Din's triumphal return in 1187. The colonial period is portrayed as the enslavement of Muslim people by Western oppressors – specifically the UK – whilst the discovery of oil in 1932 is portrayed as Western exploitation – specifically by the US – so too the dismantlement of the Ottoman Empire – the last Caliphate. The Sykes-Picot agreement, the Balfour declaration, the Suez crisis – all are seen, not as discrete moments in history, but as a continuum of a premeditated war against Islam. Wrapped around the narrative is the claim that Christianity and Judaism seek to destroy Islam, for which selective interpretations of Koranic verses help strengthen the argument. The West, so the narrative runs, proclaims values of fairness, justness, democracy and equality but undermines them whenever Muslims aspire to the self-same values. Hamas, for example, is democratically elected in the Gaza strip and yet the West refuses to recognise it and issue sanctions against the Palestinian people; the West supports Arab regimes in Saudi Arabia, Kuwait, Bahrain, Jordan, et al., where free speech is denied, where elections are rigged and where torture is a natural consequence of speaking out. The West facilitated the creation of an illegal state, Israel, by Zionist terrorists, yet refuses the creation of the state of Palestine. The European Union opens its doors to Greeks but refuses Muslim Turks. In the Former Republic of Yugoslavia, Christian Croatia is allowed by the West to break away but when Muslim Bosnia does so it is savagely attacked by Serbia. Refusing to allow armaments to enter Bosnia, the West stands by whilst Muslims are ethnically cleansed by Christians. In Iraq the West uses white phosphorous; in Abu Ghraib and Guantánamo it systematically abuses human rights; whilst in Britain Salman Rushdie's book, *The Satanic Verses*, in Denmark the cartoons of the Prophet Mohamed and in France the banning of the veil all vilify Islam, all being justified by so-called rights of free speech. These are the modern crusades and even the US president has admitted as much. The narrative's authors masterfully weave dubious 'fact' after dubious 'fact' that build to form one single argument – the West, they proclaim, is at war with Islam.

Whilst many of the narrative's 'facts' may be questionable it is difficult to deny that it is compelling. Within it is something for everyone, even the most liberal-minded and Western-leaning Muslim can find something with which they agree.

Perhaps one reason for its success is the way that it is able to harness the emotions of its audiences. In part this is due to the narrative's former 'front man' – Osama Bin Laden – who was self-evidently charismatic and who mastered a rich and flowing style of discourse that cleverly enhanced the already emotive raw power that the Arabic language is able to engender. The emotion of the discourse is successful and entirely deliberate. As US academic Karen Johnson-Cartee notes: 'Anyone interested in bringing about social and political change does well to remember this dictum: facts inform, emotions inspire.'[174] Al-Qaeda has begun a dialogue with people, not governments. Bin Laden's foreign policy, which we believe is actually a political warfare strategy, is delivered over the heads of leaders, both Western and Muslim, to voters in Muslim and non-Muslim countries alike, and it is meant to do two things: change the policies of countries allied with the United States by eroding their popular support; and strip away allies from the United States and leave it increasingly isolated. The London-based editor of *Al-Quds* newspaper, Abdel Bari Atwan, recalls a female Yemeni journalist's reaction to the 9/11 attacks:

> I didn't think that I could support violence. When I saw the World Trade Centre and the Pentagon burn, I cried, I fainted with joy ... what we see in Bin Laden is the man who was able to take our revenge, to wipe the tears that have been falling for a long time for our brethren in Palestine and Iraq.[175]

Has Bin Laden's rhetoric been successful? This is a complex question to address; superficially one might suggest that he has not. The world's 1.4 billion Muslim *ummah* have not risen up, as one, against the West. Indeed, quite the opposite. Many Muslim countries actively support the West; some, such as the United Arab Emirates, have even placed troops in Afghanistan. Neither has the 'Arab Spring' of 2011 been the result of armed Islamist uprising; just the opposite. A distinguishing feature of the protests across Egypt, Tunisia, Libya and Syria has been their secularist nature. For many of the world's Muslims, if there is a war it is one conducted in faraway lands; the business of life, happiness, families, work and prayer continue unabated. However, any casual inspection of Arabic and Muslim literature more than reveals a very great vein of discontent, that has perhaps been influenced by Bin Laden's rhetoric, but which undeniably is given greater credence by events such as the torture and abuse of prisoners at Abu Ghraib, and the detention without trial in Guantánamo Bay.

Paradoxically, however, one audience that has been heavily influenced by the single narrative is the West. The conservative, pro-US government of Spanish Prime

---

174   Karen Johnson-Cartee, *Strategic Political Communication: Rethinking Social Influence, Persuasion and Propaganda* (Rowman & Littlefield, 2003).

175   Abdel Bari Atwan, *The Secret History of Al-Qa'ida* (Saqi Press, 2006).

Minister Jose Maria Aznar was defeated in an election soon after the March 2003 Madrid attack, the victorious socialist regime of Prime Minister Jose Luis Rodriguez Zapatero withdrawing Spanish troops from Iraq soon after. In 2006, Italian Prime Minister Silvio Berlusconi's pro-US government was defeated, and Italian troops were withdrawn from Iraq later that year. And after facing a near political coup d'état, British Prime Minister Tony Blair announced that he would step down in favour of his Chancellor, Gordon Brown, in 2007. In October 2006, a group of Thai military officers staged a coup that removed Prime Minister Thaksin Shinawatra, replacing him with a Muslim Thai general who immediately announced a change in national policy on military intervention in predominantly Muslim areas of the country. In the same year it was leaked to the press that the French government was considering pulling troops out of Afghanistan. And in Iraq and Afghanistan the respective governments of Prime Minister al-Maliki and President Karzai sought to distance themselves from the US actions in their respective countries. Although a multiplicity of reasons can be given for each of these cases it seems obvious that there has been an erosion in support for the US actions – which, of course, is a key tenet of Al-Qaeda's rhetoric.

Narratives would appear to be important, then. US authors John Arquilla and Douglas Borer write that: 'The US is [also] attempting to place terrorist activities within a larger narrative: it portrays suicide bombers as destroyers of civilisation and wanton murderers of innocent civilians and American troops as freedom fighters liberating Iraq. It is in this context that US Leaders speak of the need to win the war of ideas.'[176] This may well be a narrative to which domestic US and Western audiences might relate, but it has been more troublesome with Arab and Muslim audiences. Indeed the West would appear to have no single narrative – instead it tends to be segmented by regions and changes with time. For example, the narrative for British Forces in Basra in Iraq in late 2007 began: 'The key task for the British in Basra is to help the Iraqi army build on its success earlier this year in subduing criminal gangs, which has blighted the lives of the population and the overall security of Basra city.'[177] The essence of the British presence in Afghanistan is described in a UK cross-governmental document entitled *Afghanistan: Cross Government Core Messages*. Over ten pages long, it details where the UK operates in Afghanistan, the challenges that it faces, how long the UK may be there, the problems of corruption, and progress so far. The document is not a narrative, it is a list of enduring messages and the key message for why the UK is in the country is given as:

> It is vital to the UK that Afghanistan becomes stable and secure and that it is able to suppress violent extremism within its borders. Britain's own security is at risk if we allow Afghanistan to become a safe haven again

---

176   John Arquilla and Douglas Borer, *Information Strategy and Warfare: A Guide to Theory and Practice* (Routledge, 2007, p. 28).

177   Produced by the cross-Whitehall Afghan Information Group, based in the FCO.

for terrorists. Working as part of the international community, the UK will support the Afghan government as it builds a better future, shaped by the will of the Afghan people.[178]

NATO's narrative for its presence in Afghanistan is equally detailed and covers over thirty pages. Its headline message is that: 'Afghanistan remains NATO's number one priority. This is not an operation of choice but one of necessity. We are in Afghanistan for the long term under a UN mandate for as long as we are needed and welcomed by the Afghan people.'[179] Which still leaves the reader, and as countless surveys have shown, Afghans, to ask: 'Why is NATO there?'

William Reeve was BBC World Service Correspondent in Afghanistan for nearly thirty years; he is fluent in Dari and Pashto, counts many senior Taliban and governmental figures as friends and has as intimate understanding of the country as a non-national may ever hope to achieve. He also spent most of 2008 working in Basra for the British government. His analysis of the UK narrative is not encouraging. Of the Basra narrative he states: 'it doesn't make for magical reading.' His assessment of the Afghan narrative is equally pessimistic: 'the British narrative is simply not getting across.'[180] And indeed why would it? For notwithstanding the absence of meaningful communications mediums outside the major cities, the lamentable literacy and education rates, and the sheer vastness of the country, the Afghan narrative is hardly cast in words that Afghans will understand or relate to. In a land where the events of 9/11 are still barely known, where most would be unable to place Britain on a map of the world, the fact that Afghanistan is vital to Britain's security is anathema.

One of the major problems is that the UK's narrative, for example, is written not for Afghans but for domestic UK audiences. Of course in the globalised information environment that is the twenty-first century, what is meant for the British public will spill over, often within seconds, for dissection and discussion by other audiences, whose values and aspirations are shaped by very different circumstances. For example, the *Guardian* newspaper spent some time interviewing Afghans; Kabul resident Ebrahim Faizi, an educated man in his thirties, told the newspaper that 'democracy isn't going to happen [in Afghanistan] – it says you can have sex with any woman; Islam says you're going to be punished. Democracy says it's OK to be gay; Islam says you are going behind bars. I love democracy but how can you implement it here?'[181]

As we saw in previous chapters, not only must the West be mindful of the audience but it also needs a coherent communications strategy. For Afghans to believe any messages, those messages need to have authority, they need to be trusted,

---

178   Ibid.
179   Produced by NATO Strategic Communications Division.
180   Interview with Steve Tatham, April 2009.
181   'Kabul Stories' (*Guardian Weekend* magazine, 11 April 2009).

and they need to be clear and consistent. Like a good speech, the number of key messages needs to be minimised. William Reeve believes it should be 'no more than three. If there are too many messages, the audience gets confused, cannot take them in, and will therefore not react positively'. The message should include a clear mission statement of why international forces are in Afghanistan. In Reeve's mind:

> It is strongly recommended that messages don't include any promises of aid, for instance, that cannot be delivered to all of a province. The promises can become very counterproductive if this is the case. Information campaigns have collapsed because of similar action. Afghans are too used to being promised many things that have never materialized.

Indeed, Reeve actually thinks that the key message is really quite simple: 'What Afghans have said they want above all else over the past three decades is security. They say they don't mind who provides it, just so long as they can get on with their daily lives in peace. UK Forces should say clearly that this is their primary aim in Helmand, and say how they want to provide it.'[182] Indeed simplicity was what we sought to achieve in Helmand Province in 2007. Andrew's operational design – in essence his deployment 'road map' – specifically mentioned the need for a narrative: 'Good ones reduce the complex to the simple and allow a visitor, a soldier, a new officer, an Afghan to gain an understanding and reach a point of realization much more quickly.'[183]

In work conducted in Afghanistan, former Taliban fighters were shown images of 9/11 before and after the attack. The significance of the attack was carefully explained over many days and what transpired was that the detainees began to place their own interpretation on ISAF's presence: revenge. And revenge was something that they understood, and could accept, because it was central to their own cultures. Such an idea is all but impossible for a Western politician to 'sell' but a corollary suggestion – that with 'revenge' now complete, the West was honour bound to help the country – was also accepted without comment. Like 're-venge', 'honour' is a well-understood term in Afghan culture. Yet again, honour is problematic for Western politicians; but it does not seem beyond the bounds of reason that messages that resonate with audiences can be connected to higher-level strategic themes that work in Western societies.

With so many experienced people and such a large body of academic evidence available on narrative creation, it seems quite strange that the Coalition is unable to create a single narrative of its own, one that articulates its core values whilst still keeping time-sensitive messages. Indeed for all of the sophistication of the

---

182 Interview with Steve Tatham, April 2009.
183 In common with all Brigade Commanders, Andrew Mackay writes his own plan based on the mission statement. In the UK this is called 'Mission Command'.

single narrative, Al-Qaeda is generally unconcerned about time-sensitive messaging – relying instead on imagery to convey meaning. So in a sophisticated communications society such as the West, a simple paragraph that overarches the Coalition philosophy but which allows for a series of key (and time-changeable) messages does not seem unrealistic.

Malcolm Gladwell, in his book *The Tipping Point*,[184] talks of the best stories being ones that are 'sticky', i.e. they hold deep and lasting resonance with the audience. Dr Dave Sloggett, a visiting researcher at the Defence Academy has, with the authors, undertaken much research on the idea of narratives. He is particularly interested in the 'sticky' element of storytelling and notes that the code of *Pashtunwali*[185] is:

> … handed down and defined through stories that illustrate the customs and creeds [social norms] of Afghan society. The stories act as a form of metaphor for the customs and creed; illustrating what is right and wrong. An important part of what I hope a narrative might achieve; to create *dissonance in the mind of the listener* and get them to question their support for insurgents and challenge their beliefs.

Sloggett also believes that metaphors are important parts of that process, as they help people build the 'pictures in their mind' of what the narrative is saying. In his view this is especially important when addressing largely illiterate audiences. Of course, what complicates the issue is the segmentation of audiences and different messages meaning different things to different groups. And clearly the narrative above would not make much sense to UK audiences. Indeed, as well as struggling to explain the presence of foreign troops in Afghanistan to Afghan audiences, many NATO members were struggling to retain support within their own domestic constituencies. The loss of fifteen servicemen in just ten days in Afghanistan – the deaths of eight of them in one incident being the largest loss of UK lives since the 1982 Falklands War – ignited a furious argument within government over what exactly was the British role in the country. With the British public apparently split in their support of the operation (although fully supportive of the troops themselves), the British government struggled to find words to explain the British presence. Former Foreign Secretary David Miliband said that UK forces were stopping Afghanistan becoming 'a launch pad for attacks' by terrorists – safety at home needed security in Afghanistan. 'This is about the future of Britain', he added.[186] Previous explanations of the British presence are insight-

---

184   Malcolm Gladwell, *The Tipping Point: How Little Things Can Make a Big Difference* (Back Bay Books, 2000).

185   *Pashtunwali* literally means 'the way of the Pashtuns'. It is best understood as the rules, regulations and laws of the Pashtun tribes. These rules are responsible for the survival of the Pashtun tribes for over 2,000 years.

186   'Troops Fighting for UK Future' (BBC News 11 July 2009).

ful. Hansard records a question posed to the then Secretary of State for Defense John Reid on 27 February 2006:

MR GRAY: In reply to my Hon. Friend the Member for Guildford (Anne Milton) a moment ago, the Secretary of State described the tasks faced by our troops as establishing democracy, ending terrorism, achieving security in the south of Afghanistan, helping the economy of Afghanistan and dealing with poppy destruction. Will he now tell us how he will judge when each of those tasks has been completed, how long that will take, and what our exit strategy is?

JOHN REID: We will make our judgment on the basis of changes on the ground: extension of central Government control, a reduction in insurgency, growth of the Afghan security forces and economic development. The exit strategy involves one of the entrance aims: the achievement of a degree of success in all those respects in a relatively short time—three years—in the south. As I have said many times, we do not expect the area to become Hampshire, or New Hampshire, but it will be in a significantly better state than it is now.[187]

This followed a previous answer on 7 February 2006 when the Secretary of State said that: 'Any UK deployment to Helmand is predicated upon a fully integrated military and civilian plan designed to improve security, build local Afghan capacity, address the problem of narcotics and improve development opportunities working closely with the Governor and his team.'[188] A major announcement on 26 January had outlined the objectives of the UK deployment to Helmand Province:

Just over four years ago, on 11 September 2001, we were given a brutal lesson in the consequences of leaving Afghanistan in the hands of the Taliban and the terrorists. Since then, we in this country have been at the forefront of the international effort, under the auspices of the United Nations, to defeat international terrorism, to free Afghanistan from the ruthless grip of the Taliban and to rid the country of the menace of the terrorists and the greed of the drug trafficker ... We are also working to make sure that our goals are Afghan goals, too. Assisting Afghan counter-narcotics initiatives is an obvious example. If we help them, we help ourselves at the same time. As I mentioned earlier, 90 per cent of the heroin injected into the veins of young people in this country originates in Afghanistan ... All of this has but one aim—a secure, stable, pros-

---

187   Hansard 2006 Column 1079W.
188   Ibid.

perous and democratic Afghanistan, free from terrorism and terrorist domination.

Yet there are serious difficulties associated with this justification. First and foremost there is widespread understanding that the UK is not immune to terrorist attack – the events of 7/7 clearly demonstrated that. However 7/7 originated not in Afghanistan but in Pakistan and, according to Michael Clarke, the Director of the Royal United Services Institute, it is the Pakistani connection that has featured in 'over 75 per cent of all significant terrorist activity in Britain. Afghanistan is only one problem.'[189] Indeed, despite their increasingly sophisticated information operations the Taliban probably could not, nor would they even wish to, plan and launch a terror attack in the UK – for their objective is not an attack upon the West per se but the removal of foreign troops from Afghan soil. This is not to say that the Taliban do not have a relationship with Al-Qaeda – clearly they do, for it was the presence of Al-Qaeda fighters at terrorist training camps in Afghanistan that prompted the US attack following the events of 9/11. However, most experts agree that Al-Qaeda will establish roots wherever governance has failed or is failing. At a 2009 international terrorism conference[190] the head of the US National Terrorism and Security Center was asked what kept him awake at night; his reply was 'Yemen and Somalia'. And there have been a number of newspaper reports to suggest that other countries such as Bangladesh should be added to that list. But British troops are not in Bangladesh, nor are they in Somalia, and given the history of that forsaken country there seems little chance they will operate there in the foreseeable future. Yet it is these countries that will, indeed are already, harbouring Al-Qaeda training facilities and operatives. Thus, Afghanistan is not the only 'deserving' country for Western aid and military assistance. Neither would this justification work with organic Afghan audiences who are much more focused on their own personal situation. And this explains their ambivalence about growing poppy for heroin production. For Afghan farmers it is often the only possible income. That it has such a devastating effect upon Western populations is not an issue of great concern. Besides, there are other sources for the drug trade. Pakistan, the Golden Triangle region of South-East Asia (particularly Myanmar/ Burma), Colombia and Mexico are all opium poppy exporters, but the UK has chosen not to invade them. The third strand of the government's justification for the continued British presence in Afghanistan is the need to develop Afghanistan into a functioning country – one with government, the rule of law and a civic society. This is, of course, heavily linked to the first two justifications, for on its own it simply does not stand up to inspection. The UK makes little attempt, for example, at achieving a similar presence in other impoverished nations such as

---

189   http://www.earthtimes.org/articles/show/277262,town-symbolizes-grief-as-britons-
       question-afghan-war--feature.html – website link accessible at time of manuscript submis-
       sion, but not available as at November 2011

190   International Terrorism and Intelligence Conference 2009, Washington, DC. By invitation
       only.

the Central African Republic, Guinea-Bissau and the Solomon Islands, all three of whom reside in the UN's ten most impoverished global nations.

Another criticism levelled at the British narrative is that it is purely aspirational – not a realistic assessment of the problem and how the solution may be achieved. It talks of needing to bring stability to the country, of good governance and of capacity-building, but it does not explain how these may be achieved. In fairness to the government this is not actually the function of the narrative, but it is a derivative of that narrative and should be easily explainable. Thus we may conclude that the UK government's narrative is far from persuasive.

Target Audience Analysis

> The tendency in the US Military is to talk to the guy in the suit that looks likes us. Instead they should talk to the angry old man with no teeth and a dirty gelabella – he represents the community.[191]

We think that the Pragmatic Complexity Model unequivocally demonstrates that understanding audiences is central to the communication process and it should be viewed as a preparatory phase before military operations begin. In recent years this process of understanding has become known as Target Audience Analysis (TAA). TAA is not a new discipline. Ever since the introduction of programmable computers it has been possible to micro-segment audiences into infinitely smaller categories. Many commercial market research companies have established themselves on their ability to 'measure' audience groups and customer segments. Indeed, in today's environment, few serious marketing campaigns are launched without socio-economic, lifestyle and at least some psycho-graphic analysis performed on the targeted audience. However, the research techniques developed for marketing do not directly translate to the military environment. As we will see in the next chapter, marketing communications are targeted at broad socio-economic groups and, broadly, attempt to differentiate between brands. A soap advertisement, for example, is not trying to sell soap per se, rather it is trying to sell a particular brand of soap, and to do so at the expense of competitors' brands. This product branding is based upon influencing the attitude of the customer to the particular soap product, set against other similar soap products, for example by giving it desirable qualities or juxtaposing it with celebrity figures. Marketing is attitudinal, it shapes customers' opinions of the brand to subsequently alter their purchasing behaviour. This does not translate readily to the military environment. Whilst attitude can be important (particularly in the early stages of a military operation), behaviour (particularly when violent) is manifestly more

---

191   The words of a senior US State Department Official at the George C. Marshall Center Conference on Afghanistan, 2007.

important. It is easier to conduct operations in benign environments, even if there is an attitudinal deficit, than in malevolent violent environments.

Whilst it seems intuitive to try to change the opinions of large groups – and indeed this is sometimes achieved – we believe that what is more actively beneficial is the identification of individuals within a group who are able to exercise some degree of leverage over the wider group as a whole, and in doing so influence that wider group to alter its behaviour – even if attitudes remain entrenched. Whilst it may be helpful that the wider group changes its opinion, it is not essential; behavioural change is. Not convinced? Well, there is a very instructive cartoon video that is worth watching on YouTube to illustrate this point.[192]

The Al-Anbar rising in Iraq (when Sunni tribesmen ceased fighting US forces and instead turned their attention to Al-Qaeda fighters) is an excellent example of the attitude/behaviour debate. The Sunni tribesman did not undergo any great conversion to the US cause, they simply changed their behaviour to engage a different foe for reasons that were rational to them at a specific point in time. TAA also recognises that the influencers exist within groups which are guided and restricted by norms of behaviour and attitude. A key part of the TAA must therefore be to understand how the group functions, what their primary drivers and goals are, and what triggers will cause the group to alter (or not) its existing behaviour. Without TAA, influence success is dependent upon randomness, luck and coincidence – in short, 'a fluke'. With scientifically derived, methodologically driven TAA, success in influence becomes exponentially more likely but, given the complexity of the human condition, never an absolute certainty.

So TAA is important, but how then should it be conducted, and in the military environment by whom? Received wisdom would suggest that much data can be derived from opinion polls, but in Afghanistan (which in the last ten years has become probably the most polled population on earth) we know that opinion polls can deceive and that their results are often defined not by the individual's answers but by the way the question was asked by the pollster. Opinion polls also tend to be seen as popularity or progress indicators when in reality both of these are largely irrelevant to achieving influence objectives. For example, it is the Coalition's wish that Afghans not plant Improvised Explosive Devices. In truth, whether the Afghan likes ISAF soldiers is irrelevant (although undeniably it would be an added bonus) to the influence campaign, which simply seeks to change the IED behaviour, not opinion. And so the first step in the influence process, even before TAA, is to decide what 'we' are seeking to influence and then be consistent in that objective.

What TAA reveals about groups and societies can be quite surprising. For example, a major TAA project conducted for the US Central Command[193] found that: In Afghanistan the Taliban oppose education – right? Well, some indeed may,

---

192   See http://www.youtube.com/watch?v=AB28IJbvbe0
193   Strategic Multi-layer Assessment for a Rich Contextual Understanding of PAKAF – Provisional Findings, 2009.

but the TAA revealed that this was actually a generalisation too far. In South Waziristan, for example, there were more schools under the Taliban than there are now. So how did 'we' reach this commonly held but ultimately wrong belief? Quite simply 'we' saw images of burning schools and from those made a presumption. But the presumption was wrong, for the TAA research revealed that this was a result not of religious zealotry but actually of something far more common in every society, including the West; have/have not rivalry between different socio-economic groups. Thus, if 'we' had sought to influence the local population against the Taliban by highlighting this as an endemic religious issue the whole influence campaign would have failed because it was based upon a false premise. The Kingdom of Saudi Arabia, home of the two holy cities of Mecca and Medina, has a reputation, in certain sections of the Western media at least, to be ultra-conservative. Women wear the veil, may not drive cars, and all other religions are banned. The country's justice code is famously strict, with thieves having limbs amputated and adulterers being stoned. Therefore it is not unreasonable to presume that Islam will be the pre-eminent influence on young adult male behaviour. Right? Islam is important – yes. But the TAA indicates it is simply not as important a behavioural trigger for young men as privacy from their parents, as football, and as nationalism. So an influence campaign aimed at this audience, grounded in Islamic references or context, might be less successful than one grounded in the fortunes of, say, Manchester United Football Club. In Afghanistan the tribe is the defining feature – right? Wrong. Despite the importance of tribes, it is regions and land (and the incomes and status associated with them) that are considered to be much more important. So influence campaigns vested in tribal culture may well resonate but may be less successful than ones focused on geography and land usage. Any reader unfamiliar with Afghanistan has only to read Rory Stewart's book *The Places In Between*[194] to see how his guides refused to accompany him to the next village or valley, or beyond the next mountain, because it was someone else's territory.

TAA, when undertaken properly, is an extremely complex process, and whilst its methodology is comparatively simple, its implementation is not. For it to have any chance of success, it must achieve at least four objectives:

- The precise identification of optimal Target Audiences.
- The measurement of the 'influenceability' of that audience.
- The identification of the best process to influence that audience.
- The production and deployment of the triggers that will effectively and measurably change the audience's behaviour.

---

194   Rory Stewart, *The Places In Between* (Picador, 2005).

TAA, therefore, aims to construct a robust profile of the audience and how it can be influenced by an appropriately conceived and deployed message campaign. One key feature of this approach is that messages are developed in a bottom-up fashion, with them being constructed from a process of measurement and research, and subsequently derived from reliable knowledge of the audience. This is at odds with the current way that the military traditionally conducts its business, where themes and messaging are crafted centrally and distributed downwards to theatre troops. Whitehall and Washington political messages are often a diluted and distant memory by the time they reach the tactical level, and they may actually have no relevance at ground level anyway.

It should be clear why this approach is far more effective than simple marketing approaches, or cultural understanding. There exists no universal model of communication, applicable to all groups and cultures. All communication efforts must be tailored to the local dynamics, and with respect to the behaviours one is seeking to change. Because audiences are multifaceted and cannot be grouped as a population, influencing the differing component groups of a society requires precisely targeted methods and approaches: One message – no matter how culturally relevant – does not fit all. Working out who to influence, why, how, when, and whether it is possible, constitute the first steps of TAA. Often it will be necessary to influence one group to influence another. Above all else, the process of influence is not necessarily to make a particular group like 'us' or 'our' ideas – although this is always an extra 'bonus'.

There are some further issues with TAA that merit consideration. If we think of TAA as the process of identifying the 'right' audience, we must also be mindful that there are other audiences also present. We might think of them in four groups, and the messages that we deploy may well cast a shadow upon them. They are: the target audience; a group who may react positively to the messaging applied to the target; a group who may react negatively to the messaging applied to the target; and a group who will be ambivalent and who might even be best left alone. For example, in Afghanistan the target audience may be young men tempted to join the Taliban, perhaps for payment (what the ISAF coalition refer to as ideologically uncommitted and thus tier 2, instead of the ideologically driven tier 1 Taliban). The secondary audience that reacts positively may be the Afghan central government; the secondary audience that reacts negatively may be the tier 1 Taliban; and the ambivalent audience is perhaps the civilian population who seek only survival. Indeed, understanding which audience is best left alone is perhaps one of the hardest to identify, not least because inactivity is often perceived negatively within the militaries of the West, who all, without exception, are 'can do' in their approach to operations.

6

What military operations can learn from mushy peas, soap and budget airlines

As we saw in the previous chapter, throughout the Iraq War the Coalition's strategy for success was predicated on using overwhelming military force, which from the outset became known as 'shock and awe', in place of high volumes of troops on the ground. Iraqis, it was reasoned, could easily be persuaded to support the Coalition if it meant a future without Saddam Hussein and his cohorts at the helm. Indeed, for a few short weeks that seemed a likely prospect. Nearly 80 per cent of the Iraqi population were from the Shia branch of Islam and under Saddam's largely Sunni regime had been persecuted and disenfranchised. Yet that initial enthusiasm for Saddam's departure and the US-led Coalition's arrival soon dissipated, replaced instead by anger at the breakdown of society and its infrastructure, fear at the rapid rise in sectarian-inspired killings, and collective anger and shame at having a Western occupation force within its national boundaries. Augustus Norton, Professor of Middle East Studies at Boston University, told US National Public Radio that: 'When proponents of the 2003 Iraq war argue that the Shi'i Muslims of Iraq were predominantly secular in orientation, they either ignorantly or conveniently forgot about recent history, which has had the effect of pushing the Iraqi Shi'is away from secularism, towards, if you will, higher levels of religious identification and religiosity.'[195] In short, where once there had been no religious sectarianism, now it was rife. Fear and hatred of others replaced fear and hatred of Saddam. The Iraqi people's behaviour had been dramatically changed in just a few short weeks, despite the initial prevailing attitude of relief that Saddam had been overthrown.

We saw in Chapter 4 how the work of psychologists Kahneman and Tversky on Prospect Theory had proved useful in trying to understand Afghans and Afghanistan, and how it might be used to explain the motivations behind people's behaviour when dealing with risk and uncertainty. Of particular interest were their findings about what economists refer to as the 'discount rate' – the fact that people value owning something today much more than the prospect of owning a larger quantity of the same thing in the future. This theory suggests that people are more motivated by losses than they are by gains, and as a result will devote more time and energy to avoiding loss than to achieving gain. The evidence from Iraq would appear to support this hypothesis. It was extremely difficult to convince Iraqis, of all religious persuasions, to buy into a future for 'tomorrow' when

195   Interview with Augustus Norton, Professor of Middle East Studies at Boston University, available at www.npr.org/templates/story/story.php?storyId=7411762

their 'today' was so fraught with danger and hardship. Indeed, we would argue that there are clear and obvious implications here for how we might communicate with a population that has suffered several decades of conflict – such as the Afghans. The 'here and the now' becomes critical, with people demonstrating an understandable reluctance to consider next week or next month when getting through today is such a struggle. An example of how Prospect Theory can be distorted in conflict is a tendency by both the military and development specialists to over-promise but then subsequently under-deliver. Hopes are raised and subsequently dashed, causing individuals to mistrust longer-term development plans, with the consequence that they seek to avoid further loss rather than buy in to overstated 'gains'.

An example from Afghanistan illustrates this perfectly. Many claims were made over the benefits that would be accrued if the Kajaki Dam in Helmand was made fully operational and power generation dramatically improved. This is how the BBC's correspondent Alistair Leithhead described the military operation to move a new turbine to the dam in 2008:

> Almost three thousand British troops in southern Afghanistan have successfully transported a huge hydroelectric power turbine through Taliban territory. In one of their biggest operations in Helmand, a convoy of 100 vehicles took five days to move the massive sections of the turbine 180km (112 miles). The $6m (£3.4m) turbine will produce electricity for an extra 1.9m people. Prime Minister Gordon Brown said the operation was a reminder of NATO's 'fundamental purpose' in Afghanistan. The operation to increase the output of the Kajaki Dam in southern Afghanistan is part of a development project which has been planned for two years. The convoy travelled the length of the Helmand river valley – through areas insurgents have controlled for more than two years – carrying seven 20–30-tonne sections. A spokesman said it was the largest route clearance operation the British military has carried out since World War II. Mr Brown said: 'It is yet another example of the skill and courage of our forces, but also a reminder of the fundamental purpose of why they are there – the long term development of Afghanistan, giving the people a stake in the future.'[196].

Whilst the military mission received huge media coverage in the UK, with the troops being heralded as heroes for their endeavours, for most Afghans (and in particular for the ones who had the most to gain from the dam, the residents of Helmand) there was little sense of triumph or achievement. And rationally, why should 'we' expect anything other. For a population that had seen empires come and go, building great projects which then in time fell away to nothing, the

---

perceived benefits, the prospect, of a more efficient dam and the downstream benefits of electricity that it would bring, were simply so far away that they could not possibly consider it to be a factor that might alter their current behaviour and encourage them to try to limit and refrain from insurgent activity around the dam. The lesson that has to be drawn here is that for influence to be successful and meaningful to the people who matter (and not to indirect audiences such as the UK population), the event must relate to something that is tangible and apparent and not fuzzy and indistinct, regardless of how strategically important a project such as the Kajaki Dam really is.

We know from work undertaken in Iraq in December 2003 by the Coalition Provisional Authority (CPA) that as many as 85 per cent of Iraqis had not actually met a Coalition soldier, yet by 2003 the armed insurgency was well under away. One has to wonder therefore that if Iraqis had not met Coalition soldiers themselves, and had not formed their opinions about them based upon their own experiences, why then had they taken such rapid and pronounced action to resist the presence of foreign troops? The simple answer is that they did not wish their nation to be occupied by others. This is neither irrational nor unreasonable. Yet the true answer is no doubt more complex and rests somewhere in the middle of a series of issues revolving around regional, tribal, family, religious and nationalistic cognitive drivers as well as a rapidly emerging 'free media', one encouraged by the Coalition rhetoric of freedom of speech and democracy. The hasty shutting down of newspapers by the Coalition revealed that not all speech was free – particularly when it incited violence against Coalition troops. Indeed, both the Kajaki Dam and the CPA's Iraqi survey are examples of a much larger problem that has confronted Western militaries, and will continue to do so in future operations – the over-simplification of the environment. And here an example from history is most instructive.

In the 1950s, Maximum Sustainable Yield (MSY) theory was developed to try and preserve the delicate ecological balance of waterways and rivers in and around the US. MSY involved modelling the environment from surveys which attempted to capture every possible variable, such as the number of fish species, the reproduction rate of that species, the food chain and a whole host of other data that, once captured, could be used to calculate the natural replacement rate of fish. The result of this work was that once modelling was complete you knew how much fish you could take out to keep the stocks going. Forever. MSY became the basis of international treaties over fish quotas, and for a short period of time it was a golden age to be an ecologist, since you were now in demand worldwide to work out MSYs. Or it would have been a golden age but for one important issue – fish stocks started to die out in huge numbers and at alarming rates. An ecologist called Holling identified the problem in 1973. He wrote: 'in some systems there is not a lot of change and so it is easy to keep track of things you can measure, but in places where there is lots of change, where there is often daily perhaps even explosive re-adjustment, such measurements are worse than useless'.[197] In the case of lakes, they look comparatively stable places but actually they are hugely complex and their ecosystems cannot be reduced to a few variables and some clever mathematical models. Holling felt that MSY extinctions were caused by factors outside the modelled system – factors people had never thought to measure because they were so unrelated to the problem at hand. For example, one of the things he found was that a high MSY brought a high footfall of fishermen to lakes. More fishermen equals more rubbish left behind, rubbish which disrupted the ecosystem in a way that MSY could not have imagined. In short MSY calculations, designed to preserve fish stocks, might actually lead directly to their extinction. The law of unintended consequences is an ever-present feature in conflict, and none the more so in the increasingly important arena of nation-building.

Why is this relevant to Iraq and Afghanistan? The answer is that the Coalition tried to over-simplify a complex system, one which it did not fully understand, one in which it didn't know what it didn't know. It tried, in essence, to reduce to the lowest common denominator a great deal of complexity in order to try and understand what it was dealing with. From there, poor decision-making is all too easy. Our contention is that the same problem exists in much of what 'we' try to achieve today, and that all of 'our' thinking seeks to simplify problems in complex environments in order to find answers rather than accept the complexity and work with it. Take Libya, for example. There was a widespread belief that Colonel Gaddaffi would, like the Tunisian and Egyptian rulers, topple in the face of widespread opposition. Just a little help from a NATO no-fly zone would nudge the whole operation in the right direction. And yet despite NATO's overwhelming military superiority, that took far longer than anticipated and it was not until late October 2011 that Gaddaffi and his supporters were prized from their last remaining strongholds. Even with him gone the future is by no means certain and the history books may reveal that removing him, in retrospect, was the easy bit. The Libyan ecosystem, which 'we' knew very little about in advance of operations, with all of its attendant uncertainty and unintended consequences, may yet surprise 'us'. Whilst Western leaders may congratulate themselves on his downfall, if he is replaced by, for example, a militant Islamic regime, unknown and as yet un-emerged, there may not be quite so many smiles in London, Paris and Washington. And what does 'our' behaviour in Libya, predicated as it was upon a United Nation's Security Resolution that authorised only protection of civilians not regime change, say about 'us' to other nations; specifically to nations such as China, India and Brazil?

One of the key problems in Iraq, and even more so now in Afghanistan, is that Coalition forces correctly, if belatedly, realised that the key to success lay in the hearts and minds of the population, but that its understanding of that population has been so simplified as to make its actions at best irrelevant and at worst counterproductive to the mission. The hearts and minds campaign has been focused

197   C. S. Holling, 'Resilience and Stability of Ecological Systems' (*Annual Review of Ecology and Systematics*, 1973, volume 4, issue 1, pp. 1-23).

on trying to change opinion or attitudes – not behaviour. Two case studies demonstrate this perfectly.

The NATO newspaper *Sada-e Azadi* ('The Voice of Freedom') has for some years been produced, fortnightly, for distribution around the country. The paper, of which some 440,000 copies are printed, has become the highest circulating paper in Kabul. Written in Dari, Pashto and English, it is also disseminated in Kunduz and Mazar-e-Sharif, in the north of the country. The paper, administered and run by German troops, is funded by the Commander Joint Psychological Operations Task Force (colloquially known as CJPOTIF), whose annual budget, in 2008, was €21 million (approximately £17 million). The newspaper's staff is a mix of Afghans and European journalists. The Afghans are paid around $1,000 (£650) per month – a sizable amount in Afghanistan – and there are around forty of them across the country involved in the paper's production. The European staff – known as International Civilian Consultants (ICCs) – earn a basic salary of €6,000 (£5,000) per month with incidental daily expense of €72 allowable. Team leaders typically earn around €8,000 per month.

The paper's content is provided by forward media teams (typically ICCs) and usually of the nationality of the ISAF forces in their particular area. Each team is tasked to provide four stories for the newspaper every week and four radio features for the sister radio channel also run by the German PsyOps[198] teams. However, the newspaper itself is comparatively small (the southern edition, for example, is normally no more than four pages long), so as a consequence much of the material generated by the teams is never published. The decision on what is in – or more commonly what is out – is the preserve of the editorial team in Kabul who actually put the paper together. In the words of one former ICC journalist, its editors are looking for 'fluffy stuff. New schools. New wells and happy kids'. Above all else, every copy of the paper is heavily branded with the ISAF logo.

Whilst over 400,000 copies may be produced every fortnight, anecdotally less than 10 per cent actually reach the intended audience. In Kandahar, for example, the paper is printed under contract and collected by ICCs who then divide the paper up into numbers determined by CJPOTIF staff. They are then transported to the various logistics areas on Kandahar airfield. The former ICC remembers the reaction the first time he went: 'their first reaction was to laugh and then tell you to f**k off. The pressure on air assets in Afghanistan is intense and the distribution of newspapers is as far down the priority list as it gets. More often than not the newspapers sat in shipping containers in Kandahar airfield, or in the UK's case, at Camp Bastion.' If they were ever delivered, and according to the former ICC they rarely were, they would be two to three months out of date by the time they arrived. More often than not, however, they would be burnt (an event filmed by two Austrian officers who were subsequently and mysteriously returned home)

---

198   Psychological Operations.

or sold off to locals for wrapping shopping and food in the markets.[199] The further you got away from the distribution points, the harder and harder became the logistics in distributing them, to the extent that they simply did not bother. The whole project is a 'waste of time', offered the former ICC, 'the measure of effectiveness is quantity not quality'.

He recalled one particular edition in 2008 that used an entire page to feature an Afghan woman editor, without veil or head covering, who wanted to stand for parliament. The article was extremely critical of the Afghan President, Hamid Karzai, and the ICC was deeply concerned that the image and the message were wholly unsuitable for the audience. Every paper had to be pulped. Promoting the ISAF brand is a key role for the paper, and in 2008 just under one-third of the CJPOTIF budget was spent on novelty ISAF-branded items – hats, T-shirts, school bags. Given to some of the poorest people in the world, such articles may well have been keenly valued by their recipients but, were they to be caught by the Taliban, could also spell their death warrant. As to their effect on local opinion of ISAF. Well, it is difficult to quantify but as numerous commentators have noted when studying the image of the US abroad, the wearing of a New York Yankees baseball cap may be more a fashion statement than any deep-seated admiration for or resonance with the US.

The second case study, again from Afghanistan, was graphically illustrated by Anthony Fitzherbert, a long-time Afghan hand and an agriculturalist of some note who has spent nearly forty years, on and off, in the country. Giving evidence to the Global Strategy Forum and Windsor Energy Group Seminar in the House of Lords in March 2010, he noted that:

> When working with Hazara farmers in Bamiyan in 2008 [an intrinsically poor but peaceful province] they were always remarking to me: 'Why does your government spend so much money on those murderous Pushtuns in Helmand and Kandahar who want to kill you, burn schools and throw acid in school girls' faces? While we Hazaras, who welcome a woman as our governor, do not have suicide bombers or lay road-side bombs, welcome education for our children including our daughters and long for development, receive hardly anything. Perhaps we should start to kill aid workers and lay road-side bombs and then the funds would come in our direction!' They do not say this entirely in jest.[200]

---

199   Steve didn't believe this story until he was in the British military base in Lashkar Gar in late 2010. The interpreters suggested that they would bring lunch in; it duly arrived wrapped in an otherwise pristine (and clearly un-read) copy of the NATO newspaper!

200   Anthony Fitzherbert, 'Some of the Challenges of Building Viable Rural Economy', a presentation to the Global Strategy Forum and Windsor Energy Group, Committee Room No. 4. House of Lords, Monday 8 March 2010.

In short, in attempting to 'buy off' the people of Helmand, the Coalition was isolating other more peaceful communities who could see little benefit to their acquiescence.

So where are 'we' going wrong? Let's set Afghanistan, and indeed conflict as a whole, aside for a moment and consider some good old-fashioned marketing techniques. Take, for example, a bar of soap. There are, from a walk around any large supermarket, any number of different bars of soap to choose from. Some are large, some small, some sweet-smelling, others more masculine. Some will address specific skin complaints (so the packaging tells us), whilst others will enhance our natural Ph balance. Some are colourfully wrapped, providing images of flowers and sunshine, whilst others are more sober, perhaps looking a little more scientific and professional. It is a bewildering choice for a shopper and most will tend to purchase either on the basis of cost or on the basis of past history and personal choice. Advertisers have a seemingly tough job. They have to make a consumer switch from one brand of soap to another – perhaps to one that is even more expensive. So, an average Western shopper may well buy, year in year out, the same brand of soap until they happen to notice a special offer of a different brand that offers, for example, three bars for the price of two. This may well sway them towards purchase. However, their loyalty to the new brand is now dependent not just upon the product itself (and let's be honest here, most soap seems to resemble most other soap), but also upon its price. The job of the civilian marketer is to distinguish and differentiate between soap as a commodity and soap as a brand. In short, marketing companies are employed by producers to make their product – in this example soap – different from that of their competitors by attaching some specific brand values to it. So the soap may become the 'brand favoured by James Bond' or the 'brand that keeps your skin soft and silky'.

It is through this type of marketing that products are differentiated, even if they are essentially the same. The problem for advertisers is that attitudes are very easily overcome by real-world practicalities. Let's take another example. Both Andrew and Steve would like to own their own Aston Martin sports car. Both of them, as typical males, admire the car's sporty style, its sleek looks, the roar of the engine, the exclusiveness of the brand and, if we are honest, might just, for a very short and illusionary moment, see themselves not as middle-aged men with receding hair but as suave and handsome James Bond-type figures. Of course, at some point reality surely kicks in; even if both authors could afford an Aston Martin the truth is that they probably wouldn't purchase one anyway – since it simply cannot be used for the routine family adventures, outings and trips to the supermarket that are the mainstay, not of a super spy's life, but of ordinary people. And besides, all the marketing in the world will simply not overcome the fact that neither can afford such a car. So, and this is the key bit, Aston Martin can spend all the money in the world on advertising, with the glorious knowledge that both Andrew and Steve are utterly converted to the brand, and yet that extremely positive attitude cannot be translated to actual purchasing behaviour, which at the end of the day is the whole point of the exercise.

So when would Aston Martin's advertisements have some effect? They do, after all, sell a lot of cars. The truth is that they sell most of their cars to people who have the necessary resources and – the key point – who have already decided that they are in the market for a sports car. The issue is which car? These people must differentiate between a host of exotic and tempting brands: Porsche, Lamborghini, Ferrari or Aston Martin? These are people whose behaviour is already determined – they are going to buy an expensive sports car and they can afford to buy an expensive sports car. All that the marketing people from Aston Martin have to do is make them choose their car (and its inherent brand) rather than that of the competition.

So, to return to our soap analogy, the fact is that most consumers are already buying soap. What the marketer is trying to achieve is that the shopper buys a specific brand of soap. And the truth is that this is not too difficult to achieve once or twice, particularly if you incentivise the sale in some manner. What is harder to do is to sustain a definitive change in buying behaviour and keep customers buying a particular brand. Thus marketing is attitudinal in concept – it is asking the consumer to adopt a specific attitude, view or opinion about a product type for which they are generally already in the market, and to then use that information to make them change their behaviour – in this instance to buy one brand of soap over another. What on earth does this have to do with military operations and future conflict?

In Iraq and in Afghanistan the Coalition pushed out messages, on specific channels, and hoped to achieve attitudinal change. As we have seen already, in Iraq these messages were focused on supporting the establishment of a democracy whilst in Afghanistan they were designed to build support for the government of Hamid Karzai and the continued presence of NATO and ISAF forces. It seems to us, though, that the difficulty with this approach is that it takes a far too simplistic view of the 'customer' – the Afghans. For example, it did not take into consideration that the audience may themselves already have held preconceived views about Karzai, GIRoA[201] and ISAF, views that might contextualise their attitudes and behaviours. Nor did it consider that they, the Iraqis and the Afghans, were actually messaging the Coalition as well (as we saw with the example from Anthony Fitzherbert above), and that the channels the Coalition chose may not have been the right channels for the audience. In short, the audience was not already buying into the Coalition message – in Afghanistan it was not a straight binary decision between the Taliban (let's not forget they are someone's father, brother, son) and ISAF. Afghans are savvy people; they have had to be, given the conflict that has raged in their country for so many years. They will very happily take a little bit of reconstruction aid from ISAF and GIRoA but they will just as happily accept Taliban justice if it suits them. Sitting on the fence is almost key to survival in such uncertain circumstances and they will move to the 'right side' when victory is assured. In Iraq, the same binary offer existed, and here too the Iraqis refused to accept it. For them it was not a straight choice between elements of

---

201   Government of the Islamic Republic of Afghanistan.

Saddam's former Ba'ath party and a new Western-supported government. Many Iraqis were simply not convinced by either, and nor were they even prepared to buy into an unknown future when their present was so fraught with danger and uncertainty.

We know from existing research that there are generally three ways to affect an audience. The first is informational (for example, the large fluorescent signs stating that there is a 'Closing down sale', a '50% off sale", or 'Buy three, pay for one'). The second is attitudinal (which invites us to believe, for example, that 'By wearing this aftershave you will appear sleek and sophisticated'). The third is behavioural (attitudinal behaviour resulting in behavioural change, i.e. behaviour occurs because of some rational attitudinal process or, importantly, behaviour changes but not as a tangible result of attitude). The first cannot be discarded, for it has important military applications. For example, the message campaigns to keep Iraqi and Afghan drivers 50 metres back from military vehicles are informational and make sense – most audiences would understand and would comply. So too leaflets dropped on villages in advance of kinetic military action to warn residents to stay indoors, or leaflets explaining to parents that their children must not pick up old munitions and ordnance. Again the informational component of the message will tend to resonate – provided, of course, that it is passed across a channel that the audience understands. Yet informational marketing is very unlikely to work in the wider context of military operations. For example, in Afghanistan large billboards have been erected at truck stops and on highways to try to dissuade people from becoming suicide bombers. Forgive us a moment of cynicism, but is it really credible to assume that a potential suicide bomber, with a belt of improvised explosives around his waist, and having been promised entrance to paradise and seventy-two virgins, will change his behaviour as a result of a billboards on the side of the road? He may … but it seems highly unlikely.

The second – attitudinal change (the building of brand image) – is again not to be discarded, but in a conflict environment it will have more to do with deeds matching actions then with a clever marketing campaign. For example, messages of peace and security will not resonate if the local government offices are corrupt and if Coalition air strikes accidentally kill civilians. Whilst attitude can be important (particularly in the early stages of an operation), behaviour (particularly when violent) is manifestly more important. It is easier to conduct operations in benign environments, even if there is an attitudinal deficit, than in malevolent violent environments. It is also extremely difficult to recover a brand that has become damaged. Thus the third – behavioural change – seems to us both to be the model in which 'we' must invest much more time and understanding.

Everything in the marketing model is predicated on the product – soap, sausages, Aston Martins, etc. Indeed, every single bit of research to do with marketing is predicated on that idea. But here is a thought. What happens if you take the actual product you are trying to sell out of the mix – completely? If you do – and to do so requires a leap of faith as it appears utterly counter-intuitive – then you are left with looking at the audience and asking the question: Under what conditions would a target audience engage in a specific type of behaviour? And if that behaviour meshed with our product, then we have reached our goal without regard to the product itself. OK, this is getting a bit complex so let's find an example.

Suppose you, the reader, have become the marketing manager of Mushy Peas[202] International. Just so you know, Mushy Peas International is the world's leading mushy pea company (it isn't really, but just pretend) and in recent years its sales have dropped and it has started to lose ground to other competitors (work with us on this!). So, in order to secure your large yearly bonus from the shareholders, you have been set the task by the CEO of doubling mushy peas sales in the next twelve months. How will you do it? Conventional wisdom suggests that you will employ every possible technique of advertising. You may buy double-page spreads in Sunday magazines, put adverts on TV during prime-time shows and launch viral Internet videos. And yet, intuitively, we know that this will not do the job. Why? The simple answer is that mushy peas, whilst important to you and your bonus, are simply not desirable, exclusive or exotic fare. James Bond does not eat mushy peas. Mushy peas have no particular unique medicinal quality. Mushy peas are not the choice of rock stars or catwalk models. It would seem that your bonus this year may be in danger.

But what happens if you take the mushy peas out of your advert completely? Don't even mention mushy peas in your viral adverts and centre-spreads. In fact spend your advertising budget not on your product at all but on somebody else's products. Are we mad? Well, we may be, but if you look at the profile of when mushy peas are eaten you will see that they are almost exclusively bought to accompany the UK's de facto national dish – fish and chips. So it follows that as the marketing manager for Mushy Peas International, an alternative, stronger, strategy might be for you to invest all of your advertising budget not in mushy pea promotion but ... in promoting fish and chip sales. And you might think about doing this particularly on Fridays when fish, chips and mushy peas are traditionally served for lunch in canteens and workplaces up and down the country. The point of this example is that it encourages you to think asymmetrically (and you will remember we looked at asymmetry earlier in this book in the context of bows and arrows). If you, as the marketing manager, stimulate the sales of other companies' products (fish, chips), you will automatically increase sales of mushy peas *by default* and without even mentioning them. Using this example you can see how the starting point was not the product or the advert but the *behaviour* of the customer. By asking a simple question – Under what circumstances would people buy mushy peas? – and then finding every circumstance in which the customer may consider exhibiting the desired behaviour of buying mushy peas, you can then turn all of that data into a meaningful campaign that will properly link your communication programme to the behaviour you want.

---

202   For our international readers mushy peas are a favourite dish in the UK; as the name suggests they are garden peas mashed together.

There are plenty of other examples that illustrate the point further. In the UK, successive governments have aspired to reduce smoking amongst the population for years. In 2002 the UK Tobacco Advertising Ban was passed, resulting in a three-stage implemented ban on tobacco advertising in the press, on billboards, in-pack promotions and in sporting and event sponsorship. In 2003, the European Union imposed a tobacco advertising ban in all member nations on tobacco advertising in print media, radio and for tobacco sponsorship events. Cigarette packets began to carry health warnings, which became more and more apocalyptic. Then the packets began carrying gruesome images of cancerous growths and the inside of smokers' lungs. Smoking has undeniably dropped through the years. But it has been a very slow process and, in some discrete groups, particularly teenage girls, the actual rates of smoking have risen. But the single most dramatic drop in UK smoking during that entire period has not been the attitudinal effects of cigarette packet warnings, or anti-smoking advertisements, but the enforced behavioural change of preventing smokers from lighting up in public places implemented on 1 July 2007: 'The nationwide smoking ban has triggered the biggest fall in smoking ever seen in England. More than two billion fewer cigarettes were smoked and 400,000 people quit the habit since the ban was introduced a year ago, which researchers say will prevent 40,000 deaths over the next 10 years', declared Cancer Research UK in a 2008 report.[203] Similar bans were introduced in Scotland on 26 March 2006 and in Wales on 2 April 2007. Doctors said that they were astonished by the numbers quitting. Robert West, director of tobacco studies at University College London, who carried out the study, said: 'These figures show the largest fall in the number of smokers on record. The effect has been as large in all social groups – poor as well as rich. I never expected such a dramatic impact.'[204]

'I never expected such a dramatic impact.' Really? Why ever not? With the benefit of hindsight such a dramatic impact was, of course, obvious. If you physically remove the environments where the non-desired behaviour is undertaken – pubs, clubs and other public places – then it seems logical that people will, albeit reluctantly, give up. And those that hang on, sheltering in the rain and wind on the 'naughty step' for a quick puff, suddenly seem somehow abnormal. Smoking in the wet and the cold on a Friday night whilst all your mates are in a pub or bar having a good time doesn't seem quite so attractive after a while.

Another example of the attitudinal/behavioural imbalance is with budget airlines who seem able to engender particular reactions in people. European budget airlines such as easyJet and Ryanair are very cheap and cheerful but generally manage to get passengers from A to B in the same way as their more expensive competitors. However, when something happens, such as a delay or a diversion, passengers tend to notice the difference much more. Ryanair's CEO, Michael O'Leary, said he would wait for his day in court and only reimburse travellers the original price of their air fare and no more when the plume of smoke from Ice-

203   http://www.nursingtimes.net/nursing-practice/clinical-specialisms/smoking-cessation/
        smoking-ban-in-england-has-a-dramatic-impact-on-prevalence/1703195.article
204   Jeremy Laurance, 'Smoking Ban has Saved 40,000 Lives' (*Independent*, 30 June 2008).

land's Eyjafjallajökull volcano engulfed Europe and left thousands of passengers stranded. 'There's no legislation designed that says any airline getting a fare of 30 euro [£26] should be reimbursing passengers many thousands of euro for hotel accommodation. It's absurd', he told the British *Daily Mail* newspaper in April 2010.[205] Perhaps no surprise then that budget airlines consistently achieve very low customer satisfaction scores. As the *Sun* newspaper noted in November 2010:

> Of the best known low-cost airlines, Easy Jet pleased just 59 per cent of their passengers and Ryanair 47 per cent. The survey of 30,000 consumers rated both airlines poorly for food, comfort and pre-flight arrangements. *Which?* magazine editor Neil Fowler said: 'The glamour of air travel may have gone, but there are still some classy carriers out there. As for Ryanair and Easy Jet, they might be cheap but if you want great customer service then look elsewhere.'[206]

And yet ... people still fly with budget airlines. Their attitude (to poor customer service) is not sufficient to sway their behaviours (buying budget airline tickets because they are cheap). There are countless other examples where attitudes have little or no effect on behaviour.

Now none of this is rocket science. So why then do ISAF, and indeed the UK's MoD, still rely almost exclusively on attitudinal messaging? ISAF spend millions of dollars each year on ISAF-crested footballs, on dolls, on books, on TV shows, on radio adverts and on a whole host of other largely irrelevant products designed to affect attitudinal change. We cannot and would not wish to deny that some of these have an effect, but do they prevent an IED maker from plying his trade? Do they stop young men from joining the Taliban's ranks? The answer has to be a qualified 'No'. Qualified, because if we are poor at our Target Audience Analysis (and we both think that 'we' are), then 'we' are guaranteed to be even worse at measuring effectiveness. If we don't understand the audience, and in particular its behaviour before and after 'our' influence campaign is conducted, 'we' can't possibly know, at least empirically, what 'we' have or have not achieved with 'our' campaign. But we can have a well-educated guess – and it's our guess that we have actually achieved very little. As 'we' near the end of our adventures in Afghanistan the obvious truth, after nearly ten years of our presence, is that 'we' have simply failed to bring the Afghan population on board. But actually this is a false premise because 'we' probably don't really need to bring them on board in terms of attitude. Just as in Iraq, the population is never going to think fondly of a foreign power (or for that matter forty-eight occupying foreign powers). And unless the Afghan government can demonstrate its capacity on the ground to

205   'Ryanair won't pay a penny in compensation' (*Daily Mail*, 22 April 2010). See http://www. dailymail.co.uk/travel/article-1267825/Iceland-volcano-Ryanair-wont-pay-compensation-says-OLeary.html#ixzz1KGgzLKiL

206   'Bargain Flyers not so Fancied' (*Sun*, 20 November 2010).

properly manage and resolve normal everyday Afghan problems, Afghans are not going to respond positively to that either – however much gloss 'we' in the West might collectively put on their efforts. As 'we' head to withdrawal in 2014, the reality is that we don't need Afghans to love ISAF but 'we' do need them not to engage in specific types of behaviour. 'We' need them to not lay IEDs (or to not ignore someone else laying an IED), to not provide refuge to the insurgents and to not take up arms against ISAF. And if, whilst they are steered towards that, their attitudes to ISAF or the UK or GIRoA improve, then so much the better. Of course, this process is contrary to received wisdom. Whitehall and Washington have huge press machines; in the MoD over fifty press and information officers churn out attitudinal-based work to feed the 'beast' that is the international media; whilst other organisations, for example the UK's small Psychological Operations Teams at the Defence Intelligence and Security Centre in Chicksands, are resourced to send only twelve people to Task Force Helmand to work on meaningful behavioural change.

7
Strategic communication and military enablers

Anyone who has grown up in the last twenty years or so cannot help but have noticed the emphasis, globally, that now seems to be placed to what was once called PR – public relations. The business and commercial world in particular has been devoting more time and energy to the linking together of marketing, advertising, brand reputation and company values. In part this is a response to the diversification of the information environment, which provides not just new opportunities for marketing a brand but, to the unwary or unprepared, a considerable threat as well. Take, for instance, the gagging orders issued in April 2011 by the British courts on conventional media over the reporting of the alleged extramarital activities of Premier League football player Ryan Giggs. Whilst the newspapers may not have been able to report his name, users of new media did not feel quite so constrained, and within hours of the High Court injunction his name was widely, and globally, known via Twitter.

The YouTube website has been used to expose alleged corruption in the Russian police force,[207] in the US healthcare system, in Indian food distribution; indeed, any casual search of the YouTube site using the word 'corruption' reveals over 4,000 videos. In *Time* magazine's 'Top 50 Viral YouTube Videos' of all time,[208] number 12, with over 10 million views, is US musician Dave Carroll's anti-United Airlines film. In two music videos, Carroll explains, in song, how United's baggage handlers manhandled his $3,500 guitar at Chicago's O'Hare airport and, after damaging it, offered no compensation or repair. To compound United's misery the incident then became the source of a rich vein of follow-on entertainment videos in their own right, attracting hundreds of thousands of views. And the effect? *The Times* newspaper reported on 22 July 2009 that: 'within four days of the song going online, the gathering thunderclouds of bad PR caused United Airlines' stock price to suffer a mid-flight stall, and it plunged by 10 per cent, costing shareholders $180 million. Which, incidentally, would have bought Carroll more than 51,000 replacement guitars.'[209]

---

207   See http://www.readwriteweb.com/archives/russian_cop_uses_youtube_to_expose_police _corrupti.php

208   See http://www.time.com/time/specials/packages/article/0,28804,1974961_1974925_1970 504,00.html#ixzz1O6kLkM3H

209   'Revenge is Best Served Cold – on YouTube How a Broken Guitar Became a Smash Hit' (*The Times* 22 July 2009).

However, YouTube, and indeed many other new media conduits, have also become a rich playground for advertising and marketing, and one where the ability to make a particular advert go 'viral' can potentially reap substantial profit. Take, for example, Samsung's HD camera phone trick challenge video.[210] Although with significantly fewer viewings (just 1.5m at time of writing) than the United Airlines video, Samsung went to great lengths to protect the secrecy of how the trick shown in the video was conducted, which in turn got the 'tech geeks', who happen to be the audience most likely to go out and buy the camera, thoroughly riled in trying to solve the puzzle and led to a further flurry of global online postings and blogs.

The issue of brand values has taken on particular importance because increasingly business and industry have found that values drive customer behaviour. Values are not just the differentiation between competing brands in the same marketplace (for example between British Airways and Virgin, or Aston Martin and Ferrari). Instead, they are the much more subtle and nuanced evocation of a more intangible emotional response – a 'feeling' of trust and confidence generated amongst potential customers who are invited to 'buy into' the brand and, importantly, to stay with it. For example, Apple computers pretty much do the same thing as PCs. But Apple has succeeded in building an emotional response to their products based upon ideas of lifestyle, imagination, innovation, passion, beauty and simplicity that PC manufacturers have, arguably, not been able to match. Apple seeks to make a heartfelt connection with its customers, not just through the look and feel of its products but in the way that they are marketed and sold. For example, Steve bought a MacBook in the US and asked the salesman if he could test it in the shop before his overnight flight back to the UK. The salesman was brimming over with enthusiasm and when Steve apologised for taking up his time he brushed it off, saying, completely unself-consciously, that he loved 'setting new Macs free from their boxes and packaging'.

Whilst there is clearly an art to this, there is also, most definitely, a science, and failing to understand both can have spectacular results for companies. Take the embattled BP CEO Tony Haywood, who became the fall guy for his company after the April 2010 Deepwater Horizon explosion off the southern coast of the United States. His decision to attend a sailing event at Cowes in the UK whilst attempts were still underway to stop the flow of oil, and his earlier declaration that 'I want my life back',[211] did little to endear him to an already angry international audience who expected quick action and contrition from a company which was already perceived in many quarters as being bad for the environment. It was little surprise to many that he was subsequently replaced as the company's CEO. Yet contrast him with the commanding officer of the British warship HMS Nottingham which ran aground on Lord Howe Island in Australia in 2002. Commander Richard Farrington told the media that: 'This is not a good day for me. Just as the sun comes up in the morning, if you run your ship aground you get court-

210   http://www.youtube.com/watch?v=iX8iVo5vc8o&feature=player_embedded
211   http://www.guardian.co.uk/business/2010/jun/08/bp-deepwater-horizon-obama

martialled.'[212] Yet it quickly became apparent that he had not even been onboard when the ship ran aground and, in the words of the UK's *Mirror* newspaper: 'He suggested it was his fault to protect the young lieutenant in charge. ... exemplifying the British bulldog tradition of taking the blame.' This is not to suggest that the military is some form of shining example – the kidnap of fifteen Royal Navy personnel off the coast of Iran in 2007 and the subsequent embarrassing revelation by one that he cried himself to sleep after his iPod was confiscated had a cataclysmic effect upon the Royal Navy's reputation, both internally and externally. A key part of this emerging communication process has been to generate greater understanding of the customer or audience to help find the right tone for the subsequent communication – Samsung's HD phone advert on YouTube is the absolutely perfect example of this. This is not to say that success is always guaranteed, but a key part of the corporate learning experience has been not just the ability and willingness to take risks, but the careful study of failures as well as successes. In a term first coined in the US, companies and, as we will see, governments, are increasingly referring to this as 'Strategic Communication'.

The US government first begun looking at Strategic Communication properly in 2000, but it was the attacks on the World Trade Center in September 2001 that were to galvanise its thinking about audiences and perceptions. In particular, the US started looking seriously at the manner in which it communicated its foreign policy to external audiences. Over time that self-examination has gestated into a new cross-government discipline. Such gestation has not been without problems, not least because it has occurred at the same moment, in the UK at least, that senior officers began refining their ideas about influence and its place on the battlefield.

Influence

The UK military defines 'influence' as: 'The power or ability to affect someone's beliefs or actions; or a person or thing with such ability or power',[213] and UK defence doctrine – the military's school textbooks – tells 'us' that operations are today conducted through 'Joint Action', which is the balancing of the use of force (which in doctrine terms is referred to as 'Fires'), the idea of presence and of poise (which the doctrinaires refer to as 'Manoeuvre') and influence.[214] This definition has fairly obvious weaknesses, since both Fires and Manoeuvre can exert significant influence upon a target audience in their own right. For example, we know that the visits of Royal Navy warships to foreign ports, and the traditional enter-

---

212   http://ww.telegraph.co.uk/news/uknews/1404113/Commander-who-ran-aground-revealed-to-be-ships-saviour.html

213   UK Joint Doctrine publication 3-40 available to download at: http://www.mod.uk/NR/rdonlyres/C403A6C7-E72C-445E-8246-D11002D7A852/0/20091201jdp_40UDCDCIMAPPS.pdf

214   UK Joint Doctrine publication 3-00.

taining they undertake, has been a key part of UK defence diplomacy for many years. Once upon a time a prime minister might order the dispatch of a gunboat to persuade; today, the gunboat still sails but very often its targeting revolves around soft power, not hard. Whether it is just 'flying the flag' or supporting British industry abroad, the traditional Royal Navy cocktail parties, arranged by the resident defence attaché and the embassy, have always been viewed as being highly influential, and their demise, for cost savings, has been furiously and very publicly fought.[215] The UK and the US, like many other countries, sees great value in providing military training to officers from other nations. Monarchs past and present from strategically important countries such as the United Arab Emirates, Jordan, Saudi Arabia and Oman have all been educated at various UK and US military academies; HRH Kind Abdullah of Jordan recalled with great affection his time at Sandhurst, the British Army's officer training establishment, during a visit to the UK Defence Academy.[216] Whilst of great political value, it is, however, difficult to argue its direct effect on the field of battle, particularly for the West's mission to Afghanistan, where the idea of influence has become a central part of the lexicon of battle.

The British military, in common with other nations, builds and maintains great rafts of doctrine, and indeed both Steve and Andrew, when they worked at the UK Defence Academy, were responsible for part of the chapter on influence which appeared in the MoD's guide to counterinsurgency and post-operational stability. That publication noted that: 'The Commander's role is initially to establish the effects necessary to exert the desired influence. Assisted by his staff he then derives the activities required to realise those effects.'[217] Inherent in this is the need to understand the audience. We already know that this is difficult and that whilst the West has devoted tremendous efforts to its intelligence gathering this still only tells us what an audience is doing or intending to do, not the underlying motivations behind the particular behaviour. Despite the best endeavours of doctrine centres this issue has yet to be successfully addressed. In part this is because the issue is complex and in part because for many the question is still not really understood.

Take, for example, the NATO efforts in Libya. In April 2011 a small UK team was dispatched to the NATO Joint Force Command HQ in Naples. Within four days of arriving they had submitted a substantial number of RFIs (Requests for Information) to the NATO knowledge development cell. A member of the cell came down in person to complain that his cell simply could not cope with the requests and in any event the requests were focused on Libyan civilians (which the UK team assessed was the most important audience) and not on Colonel Gadaffi's

---

215   See http://www.timesonline.co.uk/tol/news/uk/article7061362.ece and http://www.telegraph. co.uk/news/newstopics/politics/defence/7442852/Navy-told-to-scrap-200-year-old-cocktail-tradition-to-save-cash.html

216   Visit of King Abdullah of Jordan to the Defence Academy of the United Kingdom, April 2010.

217   UK Joint Doctrine publication 3-40.

military forces, where the knowledge development cell had been paying the bulk of their attention.

Philosophically, many senior officers argue that armies have been 'doing influence' for years. In part this is true. However, it is a philosophy that forgets that today's conflicts are played out in a rapidly evolving information environment where every action, every deed and every word are analysed and relayed in almost real time. Influence cannot be regarded as an add-on to military planning, it needs be at the heart of every military commander's thinking. We think that strategists and military leaders need to be more like the metaphorical marketing manager at Mushy Peas International we met in the previous chapter. They need to spend more time asking 'What effect do we want to have on a person/group?' before then considering how they may achieve it. If they do their Target Audience Analysis (TAA) right then their analysis will lead to a specific course of action, be it through the application of military force, be it through persuasion or maybe even through deception. In constructing his Operational Design, Brigadier Iain Harrison, Director of ISAF's Influence and Outreach Cell in Kabul, noted that: 'An effects based approach to operations remains wholly relevant, but applying Influence requires a more sophisticated ability to understand and use the levers of Influence; this notion is arguably as relevant for major combat operations as it is for COIN and stabilisation operations.'[218] For the brigadier, and indeed for many others, this means that the West must adopt a much more intellectual approach to future wars.

The term 'influence' for all its imperfections, has now taken hold in the UK military and is unlikely to change. This is not to say that there are not alternatives, and there are some older terms from history which still carry great resonance. Stanley Newcourt-Nowodworski, for example, recalls in his book on black propaganda in the Second World War that the Germans used the expression *Geistige Kriegfuhrung* ('intellectual warfare'),[219] whilst the British chose to use a different term – 'Political Warfare'. A very specialist skill, the deliberate placement of information, some of it false, on the battlefield, and indeed on the Nazi home front, was the responsibility of the Political Warfare Executive. We include a very short résumé of its work, not because it is necessarily a template, in operational terms, for future conflict, but because it played such a seminal role in the war and is therefore an example, in principle, of the type of attention that we think Western governments need to pay today.

---

218 JFIB/1620.04.01 dated 3 September 2009: 'Placing Influence at the Heart of HQ ARRCs Thinking and the Role of the Joint Fires and Influence Branch' (JFIB).

219 Stanley Newcourt-Nowodworski, *Black Propaganda in the Second World War* (Sutton, 2005, p. 5).

The Political Warfare Executive (PWE)

In 1938 the then future director of the British Ministry of Information, Sir Stephen Tallents, wrote a reflective memorandum about the Czech crisis.[220] He noted that the crisis had 'taught us various lessons but the sharpest and the most urgent of them was the need for properly coordinated arrangements for the conveyance of information to enemy countries'.[221] Tallents later became a key supporter of the Political Warfare Executive, a shadowy yet hugely successful information warfare unit formed in August 1941, and created to produce and disseminate both white[222] and black propaganda,[223] with the aim of damaging enemy morale and sustaining the morale of the occupied countries. The executive included staff from the Ministry of Information, from the propaganda elements of the Special Operations Executive,[224] and from the BBC. Its main headquarters was at Woburn Abbey, Bedfordshire, with London offices at the BBC's Bush House. Amongst its many activities were the creation of fake radio stations. *'Gustav Sigfried Eins'* – which alongside *'Soldatensender Calais'* – was the brainchild of one Sefton Delmer, a journalist, fluent German speaker and, as his memoires reveal,[225] eccentric patriot with a great eye for innovation and opportunity. Purporting to be German radio stations they were to prove adept at spreading confusion and sedition.[226]

However, the relevance of the PWE to this book is not so much its tactical day-to-day operations[227] against Nazi-occupied Europe but the fact that it existed at all,

220   On 1 October 1938, Czech frontier guards left their posts and German Nazi troops occupied the Sudetenland – an area inhabited almost exclusively by Germans but which had been artificially constructed in 1919 after the demise of the Austro-Hungarian Empire and the end of the First World War. It was the start of the expansion of Germany and a precursor to the start of the Second World War.

221   David Garnett, *The Secret History of PWE: The Political Warfare Executive 1939-45* (Little, Brown, 2002).

222   'White Propaganda' is generally understood to mean propaganda that truthfully states its origin – i.e. it emanates from identifiable sources and is characterised by persuasive discourse.

223   'Black Propaganda' is generally understood to mean false information of deceitful origin. Between White and Black lies Grey, the source of which is invariably impossible to identify.

224   Special Operations Executive (SOE), sometimes referred to as the 'Baker Street Irregulars', was established by Prime Minister Winston Churchill on 22 July 1940, to conduct warfare by means other than direct military engagement. Its mission was to encourage and facilitate espionage and sabotage behind enemy lines and to serve as the core of the Auxiliary Units, a British resistance movement. For greater detail see W. Stevenson, *A Man Called Intrepid: The Secret War 1939-1945* (MacMillan Press, 1976).

225   Sefton Delmer, *Black Boomerang* (Secker & Warburg, 1962); available to download at www.seftondelmer.co.uk

226   It is fascinating that the history of the Political Warfare Executive was hidden from view until the publication of *The Secret History of the PWE* by David Garnett, some fifty years after it was written.

227   Examples include: the interception of telegrams from German army hospitals to the relatives of soldiers informing them of their loved one's death. This information was used to send letters to the relatives, breaking the bad news but also adding that any valuables belonging to

and that it continued, albeit in different guises, until May 1977 when it was finally shut down by the then Foreign Secretary David Owen. The PWE was established to fill a gap by new British Prime Minister Sir Winston Churchill and his Foreign Secretary Sir Hugh Dalton, who believed that information, its power, and the need to disseminate it were of great importance to the British war effort. Typically, however, its creation was beset by trouble – not least by political infighting between the Foreign Office, the BBC, the Cabinet, Downing Street, the Ministry of Information – and by budgetary constraints imposed by the Treasury. The issue at stake was who should have control of Britain's wartime propaganda effort. Churchill was 'forced … to step in with a minute written on 21 June 1941', which brokered a compromise between competing fiefdoms to establish the PWE, and it was announced to Parliament on 11 September 1941: 'it had not been bureaucratic Britain's finest hour', recalls Andrew Roberts in the foreword to David Garnett's *Secret History of the PWE*.[228]

The PWE carried the propaganda war to the enemy – and to neutrals – via disinformation, covert radio stations, leaflets, and what came to be known as 'sibs' – false rumours which were effective because, as Paul Lashmar and James Oliver note, they 'relied on the human weakness for passing on bad news'.[229] Of key importance was that the PWE both established a forward planning capability and recognised the need to undertake proper measurements of effectiveness (MOE). One campaign that proved particularly successful was called 'Christ the King' – a black propaganda radio station which sought to pass itself off as a Vatican radio station and which denounced the Nazi Party. The rumour of its origin, note Lashmar and Oliver, appeared to travel around Europe remarkably well.[230] So too did a rumour that German soldiers fighting on the Eastern Front had had to be castrated as a result of the intense cold. Regardless, all followed the PWE's mission statement: 'to weaken the enemy's appetite for war, by hindering his ability to fight and by sustaining the occupied countries' will to resist.'[231]

What was most interesting about the PWE's work was that, whilst it engaged in both truthful and untruthful propaganda, it learnt that the most effective information operations were nearly always those which were based on accurate and factual data. Sir Douglas Dodds-Parker, a veteran of special operations and a former Conservative MP, recalled that: 'I have grave doubts whether black propaganda had an effect in any way commensurate with that of straightforward propaganda from enemy to enemy.'[232]

---

their dead relatives were to be held by officials and not immediately returned to the families. This was designed to cause a lot of bad feeling.

228   David Garnett, *The Secret History of PWE* (Little, Brown, 2002).
229   Paul Lashmar and James Oliver, *Britain's Secret Propaganda War* (Sutton, 1998).
230   Ibid., p. 15.
231   Ibid., p. 17.
232   Ibid., p. 19.

The end of the Second World War did not spell the end of the PWE. As Churchill's Iron Curtain descended across Europe there was a growing belief that the UK needed the ability to counter Soviet propaganda, and under the guidance of Christopher Mayhew the establishment of the Information Research Department (IRD) was approved by Cabinet on 4 January 1948. Mayhew declared that: 'we must be able to pass over to the offensive and not least to leave the initiative to the enemy, but to make them defend themselves.'[233] The IRD was one of the first Western information warfare units, predating even the CIA, and under British Prime Minister Anthony Eden and the then head of IRD (and future SIS[234] chief) Jack Rennie, was effectively turned into a political warfare agency against Nasser and Arab nationalism in 1956, leaving Rennie's deputy, Norman Reddaway, to keep the anti-communist operations running. IRD distributed its materials via the network of British Embassies, principally to foreign newspaper readers for dissemination to their readers, and even then in a pre-Internet world, ultimately to the British public.[235] One of its earliest successes was in publicising the existence of Soviet labour camps, which the IRD sought to compare with Nazi concentration camps. Like its predecessor, the IRD found greater value in facts than in deception and lies. Lashmar and Oliver state that its informal slogan was 'anything but the truth was too hot to handle', and note that: 'former IRD insiders say that their emphasis on the mobilisation of truth rather than black propaganda was more effective as a means of influencing public opinion.'[236]

Its end was ignominious but also noteworthy. As relations with the Soviet Union slowly thawed, its work became less relevant and it sought new avenues. Perhaps foolishly these manifested themselves in the UK with concern over the activities of trades unions and the possible infiltration of communists into the Labour Party. Such domestic interests fell outside its established boundaries and had the look of overt meddling in the British political system. And so it was shut, on the orders of David Owen, although the committee that made the recommendation did note that: 'un-attributable material had a role in creating "helpful political attitudes" in the more influential Third World countries.'[237] Its demise was recounted in a *Guardian* newspaper article on 27 January 1978, entitled 'Death of the Department That Never Was',[238] which noted that its demise did not see the end of 'government propaganda' and that a new department – the Overseas Information Department – had been established within the Foreign Office, a much smaller unit where 'no domestic propaganda'[239] was tolerated. That the IRD lasted so long, and that Garnett's book languished under the Official Secrets Act for so many years after writing, suggests that successive British governments were well aware

---

233   Ibid., p. 26.
234   The Secret Intelligence Service or, as it is more colloquially referred to, MI6.
235   David Leigh, 'Death of the Department That Never Was' (*Guardian*, 27 January 1978).
236   Lashmar and Oliver, *Britain's Secret Propaganda War*, p. 26.
237   Ibid.
238   Leigh, ibid.
239   Ibid.

of the power of information and that Garnett's book – which its jacket describes as 'a handbook of how to undermine an adversary'[240] – was just too sensitive for publication. Richard Cottam suggests why: 'clandestine political warfare of the type called for raises ethical questions … involvement in the domestic politics of other peoples is ethically offensive.'[241]

The Research, Information and Communication Unit (RICU)

Whilst political warfare may present governments with ethical dilemmas, the need for detailed and properly researched information in the twenty-first century fight against Al-Qaeda-inspired extremism, for example, appeared to have been met when, in October 2007, the British government announced the establishment of the Research, Information and Communication Unit. The Home Office publicly declared RICU's role to be 'a counter-terrorism strategic communications unit. It exists to ensure that the Government has a positive impact in its counter terrorist communications, and to both counter the impact of terrorist communications directly, and assist others in doing so.'[242] According to the Home Office, RICU has three key deliverables: first, advising CONTEST[243] partners on counter-terrorism related communications; second, exposing the weaknesses of violent extremists' ideologies and brand; and last, supporting credible alternatives to violent extremism. RICU has a staff of around thirty people and reports to three different ministers of state – the Home Secretary, the Minister for Government and Local Communities, and the Foreign Secretary.

Dr Jamie Macintosh was, between May 2006 and June 2007, personal adviser to the Home Secretary John Reid on transformation and national security. He was in part responsible for RICU's creation, which he states was a response to a perceived absence of capacity in central government. He recalled the Home Secretary's thinking: 'The Prime Minister had a Lieutenant for every other portfolio of government, except the first duty of government, national security. And that meant that the Prime Minister himself stretched across every portfolio of government and so the first duty was not getting the attention it should have. Blair agreed with that analysis.'[244] Macintosh recalled that: 'The only other time in UK history when these matters had been properly addressed and integrated was the Cabinet War Rooms of Churchill and in particular the role of PWE … the Home

---

240   David Garnett, *The Secret History of PWE* (Little, Brown, 2002).
241   Richard Cottam, *Competitive Interference and Twentieth Century Diplomacy* (University of Pittsburgh Press, 1967, p. 23).
242   http://security.homeoffice.gov.uk/about-us/about-the-directorate/RICU/ – website link accessible at time of manuscript submission, but not available as at November 2011
243   The UK's national counter-terrorism strategy is known as 'CONTEST' and is based on a policy that can be summed up in four words: Prevent, Pursue, Protect and Prepare.
244   Interview with Steve Tatham, 13 January 2010.

Secretary understood that we needed a PWE if we were serious about strategy making, and engaging in the battle of ideas, seamlessly from operational theatres abroad to the home front.'[245] Indeed, Macintosh recalls that the Home Secretary was well versed in the history of the PWE: 'He knew all about the PWE ... Yes. The historical development of it and of statecraft and governance. We debated it and discussed it in policy routinely. It was the product of an ongoing debate that stretched back to his role as Defence Secretary.'[246]

Big government departments are not known for their speed, but RICU was established comparatively quickly, despite a major handicap. Macintosh recalls that:

> If the logic was overwhelming that we were at war it should have been done quicker and more fulsomely. But you can't magic away a peacetime mentality. You can't just dispel it. In London, despite 7/7, despite Operation Overt [a terrorist plot to blow up transatlantic airliners], despite Basra and Afghanistan most people were still in a peacetime mentality (I mean senior officials and politicians). From that perspective the speed we reacted was fast ... The Cabinet Office working group formed and delivered recommendations in two months – it was chaired by John Reid. Half the Cabinet were part of it.[247]

RICU, it was envisaged, would have a very specific role. According to Macintosh it 'embodied the shared view of the Prime Minister and the Home Secretary which essentially embraced the fact that the conflict in which we were engaged was seamless so it had evolving operational theatres abroad that were interconnected'.[248] However, it was also designed to fill a gap, identified in a highly classified study of the UK's counter-terrorist strategy, CONTEST, which had found the UK lacking in several key areas. And so: 'RICU's remit was anticipated as addressing the battle of ideas. The need for a narrative, the production of content and in my language this was more about the deep battle than the close battle. We had deconflicted from the close battle of everyday political communication.'[249]

Its work was, at inception, a source of great interest to the British media, who noted that:

> Whitehall officials are being asked to draw up 'counter-narratives' to the anti-western messages on websites designed to influence vulnerable and impressionable audiences. They will set out to explain what one of-

245   Interview with Steve Tatham, 13 January 2010
246   Ibid.
247   Ibid.
248   Ibid.
249   Ibid.

ficial called the government's 'foreign policy in its totality', counter the accusations made by al-Qaida sympathisers and extremist groups and pinpoint the weaknesses in their arguments. ... The unit will also support 'alternative voices' in the Muslim community.[250]

Indeed, such commentary was not very far from the truth. In its annual Unit Business Plan, RICU identified ten key work strands, amongst them the need to highlight declining support for Al-Qaeda, the exploitation and brutality of Al-Qaeda, the incoherent agenda that it offered and its absence of Islamic theological credibility.[251] Necessarily, much of its work is conducted out of the public eye but occasionally, either deliberately or by design, it has come to public prominence.

One of RICU's first actions was to produce a lexicon of language that the British government could use to articulate its perspective. Its then head, Jonathan Allen, 'repeatedly emphasized the importance of using an appropriate lexicon informed by the audiences'. Government messages originally used the term 'Islamist terrorism' in an attempt to focus on a particular branch of political Islam, rather than on Islam as a whole. When polled, however, the vast majority of people had no idea that there was a distinction, and many in the Muslim community interpreted the term to mean 'all Muslims are terrorists'. RICU then polled the community, asking them what terms they used to describe terrorists, and from the list – which included 'idiots, sickos, bastards, and nutters' – RICU selected 'criminals and murderers'. Terms like '*jihadi*' or '*jihadist*', while accepted as disparaging by UK audiences, were rejected by Muslims abroad as associating terrorism with Islam.[252] On this latter point it is perhaps unfortunate that RICU did not extend its thinking further, for the idea of linking criminality to Al-Qaeda, rather than providing it with religious justification, as the use of *jihad* does, has been well documented. Layla Sein of the Association of Muslim Social Scientists explains:

Since the concept of *jihad* comes from the root word *jahada* (to strive or struggle for self-betterment from an ethical-moral perspective) and that of *hirabah* comes from the root word *hariba* (to fight, to go to war or become enraged or angry), an etymological and theological examination of these words provides a valid framework through which the religious legitimacy of suicide bombings in today's global community can be analyzed ... To delve into a comparative study of these Islamic concepts is to expose how *hirabah* is being paraded by terrorist groups as *jihad*. By defining *hirabah* as *jihad*, such terrorist groups as al Qaeda and

---

250   Counter-terrorism officials rethink stance on Muslims, Richard Norton-Tailor, The *Guardian*, 20 November 2007.

251   RICU Annual Unit Business Plan, Version 3. Issued by OSCT 17 March 2008. This document is classified 'RESTRICTED'.

252   Address to Homeland Security Policy Institute, 24 June 2008; available at: http://www.gwumc.edu/hspi/old/lexiconsummary.htm

others promote their terrorist agendas by misleading young, religiously motivated and impressionable Muslims to believe that killing unarmed and non-combatant civilians are activities of *jihad*, and hence a ticket to paradise.[253]

Indeed, *hirabah* is an especially useful word as it also covers both the directed and coincidental spreading of fear. It is also one of the most severely punished crimes in Islam. Thus, using the proper Arabic term could help legitimise measures by organisations such as RICU to destroy the terrorists' rhetoric and major recruiting tool. Immediately after the September 11 attacks in 2001, Dr Ezzeddin Ibrahim, the former chancellor of Al Ain University in the United Arab Emirates, noted that: 'What occurred on September 11, 2001, is one of the most loathsome of crimes, which in Islam goes under the name of *al-hirabah*. *Hirabah* is the most abominable type of murder, in that it involves killing with terrorism and intimidation.'[254] Usefully this might have been something that RICU could have persuaded the British press to take up, rather than its over-gratuitous use of the word *jihad*. However, this did not happen and *jihad* has remained the word of choice to explain deeply complicated events to Western publics and completely misrepresenting the behaviour of a very small number of Islamic zealots.

For RICU, however, such work would remain largely in the shadows, for its work has perhaps been unfairly tainted not so much by the reputation and working practices of its historical forbears but by allegations of 'spin', and not just by the British media but increasingly by the British public too.[255] And this is perhaps where RICU has struggled to explain itself. A more active disassociation from government PR for party political reasons would have been helpful, if perhaps understandably difficult for the media to accept; with in its place a better articulation of the very real and strategic mission it had in fighting Al-Qaeda's often compelling rhetoric.

Media operations

The UK Armed Forces have a long and perhaps not always glorious record of interacting with the media. Arguably, that tension is inescapable and from its earliest days was obvious. The very first embedded war correspondent, William Russell of the London *Times*, reported on the conditions that British troops lived and fought under during the 1854 Crimean War. His reports, which because of the then slow communication routes had very little effect on the real-time operational

---

253   Layla Sein, 'Editorial' (Association of Muslim Social Scientists *AMSS Bulletin* 3, no. 4, 2002).

254   Interview with Ezzeddin Ibrahim (*Middle East Policy Council Journal*, vol. VIII, no. 4, December 2001).

255   Alan Travis, 'Revealed: Britain's Secret Propaganda War Against AQ' (*Guardian*, 26 August 2008).

and tactical conduct of the battle and its protagonists, had a significant effect on the wider strategic and public understanding of the campaign and led to him incurring the wrath of the Prince Consort, Albert, who regarded his dispatches as traitorous. Yet his dispatches were to have a profound effect on one Florence Nightingale who, horrified by what she read, took it upon herself to improve the standards of care for wounded British soldiers in the field.

The immediacy of information is a significant and growing problem for the military. An incident occurring on the field of battle is reported, via mobile phone, to the news desk and is potentially on air and online immediately, with potentially profound effects. On 4 September 2009 NATO aircraft were called in by German forces on the ground to attack two oil tanker trucks they believed had been hijacked by the Taliban in Konduz, northern Afghanistan. Very quickly images began to emerge both on the Web and then in the world's media, which suggested that far from NATO having hit Taliban insurgents they had instead killed a large number of civilians. In the ensuing controversy the German magazine *Der Spiegel* claimed that the attack had been a war crime, and recriminations across the German government saw ministers and military officers falling, culminating in the German Defence Minister, Karl-Theodor zu Guttenberg, relieving Germany's most senior general, Wolfgang Schneiderhahn, of his position. Yet he was relieved of his post not for the incident itself but for what followed, and in particular for his, and the German army's, inability to provide proper information about the incident.

The confusion over the strike was an almost mirror image of the air strike on the village of Azizabad, near Herat in western Afghanistan, just over a year earlier. NATO war planes, acting on intelligence that a Taliban commander was in the vicinity, bombed the village. Within hours rumours started circulating that, far from killing the insurgent leader, a large number of civilians had instead been killed. On 25 August, three days after the strike, the Pentagon told the Reuters news agency that the 'Afghanistan attack was a "legitimate" hit at the Taliban'. The next day ABC news reported an ISAF spokesman as saying 'five Afghan civilians killed in strikes', whilst on 3 September, the US denied a UN allegation that a large number of civilians had been killed. However, on 7 September the *New York Times* published mobile phone imagery of the aftermath of the attack[256] clearly showing dead women and children. Finally, on 1 October 2008, nearly two months after the event, the US Department of Defense published the summary of a report by Brigadier General Michael Callan, which accepted that thirty-three civilians had been killed.

Why then does the military have such trouble understanding exactly what has happened as a result of events that it has itself very often instigated? Governments would put up a number of very plausible explanations; chiefly, and undeniably, conflict is an extremely difficult environment in which to seek the 'truth'. All sides will be looking to capitalise upon events to their own specific political

---

256   'Evidence Points to Civilian Toll in Afghan Raid' (*New York Times*, 7 September 2008).

and military advantage, and understanding the 'facts' is often difficult. During his time as Naval spokesman in Iraq in 2003, Steve had to deal with the media implications of two Royal Navy helicopters crashing in midair[257] just seconds after they took off from the deck of HMS Ark Royal on the first night of the Coalition attack on Saddam Hussein. The report of the crash was on the BBC news quicker than the report was received in the Maritime Component Battle Staff Headquarters (the BBC having been embedded with the Royal Navy and having a real-time satellite up-link device). The media's enquiries were instant: 'Was it enemy action?', 'Was it pilot error?', 'Was there equipment failure?" How could Steve, as the official Naval spokesman, possibly provide factual answers when he himself had heard of the incident only minutes beforehand – *and from the media itself, not from the chain of command.* Yet none of the answers would be properly determined until long after the event, and long after the 24-hour news culture had moved on to new stories. Indeed, it was not until 2007 that Oxfordshire's assistant deputy coroner, Sir Richard Curtis, recorded a verdict of accidental death on the seven aircrew, but even then, four years after the events, Alan Massey, who had been the commanding officer of the ship at the time of the incident, told the inquest: 'All I know is that the aircraft flew into each other. We can't for the life of us fathom what it was.'[258]

Such incidents lead to an obvious tension between media and military, one that has characterised conflicts such as the Falklands War,[259] the operations in Bosnia and Kosovo, and the first Gulf War.[260] The speed of news is a problem facing not just the UK Armed Forces but the British government as a whole. The issue of 'when' to comment on a news story has now become a greater issue than 'whether' the government should comment on a news story, and is carefully examined by BBC world correspondent Nik Gowing in his 2009 Oxford Reuters Institute paper 'A Skyful of Lies and Black Swans', which concludes that media engagement is close to crisis point.

Media operations, the term used by the UK to manage the relationship, is defined as the 'timely, accurate and effective provision of public information … whilst maintaining operational security'.[261] Despite having both its own Centre of Excellence and a well-defined doctrine document,[262] it is perhaps surprising that the practice of media operations remains the task of amateurs, plucked from the

257   http://edition.cnn.com/2003/WORLD/meast/03/22/sprj.irq.heli.crash/index.html

258   http://www.dailymail.co.uk/news/article-427267/Deaths-soldiers-killed-Iraq-chopper-crash-accident.html

259   The 1982 Falklands crisis is cited by many academics as a 'low point' in British media/military relations and is perhaps best summed up by an [in]famous MoD statement that the 'essence of warfare is secrecy, the essence of journalism is openness'. Readers may wish to read Robert Harris's account of the problems in *Gotcha: The Media, The Government and The Falklands Crisis* (Faber & Faber, 1983).

260   See Chapter 4, Tatham, *Losing Arab Hearts and Minds: The Coalition, Al-Jazeera and Muslim Public Opinion* (Hurst & Co (UK), Front Street Press (US), 2006).

261   JDP3-45.1 *Media Operation* published by UK MoD Defence Doctrine Concepts Centre.

262   Ibid.

ranks of the UK Armed Forces for a 'tour'[263] before returning to their core specialisation. The regular forces are supplemented by reserve forces who are more specialised; for the army this capability is known as the Media Operations Group (Volunteers) or MOG(V), and whilst they offer useful expertise they come with all the attendant issues of employing reserve forces, most notably that the Armed Forces are a secondary career and finding time to supplement and augment the regular forces will always be predicated upon civilian employment. There has also been an issue in past years when volunteers, whose civilian occupation was in the media, may have suffered a conflict of loyalties between information they were made aware of as a military officer and that which was suitable for the public domain. Given its criticality it is perhaps surprising, therefore, that the most visible and potentially politically damaging aspect of the UK's military operations is presided over by those without experience of information and media. Medical treatment would not be administered by someone without medical training, nor would rules of combat engagement be presided over by those lacking legal credentials. As we will see, however, such amateurism is a recurring theme.

Information and psychological operations

Always firewalled from their media operations cousins, information and psychological operations practitioners share one common theme: they too – at least in the UK – are largely amateurs plucked from the massed ranks of the Armed Forces. Information Operations (IO) is defined by the MoD as: 'Coordinated military activity undertaken to affect decision-makers in support of political and military objectives by influencing their will, affecting their decision-making processes and shaping their understanding, while protecting our own decision-makers and processes.'[264] Thus IO is defined as a coordinating function, but confusingly and increasingly, it is regarded as an activity in its own right. IO in the UK is parented by the Targeting and Information Operations (TIO) division within the MoD, a small group of officers embedded deep within the old War Office in Whitehall and who are part of the Deputy Chief of Defence Staff (Operations) division.

The UK's psychological operation capability is maintained by the 15th Psychological Operations Group (PsyOps) and is based at the Defence Intelligence and Security Centre (DISC) in Bedfordshire. The unit's title is perhaps somewhat illu-

---

263   In the UK Military a tour is typically of around 18 months' to 3 years' duration and may be best explained as an attachment to a unit or group. Some tours may be within core competency areas – for example a Naval engineering officer may undertake a tour as the engineer on a ship at sea. However, some are more general and will take personnel of any specialisation – this is typically the case for media operations where often the officer will have no prior experience of the subject and, since it is away from their core expertise, is unlikely to return to it in the future. Often these are referred to as 'broadening' appointments to aid an individual's career development and test competency away from core specialities.

264   JDP3.80 *Information Operations* published by UK MoD Defence Doctrine Concepts Centre.

sionary – there are no 1–14 PsyOps units but, as the stag's head logo[265] of the unit testifies, there were once. During the Far East campaigns of the Second World War, PsyOps battlefield activities in support of 21 Army Group were conducted by Amplifier Units (numbered 10–14). Indeed, one of the very first units on the scene at the liberation of the Belsen concentration camp in 1945 was the 14th Amplifier Unit, which announced to the prisoners that whilst they were free from their tormentors they most certainly were not free to leave the camp, because of its outbreak of cholera.

As well as deploying Psychological Support Elements (PSE) on operations, 15 PsyOps trains both strategic and tactical PsyOps. The MoD defines the purpose of psychological operations as to 'influence the perceptions, attitudes and behaviour of selected individuals or groups'.[266] It might be argued that there is little difference between the aim of media operations and that of psychological operations, since both seek to influence a target audience in a specific manner. Yet media operations is essentially a facilitator for the media who actually produce the finished product, and over which the military typically have little or no control.[267] Psychological operations, however, retains direct control over its products, be they print, radio, new media, TV or loudspeaker broadcasts. There is, of course, some crossover; the MoD's military combat camera teams often film events which the civilian media cannot attend. (The early years of the Afghan conflict were examples, the sheer difficulty of getting media to the high altitude and remote operating grounds in which the battle was taking place meant that the combat camera team footage was extremely popular.) However, the MoD has no TV service of its own (website notwithstanding) and thus the footage is still passed to the media for dissemination. This is not the case for PsyOps products.

It has already been noted that the US chooses different terms from the UK for its information activities, and this is also true of PsyOps, which the US refers to (as of a 2010 directive) as MISO (Military Information Support to Operations). Although many of its personnel are reservists, it is a far larger organisation than its UK colleague and indeed is commanded by a major general. Created in 1952 and based at Fort Bragg, North Carolina, (the home of both the US Airborne Regi-

---

265   The group adopted as its logo a stag's head which had been used by Indian Field Broadcast Units (IFBU) – reputedly the deer's antlers symbolise both the combat support function of PsyOps and the antennae associated with a major means of dissemination of psychological warfare messages.

266   JDP3.80 *Information Operations* published by UK MoD Defence Doctrine Concepts Centre.

267   This is for many a moot point. There is a well-developed line of academic thinking (see in particular Carruthers, *The Media and the Military*) that suggests that when journalists voluntarily embed with military units, and submit their work for approval prior to release, they are in fact submitting editorial control to the military. This author denies that allegation as there are plenty of documented examples of very pejorative and damaging material being filed by journalists through the military embedding process and it being published without amendment. However, the allegation that journalists become reliant upon the military during extended embeds, and build empathy with them that might adversely affect their editorial view, is more compelling.

ments and its Special Operations Forces) the US PsyOps capability was originally designed 'to organize, train, and support indigenous personnel in behind-the-lines resistance activities to "retard" a Soviet invasion in Europe, the Group's true historical forerunner was the Office of Strategic Services'.[268] Today, it is divided into two groups – the 2nd and 7th Psychological Operations Groups. Their website cites their objectives:

> Psychological operations support national security objectives at the tactical, operational and strategic levels of operations. Strategic psychological operations advance broad or long-term objectives. Global in nature, they may be directed toward large audiences or at key communicators. Operational psychological operations are conducted on a smaller scale. They are employed by theatre commanders to target groups within the theater of operations.[269]

Each group is sub-divided into sixteen companies. Since a company is between 100 and 200 personnel in size, this suggests the US military has a total size of around 3,500 psychological operations personnel – the UK is able to field less than 2 per cent of that number.

In *Leaflets of the Persian Gulf War*,[270] the 4th Psychological Operations Unit highlighted its work between December 1990 and February 1991. Dividing its work into three areas – leaflet drops, radio broadcasts and loudspeaker operations – the unit dropped over 29 million leaflets, deployed 66 loudspeaker teams and broadcast 'Voice of the Gulf' – a Coalition radio news station targeting Iraqi soldiers. In the 2003 invasion of Iraq, similar techniques were used, with the British frigate HMS Chatham, in particular, broadcasting over 296 hours of radio broadcasts directly into southern Iraq,[271] whilst the US flew specially converted C-130 aircraft of the 193rd US Special Operations Wing, the curiously named 'Commando Solo' plane able to transmit high-quality radio and TV signals as well as deploying sophisticated jamming devices.[272]

Superficially, then, one might conclude that psychological operations is a well-established tenant of the contemporary battlefield. And so it is. Yet its deployment, at least in the UK case, is not without difficulty. The House of Commons Defence Committee published its Third Report of Session 2003–04 on the lessons of the

268   A. Paddock, *Psychological and Unconventional Warfare, 1941-1952: Origins of a Special Warfare Capability for the United States Army* (Army War College Paper, Carlisle Barracks, 1979).

269   http://www.usacapoc.army.mil/facts-psyop.html

270   4th Psychological Operations Group (Airborne), *Leaflets of the Persian Gulf War*, Unit Publication produced by Colonel Layton G. Dunbar, US Special Forces.

271   Tatham, *Losing Arab Hearts and Minds*, p. 161.

272   Ibid., p. 157.

Iraq war on 16 March 2004. The report noted that: 'We believe that the British information operations campaign did not begin early enough. We are concerned that the lessons of the Kosovo campaign were not better learned in this important area. It is disappointing that the Coalition is widely perceived to have "come second" in perception management',[273] and further commented that: 'We believe that the importance of the media campaign in the modern world remains under-appreciated by sections of the Armed Forces. The early establishment of a robust media operations capability in theatre must be a priority for any operation.'[274]

There is one hugely important component on PsyOps (or MISO) that is easily overlooked: PsyOps is the only line of activity in contemporary conflict that actively uses the techniques of TAA as a precursor to operations. Both 15 PsyOps and the US MISO teams have dedicated TAA practitioners, often but not exclusively taken from military intelligence backgrounds, backed up by civilian scientists from research agencies such as the Defence Science and Technology Laboratories (DSTL) in the UK, an agency of the MoD, and in the US, the Defense Advanced Projects Agency (DARPA). TAA is a vital and under-resourced capability, but one that we believe is utterly key to understanding future behaviour-based conflict, and in recognition of that, the UK's military Doctrine Centre agreed to include behaviour in its 2011 document on Strategic Communications.

The US Human Terrain System (HTS) and The UK's Defence Cultural Specialist Unit

US Major General Ben Freakley, Commander of Joint Task Force 76 in Afghanistan, has said:

> Cultural awareness will not necessarily always enable us to predict what the enemy and non-combatants will do, but it will help us better understand what motivates them, what is important to the host nation in which we serve and how we can either elicit the support of the population or at least diminish their support and aid to the enemy.[275]

In a bid to understand the cultural dimension of twenty-first-century warfare, the US military's Foreign Military Studies Office began the task of establishing and deploying the Human Terrain System (HTS) – five-man teams, comprising social

---

273   http://www.publications.parliament.uk/pa/cm200304/cmselect/cmdfence/635/63506.htm

274   House of Commons Defence Select Committee Report on Iraq. Third report of Session 2003-2004; available to download at http://www.publications.parliament.uk/pa/cm200304/cmselect/cmdfence/57/57.pdf

275   J. Kipp, L. Grau, K. Prinslow and D. Smith, *The Human Terrain System: A CORDS for the Twenty-First Century* (Military Review, 2006, p. 9).

scientists and military personnel, who could advise commanders at operational and tactical levels on cultural awareness shortcomings. It was not a new idea; in the Vietnam War the US military established, together with the South Vietnamese government, a Civil Operations and Revolutionary Development Support programme (CORDS), designed specifically to 'win hearts and minds'. CORDS was premised on the belief that the war would be won (or lost) not on the battlefield but in the struggle for the loyalty of the people.[276] Indeed, as one of the scheme's instigators, Jacob Kipp, observes: 'While history offers many examples of insurgencies worthy of study, the HTS concept has been largely inspired by lessons drawn from the US experience in Vietnam.'[277] A 2007 Department of Defense report on HTS noted:

> The local population in the area of conflict – the human terrain – must be considered as a distinct and critical element of the battlespace. Therefore, the Human Terrain Team [sic] seeks to integrate and apply socio-cultural knowledge of the indigenous population to military operations in support of the commander's objectives. In the words of one HTT [sic] member, 'One anthropologist can be much more effective than a B-2 bomber – not winning a war, but creating a peace one Afghan at a time'.[278]

By 14 April 2007, thirty-eight HTS personnel were deployed in Iraq, distributed among five teams. Of those, eight were social scientists and thirteen spoke Arabic. Their deployment was clearly popular, and they sought to manage some key issues. First and foremost was to provide commanders with relevant socio-cultural knowledge and understanding, and to extend that further by providing specialists able to help integrate that understanding into the military decision-making process. Second, and of key importance, the HTS teams sought to minimise the loss of knowledge and local understanding which occurred every time a unit rotated out of theatre. The DoD report noted:

> That soldiers on their second – or third – tours possess inestimable knowledge about the area in which they are operating is undeniable. Yet, as currently organized, combat brigades do not possess the organic staff capability or assets to organize this knowledge ...Therefore, it is the job of HTS to take the knowledge these soldiers have gleaned, to examine the information already being gathered on the ground on a daily basis, engage in original research, and consider this information in

---

276   Ibid., p. 10.
277   Ibid.
278   US DoD: Human Terrain Team Preliminary Assessment: Executive Summary July-August 2007. Director, Human Terrain System Assessment Team.

terms of broader issues from a different perspective in order to add to the brigade commander's situational awareness of the social, economic, political, cultural and psychological factors at work in the environment.

The HTS scheme has not come without considerable criticism, chiefly from the American Anthropological Association, which expressed deep concern at their ability to 'fulfill their ethical responsibilities'[279] as anthropologists. Indeed, criticism of the issue has formed a whole sector of academic writing, not least *The Counter, Counter-Insurgency Manual*, written by the Network of Concerned Anthropologists.[280] Unsurprisingly, the reaction in the US military has been somewhat different. Colonel Martin Schweitzer, Commander of the 82nd Airborne, told the *New York Times* that his unit's combat operations in Afghanistan had 'been reduced by 60 per cent since the scientists arrived in February [2007]',[281] whilst Colonel David Woods of the 73rd Cavalry told the paper that 'you have to evolve, otherwise you are useless'.[282] In a fascinating exchange in *Survival* magazine, a US marine relays his personal experiences of cultural awareness from operations in Bosnia, Fallujah and the Horn of Africa, which are then dissected by four anthropologists.[283] At the crux of the marine's view was that: 'Anthropology and ethnography teach us to listen well, ask good questions and develop a broad yet critical understanding of ethnic conflict.'[284]

The UK has taken a slightly different tack, deploying not anthropologists but, instead, cultural advisors from the Defence Cultural Specialist Unit. Established in 2010 at RAF Henlow in Bedfordshire, DCSU is parented by the 1 Military Intelligence Brigade. The unit exists, so its mission statement proclaims, to 'deliver military cultural specialism'.[285] Its staff are all British military officers and all are linguists, each having completed the fifteen-month long Pashto language course at the UK's Defence School of Languages, as well as a series of specialist courses in anthropology at Cranfield University. Now comprising forty-two regular servicemen and women, and a growing number of reservists, the unit seeks to deploy one cultural advisor (colloquially known as a 'Culad') to every battle group, and one to the deployed Brigade Commander Headquarters.

---

279   Statement on HTS made by the American Anthropological Association, 31 October 2007.
280   Network of Concerned Anthropologists, *The Counter-Counter-Insurgency Manual or, Notes on Demilitarizing American Society* (Prickly Paradigm Press, 2009).
281   David Rohde, 'Army Enlists Anthropology in War Zones' (*New York Times*, 5 October 2007).
282   Ibid.
283   'Anthropology in Conflict: An Exchange' (*Survival*, June-July 2008, pp. 127-162).
284   Ibid., p. 138.
285   http://www.mod.uk/DefenceInternet/DefenceNews/DefencePolicyAndBusiness/SpecialistU nitToAdviseCommandersInHelmandOfCulturalIssuesLaunched.htm

Strategic communication

In April 2011, the UK MoD's Defence Concepts and Doctrine Centre (DCDC) is-sued JDN1/11, a doctrine 'note' (and therefore a discussion document) rather than a JDP (a 'publication', and therefore agreed and prescribed military doctrine). In this document strategic communication was defined as: 'Advancing national in-terests by using all Defence means of communication to influence the attitudes and behaviours of people.' Critically, it later explains the three principal types of communication:

> ... informational, attitudinal, and behavioural. Informational communi-cation seeks simply to impart (for example, a news item such as HMS Manchester Visits Merseyside before Decommissioning on the MOD website). Attitudinal communication seeks to positively influence peo-ple's opinion on a particular issue. This is a key component of routine political communication (for example, the Government's efforts to im-prove internal and public confidence in the medical support provided to Armed Forces personnel, particularly those wounded on operations). Behavioural communication seeks to induce a particular type of behav-iour, either reinforcing or changing it (such as the laws to make people wear seatbelts or increasing the tax on cigarettes to reduce the numbers of smokers in the country). The three types of communication can be linked together but are not necessarily dependent upon each other. For example, attitudinal and behavioural campaigns can be combined (such as in the Give Up Smoking campaign), while informational campaigns may seek no attitudinal or behavioural change at all.[286]

That behaviour should figure so prominently is by no means an accident; the re-sult of concerted lobbying by Steve, it was included despite resistance from other officers, who remained of the view that strategic communication was all about attitudes, and British taxpayer attitudes at that. This was not helped when stra-tegic communication officials from other government departments were brought together for a round-table discussion on the issue. Almost all came from govern-ment press organisations and, sat as they were amongst a number of senior jour-nalists and academics, it is perhaps understandable why strategic communica-tion is seen principally as a presentation, and therefore media, issue.

And this is the problem with strategic communication, for whilst it inherently embodies the principles of influence and behavioural change, it does so counter-intuitively. The assembled contributing members of the DCDC panel were very much divided over the issue of TAA, and as a result it has received only the

---

286   JDN1/11 Strategic Communication 'The Defence Contribution', available to download at http://www.mod.uk/DefenceInternet/microsite/dcdc/

most cursory mention in the note, and a detailed proposal to include a chapter on measures of effect failed to find any traction at all. We would like to think that the fact that such a forward-thinking publication could even be printed was ideally indicative of the pace of change in thinking over the past few years. Regretfully, this would be a step too far, for in reality JDN1/11 owes its creation to the personal direction of the UK's Chief of Defence Staff, General Sir David Richards, who admitted to Steve at a recent event that his entire thinking about conflict had been changed by his experiences of commanding operations in Sierra Leone and Indonesia. Yet even with such powerful backing, the document could still only reflect a consensus – truly innovative thinking was, on this occasion, too much for the market to bear, and is illustrative of the manner in which the UK military evolves its thinking – slowly and with the utmost conservatism.

Dr Ken Payne is a King's College academic who specializes in influence and strategic communication. A former producer on the BBC's flagship investigative journalism programme Panorama, he is well placed to comment. He writes:

> If Strategic Communication is to be anything more than a poorly conceptualised buzzword or slogan, then those interested in the problem of persuasion in wartime must deepen and broaden their understanding of the means through which influence is attained. Social psychology, indeed psychology more broadly, has plenty of robust findings that can be utilised by practitioners. The dilemma for the military is whether and how to engage with this literature – is it the stuff of specialists, or generalist officers? The thrust from DCDC suggests the latter. In which case, DCDC must lead the move away from naive understandings of truth and credibility – acknowledging that there is a world of difference between lying and constructing a persuasive narrative is a promising start.[287]

---

287   Dr Kenneth Payne, 'Thoughts on the Psychology of "Strategic Communication"' (Defence Studies Department, King's College London).

8
Influence and perception

> The best policy is to use strategy, influence and the trend of events to cause the adversary to submit willingly.
>
> Sun Tzu[288]

Let's summarise where we have got to so far. We have looked at the conflicts that shaped our joint thinking; we looked at the very nature of communication itself; we examined ideas of advertising and marketing; and we looked at the structures (we called them 'enablers') that currently exist, or have existed in the past, in the governments of the UK and of our allies. We even looked at mushy peas and sports cars. Central to all our ideas has been the need to understand audiences and, with that knowledge, effect properly constructed influence campaigns, perhaps dislocating the urge to apply force, as the primary activity, from the epicentre of military thinking to the periphery. The former Australian soldier David Kilcullen has rather famously noted that:

> [We] typically design physical operations first, then craft supporting information operations to explain our actions. This is the reverse of al-Qaida's approach. For all our professionalism, compared to the enemy's, our public information is an afterthought. In military terms, for al-Qaida the 'main effort' is information; for us, information is a 'supporting effort'.[289]

The French strategist David Galula was perhaps more succinct: 'If there was a field in which we were definitely and infinitely more stupid than our opponents, it was propaganda.'[290]

To be clear, neither of us is suggesting that propaganda is the key to success in future conflicts. The word itself is highly contentious and probably inextricably linked to both totalitarian regimes of the twentieth century and to an era when even a non-totalitarian state could effectively control public discussion (or at least effectively suppress certain elements of it). However, we are attracted to Galula's

---

288   Sun Tzu, *The Art of War* (Filiquarian, 2006).
289   David Kilcullen, 'Counterinsurgency in Iraq: Theory and Practice 2007'; available at http://www.smallwarsjournal.com
290   David Galula, *Counterinsurgency Warfare: Theory and Practice* (Praeger, 2006).

words because, first, it is clear that the challenges that face the British military in Afghanistan in 2011, for example, are similar to those that faced the French military in the Algerian civil war over fifty years ago – i.e. an adaptive and innovative adversary – and second, because in its root, the Latin term *propagare*, means the pinning of fresh shoots of a plant into the earth to reproduce and take on a life of their own. We believe that this is a not unreasonable analogy for promoting and growing new ideas and thinking values. We think that the West desperately needs some new thinking and we believe that needs to be based upon harnessing the potential of influence to achieve military, civil and political objectives. Cynicism abounds, but that it should be attached to a process that seeks to reduce the need for hard military force is, we believe, illogical, and particularly so in environments where collateral damage is so obviously damaging to the mission, and where body bags, be they friendly or hostile, are a corrupt and distasteful measure of progress. We think that contemporary and future conflicts demand that 'we' are able to initiate behavioural change in combatants, in the populations from which they garner their support, and with those who, or who may in the future, exercise or seek to obtain power. We make three justifications for this assertion.

First, defence forces are expensive assets and the taxpayer rightly demands best value for money. In a highly challenging fiscal environment, with competing demands from across the spectrum of public services, defence needs to be realistic. It may be that in the future the defence budget will not sustain a capability to conduct the full spectrum of military operations that have been undertaken in the past – we saw this, in the UK, in the Strategic Defence and Security Review announced in November 2010. The military can bemoan and bewail, or it can adapt. We believe it must adapt, and that it will be necessary, and certainly desirable, to be thinking now of perhaps hitherto non-military ways of deterring and defeating an adversary. The issue of deterrence will be touched upon later, but it seems obvious to us that preventing conflict is infinitely more desirable than engaging with it. Influence, and its role in changing behaviour, can have a direct impact on the nature of how a conflict is planned, fought and sustained and therefore must be regarded as being central to military campaigning.

Second, public perception can have a long-term and decisive effect upon the nature and success of foreign policy and military operations. Conveying information messages to specific audiences, in order to influence behavioural change for specific political or military objectives, may well prove more decisive in future conflicts than just the placement of bullets and bombs upon a target. Neither civilian nor military leaders can afford to take a passive view of public opinion, for in foreign policy in particular it can constrain and limit action. As a result of opinion, which for many in the world will form perceptions of reality, people will make choices. Our preference should be that people make the 'right' choice – one that supports 'our' objectives. In Afghanistan, and perhaps in future conflicts, the task of nudging people towards that choice, either by design or consequence, should become a function that the military perform in conjunction with civil actors.

Third, influence is actually a concept well understood by other government departments (OGDs). All departments of state have an interest in influence and it might be seen as a tool for unifying cross-governmental activity, one that is far less intimidating than conventional military tools. This is important, for whilst the military will continue to have a seminal role in future complex operations, as we noted earlier, lasting solutions do not come at the end of a gun barrel. Former British Ambassador to the United States, Sir Christopher Meyer, noted: 'there has been scant joined-up government between the soldier, the aid worker and the diplomat' – which suggests that the so-called 'comprehensive approach' (a strategy designed to link together thinking and actions across government departments) has not yet become a workable methodology. The allure of the comprehensive approach – what it promises – has not been matched by an effective outcome. Indeed, its ability to create competitive rather than creative tensions across OGDs has resulted in levels of bureaucracy being attached to it that actively inhibit adaptation rather than encourage it. This is largely due to each department having differing aims, different cultures, applying alternative solutions and each suffering the inadequacies of the other. By making the role of influence far more central to ways, means and ends it might encourage departments of state to deal more effectively with those competitive institutional tensions that abound and in its place look to creative tension as a more effective catalyst to decision-making.

Experience tells us that perceptions are formed from a complex mix of sources. Sometimes they may be based upon first-hand experience – very often they are not. They may be formed as a result of interaction within complex societal networks – family, tribe, ethnic group, religion. They may perhaps be formed as a result of interaction within the new informational environment of bloggers, YouTube and social network sites. Or, as we have learnt from Afghanistan, they may emanate from other stimuli – some centuries old, such as *shuras*, storytelling and codes of conduct such as *Pashtunwali*. What we do know in the current conflict that so taxes the West's armed forces is that Afghans are fundamentally pragmatists, an attitude forged through conflict, geography and sacred values. Few have any wish to return to the excesses of the pre-2001 Taliban government. Thus Afghanistan, at its heart, is about stopping a deeply unpopular former government returning to power – for Afghan interests, for UK interests and for regional and global security interests. Indeed, the insurgency is unique in that is probably the only one ever to be conducted by the previous government of the country. Inherently this should make the West's task conceptually easier, since all that has to be done is to deny the Taliban popular support. Yet set against the reality of the environment it is, of course, hugely complex. In a land so scarred by conflict, nudging pragmatists in a specific direction by getting them to make different choices is far easier said then done. Subsequently, we have also learnt that 'our' enemy (in Afghanistan 'we' have perhaps unhelpfully conflated it into one group which 'we' call 'Taliban') also makes choices. For the diehard ideologist, removing the 'infidel crusader from Muslim lands' may be the single goal of the conflict. Yet the 'Taliban' are not all ideologues; dispossessed young men, drug barons and criminal elements are all in this mix and all make choices on a range of issues from repelling foreigners to poverty, to drugs or seeking out power. In the grinding poverty and hopelessness of Afghanistan such people will make any number of choices – pragmatism – if what is offered is better than what they have. Perception is a powerful and motivating aspect of making choices. This is important. What might seem to Coalition forces as profoundly irrational behaviour may actually be entirely rational to an indigenous population. Equally that same indigenous population behaving in an entirely rational manner to them may appear to us as entirely irrational. The subsequent consequences are obvious – our own perceptions can be profoundly wrong, which in turn can lead to poor decision-making. The first paragraph of Chapter 1 is as fine an example as any.

For the committed and long-term ideologues, we know that Taliban commanders are very good at intuitive decisions. They have honed their skills on years of experience of fighting one enemy after another. Since the ISAF Coalition is not, in essence, presenting significantly new military challenges from those of the Soviet army, the Taliban can afford to rely on intuition and agile decision-making rather than long-term strategic plans. Indeed, it is striking that the Taliban have presented almost no proposals on what an Afghan government, under their control, would do were their insurgency successful; this is in stark contrast to the multitude of plans and policies presented by GIRoA[291] and ISAF. If 'we' were to consider the idea of presenting complex choices to Taliban commanders as part of 'our' operational design, 'we' may be able slow down their decision-making process, perhaps force group decisions, perhaps indecision, and therefore begin to drive wedges between the reconcilable and the irreconcilable. This is a concept that has occasionally been referred to as 'reflexive control', and the Soviet Union used this, albeit imperfectly, during its own occupation of Afghanistan in the 1980s and, with much more success, in the conflict in Abkhazia in 2008, where the enemy was presented with a range of thought-through options and steered towards a calculated decision, one that was predicted in advance by Russian forces and used to their best advantage.

Coupled to this will be a capability to slow down or stop the enemy's ability to adapt. As we have previously observed, Joshua Cooper Ramo saw how Hezbollah paid scant regard to success but obsessed over failures.[292] The key to constant adaptation therefore lies in recognising failure or poor performance, not self-satisfaction with gaining or winning. Similarly, Ramo relates the story of Michael Moritz, a phenomenally successfully venture capitalist (who invested $12.5m into Google very early on), and how he constantly pushed for quick pivots because no plan should last longer than was necessary. We argue that the role of influence is central to this approach as it ensures that the fundamental requirement of context is addressed, provided that commanders, at all levels, are prepared to revisit it time and time again.

---

291   Government of the Islamic Republic of Afghanistan.

292   Joshua Cooper Ramo, *The Age of the Unthinkable* (Little Brown, 2009).

It is clear that understanding societal landscapes is important, and the armies of the West have made some improvements in their cultural understanding and, more importantly, in turning that into useful training for deploying soldiers. What we wonder, however, is whether 'we' are making the necessary commensurate investment in education, for, in conducting wars amongst the people, what Kipling in 1899 referred to as 'the savage wars of peace', commanders will need to make a substantial investment in their own cerebral appreciation of not just the tactical environment but also the strategic and cognitive one. We are concerned that this is not currently placed at the forefront of military thinking, and nor are we convinced that the military – indeed the whole of government – is philosophically, culturally and organisationally able to assist in its development.

For example, we showed in Chapter 5 that successful influence is predicated on robust and scientifically derived Target Audience Analysis (TAA). Who in the military is qualified to undertake this? How would they even try? Let's think about this for a moment. 'We' need to undertake rigorous qualitative and quantitative data collection amongst target populations. 'We' want to sit down and interview individuals, in their own languages, and ask them detailed questions about their lives. The military simply can't just do this in advance without attracting attention, and we are not even sure that the military has the capacity to undertake such work anyway. Once conflict has begun, it is even less easy to undertake such research. People will be naturally suspicious of strangers in uniforms, carrying weapons and arriving in armoured vehicles to ask them questions about their motivations for specific behaviour. This presents very sizable problems. To an extent the US armed forces have attempted to address this with the creation of the HTS we discussed in Chapter 7. In Afghanistan, the US has thirty such teams deployed, each consisting of around five or six research scientists. But even they have limitations. How then are 'we' to gather the information necessary for meaningful behavioural change?

The US and its allies have invested heavily in the last few years in various intelligence-gathering capabilities. Quite aside from the well known unmanned aerial vehicles (UAV) that can track, from great heights, individuals of interest, and the incredible electronic intercept capabilities that can pinpoint mobile phone calls anywhere on the globe, there has been a huge increase in HUMINT (human intelligence) assets, both in collection and analysis. Understandably, therefore, with such large-scale investment, commanders are unwilling to accept that TAA may be beyond their capabilities. Regardless, it is our view that, if we are to undertake influence successfully, we need TAA, and TAA at the moment is an expertise that currently resides best in the domain of a few specialist private military companies (PMCs). Spending additional money on PMCs is a bitter pill to swallow, a tacit admission that past expenditure has not been in the right areas.

What might influence look like in future conflicts?

In April 2011, the US-based Social Science Research Network published a study which suggested that there was almost no link between poverty and support for violent militant groups. This is not the first time such ideas have been raised, and indeed even the UK government's own Behavioural Science Unit, hidden within the bowels of the security service, MI5, concluded that there was no single and identifiable pathway towards terrorism.[293] Scott Atran in his book *Talking to the Enemy* relates time and again how people do not simply kill for a cause, they kill and die for each other and the roots of much of the support to jihad can be found in school classrooms, school football teams and childhood friendships. Just like the research which disproves any strong connection between attitudes and behaviours, this is contrary to prevailing wisdom and, if true, has serious implications, in particular for international aid. In the UK, international aid has proved a contentious issue; whilst few would disagree that wealthy first-world countries have a moral obligation to assist those from the third world, the nature of the donation (and, in cash-strapped Britain, its size) is always hotly debated. Why, for example, should Britain provide aid to India, a country that operates its own space programme, is itself a foreign aid donor (providing more than £300m to poorer countries in 2008) and which spends $36 billion a year on defence. Why should the UK provide aid to China, when China's economy is far out-performing that of the UK? Why should aid budgets be ring-fenced when almost every other aspect of the British exchequer is being cut or trimmed in the wake of a world financial crisis and a profligate former UK government?

One of the arguments that is raised in defence of international aid is that it is part of a strategy to protect the UK from future terrorist attack. The UK's Home Secretary Theresa May is on record as saying that: 'If you get aid right in certain parts of the world, it will reduce the possibility of terrorism on the streets of the UK.'[294] But here is a study, one undertaken by reputable scientists, that suggests that poor Pakistanis were actually *less* likely to support extremist groups than the more affluent and better educated. In fact, if you think about some of the most (in)famous terrorist leaders from the past, for example Osama Bin Laden, Ayman Al-Zwahiri, Carlos the Jackal, Abu Nidal, Mahmoud al-Zahar and Ulrike Marie Meinhof, they have one common and obvious similarity – they weren't poor. Neither, for that matter, were they poorly educated. For the British government and its £1.4bn aid budget to Pakistan this, then, should perhaps be ringing some alarm bells. More importantly, for us, it provides a starting point for the question of what influence might look like in the future.

If we think conceptually about conflicts, there are certain phases that most, perhaps all, will go through. We might model these as: peacetime, pre-conflict, initial conflict, steady-state conflict and finally, we hope, post-conflict. In each phase

293   'MI5 Report Challenges Views on Terrorism in Britain' (*Guardian*, 24 May 2011).
294   'British Cash for Pakistan will not Reduce the Terror Threat, Experts Say' (*Telegraph*, 21 April 2011).

there are certain key groups who potentially hold disproportionate sway over the evolution of events depending upon their perception of circumstances; some 'we' will know, others, as we saw in Iraq, will not. Table 8.1 shows some examples of two past conflicts to illustrate this.

Phase	Key events	
	Iraq	Afghanistan
Peacetime	UN sanctions on Saddam Hussein's regime: effect on Iraqis	Withdrawal of US / Western support after Soviet occupation
Pre-conflict	UNSCR 1441. Compliance or material breach?	Assassination of anti-Taliban leader Ahmad Shah Massoud on 9 September 2001
Initial conflict	'Shock and Awe' bombardment of Iraq	Taliban consider handover of Bin Laden for cessation of bombing
Steady-state	Dismantling of Iraqi army	Taliban insurgency
Post-conflict	Capacity-building	Creation of GIRoA institutions

Table 8.1 The application of Target Audience Analysis before, during and after conflict.

In each case properly conducted TAA would have provided 'us' a degree of insight not just into the prevailing conditions of the time, but into how behaviours might develop as circumstances change. For example, UN sanctions were imposed on Iraq in August 1990 and not finally lifted until late 2010. In that intervening period of twenty years there are contrasting views about the number of civilians who were affected as a direct result of the embargos. Whilst different studies can't agree on the numbers, they are all united in their assessment that the Iraqi people, rather than the ruling regime, were hit hardest. So what would a TAA have revealed? Anger at the regime? Almost certainly, but so too would there have been anger at the West for punishing the Iraqi people for their leader's behaviour. Arguably, it might even have revealed that far from the post-9/11 sanctions splitting the country, they actually hardened attitudes. As in Afghanistan, people were offered a binary choice – Saddam Hussein or the West. Their decision, unsurprisingly, was often more complex, with them deciding, as we saw in the insurgency, to choose neither. Had we undertaken a TAA of the Iraqi people in advance of the dismantling of the Iraqi army we may have learnt that it was an exceptionally cohesive element of Iraqi society – one of the few aspects of society that functioned. We now know, with the benefit of hindsight, that the removal of Saddam's security apparatus, and particularly its army, was one of the most significant errors of the immediate post-Saddam period. A proper TAA might also have revealed that Ahmed Chalabi and the Iraqi National Congress held nowhere near the level of popular support within Iraq that it claimed, and might perhaps have changed the course of that particular conflict.

And what of Afghanistan? Had a proper TAA been undertaken of Afghan sentiment when Ahmed Shah Massoud was assassinated in 2001, just days before 9/11, it may have provided a greater understanding of the faultlines that already existed within the country, but which had largely been ignored by the West since the Soviet army had finally pulled out in 1989. So, too, with the benefit of hindsight (and as we have illustrated in the chapter on operations in Afghanistan), would a proper TAA have helped us understand the Afghan population, its imperfections and rivalries, and perhaps have allowed the West to adopt a more nuanced approach to its ISAF mission, one far less black and white than the term 'War on Terror' allowed.

In short, proper TAA of nations of interest, taken at regular intervals, would build up far more data for use in conflict and, better, would perhaps deter conflict better than conventional intelligence about guns, bullets and networks ever could. Such thinking has application not just in the military environment but across government departments. Indeed, we started this section with a debate about the utility of foreign aid as a prophylactic for terrorism. On what basis was that policy decision taken? Was it because a bunch of senior civil servants and politicians got in a 'group-think' huddle and decided that, intuitively, this was a good idea? Or was it the result of carefully distilled and sifted data, where the motivations of a population were carefully analysed, and from which data sensible foreign policy was created?

It is not enough just to write about influence in military doctrine. Influence as a concept, in the way that Andrew sought to define it in Helmand, does not have a clearly visible academic or doctrinal background. When Andrew identified the need to introduce thinking about influence operations during pre-deployment training, it became clear that there was a significant lack of previous writing on the subject. There is a great deal of doctrine available regarding the application of information operations, psychological operations and similar concepts. It was generally agreed within 52 Brigade that this was of little value at the tactical level; it did not tell soldiers how to execute influence. What was needed was a tactical non-kinetic effects doctrine that would explain how a company, battle group and brigade could deliver non-kinetic effect. It is very much more than simply passing a message. As we saw from the doctrinal definition of joint action, influence is achieved using a combination of kinetic and non-kinetic activity. For it to stand any chance of enduring success it needs a thorough understanding of audiences. Successful information operations, on the other hand, are those (generally non-kinetic) actions that are focused on exploiting the effect of military or civil activity, or explaining why we are conducting that activity. Influence, therefore, differs from information operations; it is more holistic in approach and has a higher purpose. Quite simply, it is a way of thinking, and in an operational context it is multi-dimensional – necessitating second- and third-order consequence thinking. This involves consideration of what is to the left, to the right, above and below your immediate target. It must also include an absolute recognition that conflict remains an extension of politics, and that all military effort and activity must contribute to the achievement of politically generated policy goals. And it can be difficult to navigate these choppy waters, given the high stakes and the obvious consequences of getting it wrong. David Galula observed that in counterinsurgency operations: '[P]olitics becomes an active instrument of operation. And so intricate is the interplay between the political and the military actions that they cannot be tidily separated; on the contrary, every military move has to be weighed with regard to its political effects and vice versa.'[295]

An influence strategy is therefore central to any political strategy, which in turn must provide the foundation for an effective means of conducting influence at the tactical and operational levels without necessarily seeking to constantly control or direct that effort. In Iraq in 2007, for example, the higher influence strategy was designed to move the various communities towards a political accommodation that would reduce communal violence. At a lower level, it was about jobs, economic development and isolating the insurgents from the population. No one would suggest that in this multidimensional layering of applying coherent influence, generic messaging was either workable or appropriate.

One of the reasons why this was so problematic for 52 Brigade, and why this concept is relatively new, is that traditional army training points commanders towards kinetic solutions. Perhaps of more relevance is that successful military careers – particularly at the junior officer level – are built on hard power. As former US army Colonel Norvell De Atkine notes: 'The death knell of a career is to be identified by the career makers and breakers as being out of the mainstream.' Thus, the UK Armed Forces have no professional information operations practitioners, no professional media or psychological operations specialists. The UK believes that its armed forces are too small to justify such specialities and yet we argue that it is precisely because the UK's military is so small that such skills are needed. In their place, well-meaning and enthusiastic amateurs are seconded from every branch of the military for two- or three-year tours. They do their best with minimal training, but they are unlikely to return to such duties again. To make matters worse many of those who fill these appointments are, in fact, 'individual augmentees' (IAs) and often make their first appearance in a brigade's or division's preparation at the Mission Rehearsal Exercise – in other words, a few weeks prior to deployment. We argue that no commander would accept his Chief of Staff, for instance, appearing at this stage, and neither should he accept IAs

---

295 David Galula, *Counterinsurgency Warfare: Theory and Practice* (Praeger Security International, 1964, pp. 54–56).

appearing either. Whilst ideas of soft power are raised at staff colleges, what to do with those ideas is not. Hard power retains supremacy, reinforced by professional training courses throughout a soldier's career and by core texts such as the 'Principles of War'[296] (for example, tenacity in the face of the enemy, moral and physical courage). Yet in today's multipolar and highly complex world, winning kinetic battles is comparatively easy, but losing the peace is even easier.

We saw in chapter 2 the work of Ivan Arreguin-Toft on the nature of conflict and how the underdog can succeed. He has shown that the outcome of conflict will in the future not be so much a function of a stronger actor defeating a weaker one but of an actor that uses the most strategically useful techniques of battle – be they soft, hard or asymmetric – that will prevail, and he demonstrates that, since 1800, the results of conflicts have increasingly favoured the actor willing to make conceptual jumps in thinking. This places considerable emphasis on a willingness to continually refine, reorganise, adapt and transform, contingent on how the character and dynamics of a particular conflict evolve over time. What does this mean for Western armies? Essentially it calls into question the basis of the educational process that underpins training. For example, in a typical senior British army officer's career, perhaps spanning thirty years, a general may, after completing basic training, spend around two years in staff colleges. As a junior major he is required to attend the recently introduced nine-month Initial Staff Course. Again, as a major or lieutenant colonel, he *may* be selected for the forty-week Advanced Staff Course, and as a one-star he *may* attend either the twelve-week Higher Command and Staff Course and/or the longer Royal College of Defence Studies programme. Yet almost none are guaranteed and almost all are dependent upon operational tasking and the perception of career needs. In between these comparatively short periods of intellectual broadening lie long and extended periods of either operations, support to operations, training or protracted periods in the MoD central staff fighting political wars of budget attrition and programme procurement. Now in comparison to the civil service, or indeed to the commercial sector, this is actually quite a long period of education. However, unlike industry, the army's success is measured either by its lack of use (its deterrent value) or it is defined by its ability to respond quickly and successfully to an instability, noting that every instability is different, invariably in different parts of the world and involving people with a myriad of different values, beliefs, cultures, et al. How, then, do the commanders of tomorrow, and their troops, prepare themselves for the challenges of future war? There is no quick-fix solution but, as we note later, lifelong learning and education must be considered key. However, it is not sufficient to simply send people on courses, we have to send them on the right courses, and we question if the existing staff colleges are able to adapt quickly enough to meet the needs of their students.

---

296   The 'Principles of War' were first properly articulated by Carl von Clausewitz in his nineteenth-century essay *Principles of War*, and later expanded upon in his book *On War*. Even today they form the philosophical basis of military doctrine and operations.

The words of US futurist Alvin Toffler ring true: 'The illiterate of the future are not those that cannot read or write. They are those that cannot learn, unlearn and relearn.'[297] Toffler speaks of the Western world's educational system being designed to meet an industrial discipline of a past age, one unprepared for the future. We fear that the West's Armed Forces may be similarly predisposed and, from the top of the shop through to the Army's staff colleges, the structures, despite the best will in the world, are institutionally incapable of keeping pace with rapid change and the associated willingness to adapt – and quickly – at the same time. Numerous examples illustrate the point. In 2009, the then soon to be Chief of the General Staff (CGS) returned the British Army to a campaigning philosophy with the issuing of the 'Operation Entirety Op Order'. This was a quantum change in the way that the British army conducted its operations abroad, but at the time of writing its implications (for the army, for the other services and across government) receive almost no attention on staff course syllabuses. A second example is the absence of proper research within the MoD. Research forms the basis of education and learning, education and learning the basis of training. Yet even at the most senior levels education and training are often mistaken as being the same or, perhaps even worse, education is wrongly seen as a 'luxury' and second to training[298]. We believe that training develops an individual's knowledge, skills and behaviour for particular roles through regular practice and instruction, but that education develops an individual's intellectual capacity, knowledge and understanding; it equips them to come to reasoned decisions, judgements and conclusions, including in unpredictable and complex circumstances and situations. Western militaries rightly pride themselves on the quality of their training, but we fear that careers are increasingly built on budgetary and management competence in place of the necessary education to conceptualise tomorrow's challenges. An analogy may be helpful. A patient requiring surgery will take more confidence from being operated upon by a surgeon with recent surgical experience than one who last undertook the procedure some years past. But in the case of a rare condition, the patient will be happy to be operated on by anyone qualified to remedy the malaise. The military, if the UK's foreign policy works, should be the surgeon that works every few years, not continuously. But that 'surgeon' needs to retain currency, and capability, for future difficult operations, not past ones. And in doing so they need to inspire confidence in the patient that they will perform to the best of their abilities by being cognisant of the latest thinking and research. This is the role of education, and the provider, for the military, must be various Western defence academies and staff colleges. Of course, in conflict we know that the military is seldom the sole participant, so education needs to

---

297   Alvin Toffler, *Rethinking the Future: Rethinking Business Principles, Competition, Control and Complexity, Leadership, Markets and the World* (Nicholas Brealey Publishing, new edition 1998).

298   Our favourite way to illustrate the difference between the two is to ask if a parent would be happy for their child to have sex education at school; invariably the answer is 'yes'. But ask them if they would like their young son or daughter to have sex training and the answer will be, for sure, a resounding 'no'.

extend across government, and its educational academies such as, in the UK, the National School of Government, and, perhaps most critically, to politicians.

The issue of 'Lessons Learned' (LL) presents an interesting case study. The military places great stock in generating Lessons Identified (LI) after each operation or exercise. Some of these are anecdotal, others are more empirically derived. Invariably, because they point to military shortcomings, their detail is classified; this means that their distribution is necessarily limited to those who have the necessary clearances and mechanisms to read, store and protect the data. We are not arguing for the wholesale release of classified documents (many of which are, we believe, over-classified anyway), but we do wish to see a better connection between LIs and the military education process – such that LIs (if they are indeed the right lessons, and we note the disparity between the ability to collect LIs and the ability to analyse LIs) are genuinely turned into LLs. We contend that in the important area of influence and, indeed, in a number of other important operational areas, this does not currently happen. For example, the major tools of military influence are media, information and psychological operations. Yet we know from our own experiences that it is precisely these areas where 'we' have struggled. The issue then is how, and who, will turn those LIs into meaningful LLs. For we contend that if 'we' had truly learnt and not just identified lessons, we would not see the same reports emanating from Afghanistan in 2011 as 'we' did, for example, from Kosovo twelve years previously. These points are indicative of the problems of innovating and facilitating change in a highly complex organisation, particularly one where budgets have become the key driver and where process very often prevents innovative thought. This, however, is an explanation of, not an excuse for, lack of action, and is entirely counter to Toft's research, which shows that winners will often be those best able to make conceptual jumps in thinking – innovation – in complex environments.

As Lieutenant General William Caldwell, Commander US Combined Arms Center, US Army, observed in a recent article on the *Small Wars Journal* website:

> We need to educate Soldiers ... and how their actions can have strategic implications. They need to know what the second and third order effects of their actions are. There are very few soldiers out there who would intentionally harm the mission ... when many of these incidents occur it is because they just don't know that it is going to have that kind of effect and cause that kind of damage.

Or, as US academic Stephen Rosen notes, the speed of change in the information age aggravates the 'procedural conservatism' of the military.

Winning tomorrow's conflicts

In July 2011, the BBC's flagship radio news programme, 'Today', broadcast an intriguing article about the use of behaviourally based programmes to reduce the number of missed appointments at UK National Health Service (NHS) doctors' surgeries – missed appointments are costing the NHS over £24m every year.[299] The programme featured Professor Robert Cialdini, author of the seminal textbook *Influence: The Psychology of Persuasion*.[300] First, Cialdini asked patients to re-state aloud the date and time of the appointment they had just been given over the phone – reducing no-shows by 6.7 per cent. Second, for those who came into the surgery, they were asked to write down themselves the time of the new appointment – reducing no-shows by 18 per cent. But perhaps most stunning was the final measure he introduced, which was to change the wording of posters that noted that the previous month sixty-seven patients had missed their appointments. Instead, it said that 97 per cent of patients last month made their appointments – this reduced no-shows by 30 per cent. If basic techniques such as this can be used by the Department of Health to save money and to improve service, surely similar techniques have application in conflict?

The image of war perpetuated in Hollywood movies is often very far from reality. Ask any old soldier and they will tell you that war is characterised by prolonged periods of boredom, punctuated by short moments of abject terror. War is cruel – not least to those caught up by fate within it. In Iraq, the estimates of the number of non-combatant casualties and deaths vary widely. IraqBodyCount.Org estimates between 90,000 and 100,000 civilian deaths; the British medical journal *The Lancet* suggest the figure is closer to 600,000. It is unlikely that the true death toll of that conflict will ever be accurately charted. In Afghanistan, the UN suggests that 600 non-combatants were killed in 2009 alone. Whilst the vast majority may well be the victims of insurgent actions, a number of those, by the US military's own admission, were caused by the poor judgement and error by Coalition troops.

The financial cost of post-11 September 2001 military operations is equally problematic. Joseph Stieglitz, the renowned US economist, has suggested that the total bill may be close to $16 trillion – the cost of the operations in Afghanistan costing the UK taxpayer alone approximately £18bn.[301] However you judge war – be it by body count, by cost or by achievement (the last perhaps being even harder to accurately assess) – it is hugely costly. Yet is it possible or even realistic to consider a future society untouched by conflict? In the creation of the UK's National Security Strategy 2 (NSS2), in which Steve was directly involved whilst on attach-

---

299   The programme can be listened to at http://news.bbc.co.uk/today/hi/today/newsid_9551000/9551149.stm

300   Robert Cialdini, *Influence: The Psychology of Persuasion* (HarperBusiness, revised edition, 2007).

301   Richard Norton-Taylor, 'Costs of British Military Operations in Afghanistan Estimated at £18bn' (*Guardian*, 28 July 2011). See http://www.guardian.co.uk/politics/2011/jul/28/afghanistan-libya-costs-military

ment to the Cabinet Office in 2009, the inevitable answer was 'no'. In developing NSS2, the Cabinet Office held thirteen workshops across government, inviting government departments and agencies to forecast out to five and twenty years. If the five-year period was troublesome, the twenty-year period was exceptionally problematic – the range of unknowns and variables expanding exponentially. And these were forecasting what former US Secretary of State Donald Rumsfeld called the 'known unknowns' – issues such as climate change, migration and economic collapse. What of Rumsfeld's unknown unknowns? NSS2 required a thirteenth workshop – called simply 'Challenge XIII' – to consider the unexpected. And this is not just academic vanity. We saw in the 1930s that the Soviet Union practised almost exclusively for offensive operations and yet was very nearly defeated when Hitler's Nazi Germany (a former ally) attacked in 1941. This is the new paradigm and it is a revolution of economics, politics, information – indeed, we have given it a name: globalisation. And history tells us that revolutions outpace institutional adaptation.

Even as the cost of the first wars of the twenty-first century are calculated, so contingency planning for likely future conflicts is taking place. And these are likely to be very different from those that characterized the twentieth century. Today, Western governments worry not about expanding empires but about failing states, of the competition for natural resources such as oil and water, and the nightmare scenario of extreme ideological groups attaining, and using, weapons of mass destruction. To suggest an alternative, peaceful, future seems overly optimistic. For centuries man has found reason to wage war on fellow man, and there seems little possibility that this will change.

American Russian analyst Timothy Thomas wrote in his 1997 study of Russia:

> A battle is waging somewhere on Russia's southern border. During a lull in the fighting Russian loudspeakers emit provocative messages designed to influence or hypnotize the enemy forces. Holograms designed to induce fear or uncertainty display messages and images embellished with cultural and religious connotations ... As the fighting resumes, multiple rocket launchers and artillery rocket attacks pose yet another type of psychological war – one based on the shock effect of tons of explosive ordnance.[302]

An unlikely proposition, or prescient look into the future? Given the uncertainty of the future, foretold by NSS2, and the speed of technological advance, the latter does not seem unreasonable and gives credence to the front cover of Philip Bob-

---

302   Timothy Thomas, *The Russian Armed Forces at the Dawn of the Millennium* (US Department of Defense, 2000).

bitt's book, *Terror and Consent*,[303] which ambitiously proclaims that: 'every widely held idea we currently entertain about twenty-first-century terrorism and its relationship to the wars against terror is wrong and must be thoroughly rethought.' Bobbitt's central thesis is that the war against terror represents a new phase in the development of warfare and that there must be dramatic political, military and ethical developments to fight it successfully.

As the UK's Defence Academy noted: 'the UK cannot sustain the capability to conduct the full spectrum of military operations undertaken in the past … we need a drastic change in the way we do things.' What is that drastic change? We have already noted the very substantial changes to society that the 'information age' – however imperfect that term may be – has brought. It has highlighted the effect that information can have on people – and how perception (or perhaps more accurately, misperception) can cause very substantial change not just to people's opinions but also to their actions. It has also suggested that 9/11 necessitated a fundamentally rethink of the war and peace paradigm, of war in faraway places but of violence and terrorism at home. As 7/7 showed, internal threats are now very much part of external wars, and we must therefore now consider issues such as defence in a coupled manner with ideas of security. And, as we have seen, we are increasingly learning that in this new paradigm weaponry is not exclusively that which kills or maims. Today, information – electronic, economic and political warfare – all play increasingly important parts in conflict. More importantly, the sheer range of potential weapons means that the nature of future conflict is absolutely uncertain. As Bobbitt wonders, what would happen if terrorists could in the future interrupt the communications of airplanes and ships; if by remote control they could alter the chemical construction of medicines under manufacture; or if they could change the pressure in gas pipelines headed from Russia to Europe? Far-fetched? We have already seen how the huge technological advantage of the US can be comparatively easily subverted by a far weaker enemy. The *Wall Street Journal* revealed in December 2009 that US reconnaissance drones had been hacked into by insurgents in Iraq, using equipment that cost less than US$30 on the Internet.[304]

In his book *The Age of the Unthinkable*, Joshua Cooper Ramo describes a world of inherent unpredictability and constant 'newness'. To Ramo it is a world where those that we entrust with the management of its problems will constantly fail. Indeed, their endeavours may actually achieve the opposite of that which was intended at inception, *unless* they are prepared to adapt. We do not have to watch whilst history collides with our lives but can step forward and change history, although, Ramo argues, to do so we must be prepared. From our shared experience of military operations and of working within intractable environments, military,

---

303   Philip Bobbitt, *Terror and Consent: The Wars for the Twenty-First Century* (Allen Lane, 2008).

304   Siobhan Gorman, Yochi J. Dreazen and August Cole, 'Insurgents Hack US Drones. $26 Software is Used to Breach Key Weapons in Iraq: Iranian Backing Suspected' (*Wall Street Journal*, 19 December 2009).

governmental and civilian, we believe that there is one fundamental certainty confronting the armed forces: uncertainty. The question we must therefore address is: How do we prepare our people for the kind of challenge that such uncertainty will bring? We called our book 'Behavioural Conflict' because it is our unequivocal view that changing the behaviour of individuals, groups, governments and societies will be the key to future success. If subtle behavioural campaigns can have proven success in improving the health service, as we saw earlier in this chapter, why on earth are we not investigating their utility in the military and security environments?

When the Armed Forces dealt in heavy attrition or manoeuvre warfare the attitude and behaviour of the enemy was placed largely at the periphery of a commander's thinking. But heavy attrition and manoeuvre warfare does not, we believe, characterise future conflict – although we also accept that it cannot be ruled out. In behavioural conflict – particularly in the information age – we will need to confront very cerebral issues. For example, we may have to reassess notions of victory. What does 'victory' in Afghanistan look like? Have we achieved 'victory' in Iraq? We would not presume to have an answer to either question, but we do have an observation: we believe that 'victory' today, and in the future, will look very different from signature ceremonies on Lüneburg Heath in 1945 or Port Stanley in 1982. Indeed, 'victory' may not even be immediately apparent in current and future conflicts. During 52 Brigade's deployment we chose to avoid using words such as 'winning' or 'victory' as they are too absolute and do not engender confidence when considering, for example, reconciliation initiatives. We settled instead on 'succeed' or 'success', as everyone can interpret their role in success. Success has many fathers, failure is an orphan. Also, if we accept from the outset that victory may prove illusory, then we may also have to ask questions of our objectives, and what is, or more specifically what is not, achievable. In short we will have to come to terms with an absence of absolutes.

To accelerate our preparedness, we believe that three key areas of work need to be undertaken if we are to expect the West's Armed Forces to succeed in what Alvin Toffler calls the 'third revolution to befall mankind' (the first two being the agricultural and industrial revolutions) – the information revolution. First, and foremost, we need to broaden and expand the minds of all our people, from the strategic corporal to those who will command and lead. We therefore propose a wholesale broadening of western military education programmes. Second, we wish to see the expansion and professionalisation of certain key information-age enablers – notably information, media and psychological operations practitioners and, of equal importance, their directing and command arrangements within the hierarchy of Western militaries. Finally, we believe an expansion of organic research capability is vital if 'we' are to respond meaningfully to future Rumsfeldian 'unknown unknowns'.

Education

As we have already noted, the UK MoD, and indeed the US DoD, is deservedly a world-renowned training organisation, welcoming each year thousands of British and international students to its many courses and programmes. We do not denigrate their value. However, we are concerned that education is the poor relation of training, particularly when looking to make cost-savings. We believe we must prepare our people for the complexities of the future and that life-long learning is the key. There are many ways that this can be achieved, at both macro- and micro-levels. Some examples illustrate the point. At the macro-level, we would wish to see a return of the strategic estimate process, which was effectively dismantled in 1994. The corporate appreciation of world events has, we believe, been hindered by the reduction in the defence intelligence staff (shortly before the 2011 Libyan crisis the MoD cut its North African intelligence desks as a cost-saving measure), by the removal of many Defence Attaché (DA) posts, and by an absence of deep specialist expertise. For example, during operations in Bosnia, Iraq and Afghanistan the UK MoD had to surge personnel through language-training courses – a process that in some instances can take years. Whilst we recognise that it is impossible to retain a corps of global linguists, it is possible through proper research to determine those areas of the world where the probability of future conflict or intervention is highest and to properly prepare at least a small seed-corn cadre of individuals. This may mean linking such expertise to the DA circuit, which is currently regarded as the preserve of older officers nearing retirement. For young officers, the DA circuit is seen as a hindrance to career development; we believe this notion to be wrong. The UK Defence Academy currently welcomes students from over forty nations to its courses, but sends British officers to considerably less than half that number of international staff colleges – it being regarded as an expensive luxury. We believe that this too is unhelpful and we note the very positive experiences and lifelong relationships that are built through such attachments. These do not necessarily have to be abroad. We welcome the placement of senior government personnel on military staff courses and would wish to see this expanded. On the subject of Britain's Defence Academy, we wish to see officers returning from theatre routinely being posted to the Academy staff to mentor those on courses and to codify the knowledge that they have gained. In many training schools, recent operational experience is keenly sought, but this appears less the case in educational environments. Such a move would help provide a bridge between operational adaptation and deeper institutional learning. Indeed, learning and the acquisition of knowledge – by both individuals and groups – is, we believe, an issue paid only scant attention. It is not helped by regulations that hinder senior officers from sharing information and ideas through external new media such as blogs and websites, and the architecture of internal MoD computer networks that do not facilitate blog-type discussion. We would also add a word of caution over too prescriptive a reliance upon operational experience; operational experience can be invaluable – but only if it is right. We have observed US efforts to develop 'wiki-doctrine', an initiative that envisages web-based army doctrine being updated directly by certain forward-based units and formations, therein negating the necessity of time-consuming referral to higher-level command through a tortuous staffing process. This is not perfect, but it does facilitate comparatively immediate exchanges, by practitioners in operational theatres, and will allow the 'right' operational experience to rise to prominence.

We also note with envy the freedom senior US officers enjoy to engage with both external and internal communities in their decision-making processes. Indeed, the inclusion of external organisations – particularly academic ones – is, we believe, vital. We welcome the decision of the MoD's strategy unit to post on King's College London *Kings of War*[305] blog – inviting comments and views on future strategic threats. The quality, range and number of replies they received were indicative of the huge pool of talent that the MoD can tap into. We also note that the US publishes many of its military students' thesis and staff papers online, making them freely available to the general public and, more particularly, to each other for reference, comment and debate. The UK does not share defence research papers, and key journals such as the *British Army Review* have only in 2011 finally been given an internal In*tra*net presence. Compare this conservatism with the US, where almost every discussion journal is openly available on the In*ter*net, and serving officers freely engage in debate on websites such as the *Small Wars Journal*[306].

In his 2009 lecture to the Royal United Services Institute, the UK's Chief of Defence Staff, Air Chief Marshall Sir Jock Stirrup, commented that: 'we have lost an institutional capacity for and culture of strategic thought.'[307] We contend that expanding the UK Armed Forces educational and learning programme, which in many instances does not need large-scale capital investment but rather a shedding of the shackles of process management and 'conventional wisdom', will contribute to this significantly.

Professionalisation

We believe that we have demonstrated that, whilst the job of Information Operations (IO) or Media Operations Officer is extremely hard, it is also, potentially, one of the most important appointments to any battle group or staff. That it should be routinely filled by an augmentee with little or no experience is ridiculous. We propose that IO, PsyOps and Media Ops be professionalised under the banner of a strategic communication organisation, and one which reaches across government. Intrinsic to this restructuring should be the recognition that in complex societies the military may well not hold all the answers and outside assistance will need to be sought. For example, despite all of 52 Brigade's research and learn-

305   http://kingsofwar.org.uk/
306   http://smallwarsjournal.com/
307   Sir Jock Stirrup, CDS lecture to Royal United Services Institute, 3 December 2009; available to download at: http://www.rusi.org/cdslectures

ing, the various ideas presented above still did not properly prepare the Brigade for its deployment because the motivators and opinions of the population were still not clearly and scientifically understood. Although the MoD and OGDs have commissioned countless surveys and opinions polls, these did not identify the real psychological drivers and influence levers of the very diverse nature of Afghan society. Indeed, their findings were often counterproductive because they summarised views and opinions held in the past, not motivations for the future. These must no longer be key drivers for military and political policy. Only in late 2009 has this seminal requirement been properly funded and undertaken, by the US, and we note the work of the UK-based Behavioural Dynamics Institute with the US DoD and the State Department in its proven Target Audience Analysis programme. But we also note the use of many other contractors – some good, some considerably less so – in units, commands and departments – invariably without any correlation to each other and often providing conflicting advice. Professionalisation will facilitate the proper understanding and scrutiny of contractor support. Simultaneously we question the efficacy of continuing to combine hard power targeting with soft power information deployment under the same organisation. We note that the creation of any new manning structure is often fraught with difficulty – the Royal Navy resisted for many years the creation of a bespoke intelligence specialisation – the only one of the three services not to be so equipped – despite seemingly compelling evidence of its need. We envisage that resistance to a broader information specialisation would be just as strong. However, we also note that with some small degree of innovation it might be achieved without any cost. Military officers typically change their appointments (postings) every two to three years. At least once on every rank and often more they move away from their core specialisation for a broadening appointment. We believe that with clever manning processes it should be possible to grow selected individuals on a twin career ladder, where the broadening appointment is replaced by an information-related one. The model for this already exists with Royal Navy barristers, who are mainly logistics officers by training but who focus their out-of-specialisation time on legal appointments. This process simultaneously grows lawyers and logisticians, providing them with experience, training and increasing seniority, and allows them to hold down positions of great responsibility in either domain. Even with professionalisation, and external support, we recognise that in the field commanders often have to make difficult and time-critical decisions. We note the US use of deployed Human Terrain System (HTS) personnel – psychologists and anthropologists – able to advise the command on cultural and human behavioural issues. As we have seen, the UK has no such direct model, relying instead upon Culads, and we would like to see urgent attention paid to their development and deployment. We note that HTS have not been without controversy, and we understand many of the objections that have been raised. However, we firmly believe that any process that reduces the need for hard kinetic power is worthy of trial. It cannot be appropriate that individual military commanders have to engage in detailed, self-initiated, self-study – there must be the same level of external support as there is for any other aspect of conflict.

Research

We are firmly convinced that only through research will the West's militaries be prepared for the future. Whilst the US has a long-developed and well-funded research programme, the UK is not so fortunate. The UK MoD's in-house research capacity was almost eliminated by the privatisation of the Defence Evaluation and Research Agency (DERA) into QinetiQ in 2001. We cannot help but note that the change occurred at the exact same time that the nature and complexity of the problems the UK military will face, and the need for equipment to meet those challenges, changed forever. At the micro-level we are deeply concerned that the fundamental understanding of the need for the UK's Defence Academy may be to provide selection courses for promotion rather than embracing new concepts, innovating and researching. We note that the UK's military staff courses are, at their core, 'taught' courses, whilst US military staff courses are significantly more research-based – the sheer volume of highly original research undertaken and published by US students is indicative of this. So too the huge number of US military officers that gain PhDs. We note that the UK defence budget at one time funded seven research chairs in UK universities; today there are none. Although the UK defence community nominally has access to a large number of King's College London academics based at the Defence Academy, we also note that the Academy has no ability or remit to direct their research. We note the 2009 dissolution of the Defence Academy's Advanced Research Group – as a cost-saving measure – which in 2007 was the only organisation across the MoD able to support 52 Brigade's operational design. Research, we believe, needs a champion, and in the US we see just such a vehicle: the establishment of the US Center for Complex Operations (CCO) at the National Defense University (roughly analogous to the UK's Defence Academy), which networks civilian and military educators, trainers and lessons-learnt practitioners dedicated to preparing for complex operations, including stability operations, COIN and irregular warfare. We believe that a similar capability is urgently required in the UK. This is not to say that we see that all the answers lie in the US; the UK has its own rich tradition of innovation – the Political Warfare Executive and Special Operations Executive provide good historical examples. Australia too has been particularly proactive in its development of complexity understanding. However the US, with its vast budgets, seems increasingly willing to speculate and then invest in research. The nature of the 'special relationship' should allow us to quickly learn rather than begin long and costly development processes of our own.

Our book accepts, at its very heart, the Clausewitzian premise that conflict is a clash of wills. We have sought to advance the idea that alongside kinetic power there is potentially a more behavioural approach which, we believe, can affect the enemy's will and be as, arguably more, effective than kinetic power in future conflicts. Andrew's success in recapturing the town of Musa Qala – a key Taliban stronghold – indicates that this does not have to be at the expense of military effectiveness. We believe there to be multiple benefits to such an approach. Although we cannot prove causality (the absence of figures for enemy and civilian deaths preventing more granular analysis), there appears to be a strong correlation between the nature of a deploying commander's operational design and its effect on UK casualty figures in Afghanistan, as shown in Table 8.2.

Deployment name	Deployment Brigade	Size of deployment in personnel	UK deaths during deployment	% UK deaths to size of deployment
Herrick IV	16 Air Asslt	4500	33	0.73
Herrick V	3 Cdo	5200	13	0.25
Herrick VI	12 Mech	6500	28	0.43
Herrick VII	52 Bde	7750	13	0.16
Herrick VIII	16 Air Asslt	8530	26	0.30
Herrick IX	3 Cdo	8300	32	0.38

Table 8.2 UK casualty figures, Afghanistan 2006-2009.

Intuitively, this seems obvious. However, the absence of contemporary research and the capacity to undertake it means we cannot prove this. In order to do so there needs to be proper research and education, and our view is that this does not currently exist nor, if current trends prevail, will it ever do so. What we are advocating in this book cannot be realised within the current structure of the MoD, which has to adopt a far more adaptive and innovative capacity. As the Commanding General of US Training and Doctrine, General Martin Dempsey recently suggested, military power, in the future, will be measured in terms of the 'Ability to Adapt'. We regard it as essential that the capacity to do so now be given serious attention by the MoD if we are to meet the former British Chief of Defence Staff, Sir Jock Stirrup's, idea of becoming 'nurturers' of strategic thinking rather than 'hunter gatherers'.

The old saying 'live and learn' must be reversed in war, for there we 'learn and live'; otherwise we die.

9

The science of influence

by Lee Rowland

No man is an island, entire of itself.

John Donne[308]

Have you ever looked to the sky on a clear autumn day and wondered how that flock of birds managed to hang a left, all at precisely the same time? The movement seems so cohesive, so slick and fluid, that one could be forgiven for thinking that there are strange forces at work, as though some kind of energy field binds the group together. Yet nothing so mysterious is at play. Although a fascinating phenomenon, the flocking behaviour of birds, like that of buffalo herds and schools of fish, is an example of the natural process of emergence. Often, just a few simple rules underlie the seemingly complex behaviour that arises at the group level. In the case of flocking, as few as three rules – such as 'steer to avoid overcrowding of flockmates' – may explain the observed movements of the flock. The crucial thing to understand about these behaviours is that they do not arise as the property of any individual. Rather, the swift decisions of each bird are dependent upon other members of the group, such that the overall effect is of supreme group co-ordination.

What can the flocking of birds tell us about how to do influence? Actually, quite a lot. Flocking is an evolved adaptation that ensures a greater chance of survival for the members of a species. Humans are not so vastly different, having improved our survival prospects by evolving in complex social groups. It naturally follows that the human group powerfully shapes the motivations behind our behaviour.

Whilst the rules that govern our social behaviour are not as simple nor yet as formally specified as those of birds, social scientists are making extraordinary advances in discovering the rules and how they might be applied to understanding and improving human affairs. The principle of *social proof*, for example, states that in ambiguous situations people will observe what others are doing as a guide to what they themselves should be doing. Consider the first thing that people do when they hear a fire alarm: they look out into the corridor and see what everyone else is up to. The alarm's message is loud and clear – it could not be more resonant. It has our best interests at heart: to save our lives. Yet still we are most concerned with the behaviour of those around us. No one wants to be the goon standing out in the parking lot alone. For the purposes of influence it is impera-

---

308   John Donne, 'Meditation XVII Devotions Upon Emergent Occasions and Death's Duel' (1624).

tive that we understand the importance of group norms, the social and behavioural dynamics, and the pressures of minds on minds that shape the totality of our behavioural interactions. Our reality is determined in large part by what we think others are thinking, and why we think they think it. Influencing people is about group psychology – and the behavioural rules that govern us.

Andrew and Steve discussed the application of Kahneman and Tversky's work in the field of behavioural conflict (see Chapter 4), and these are the kinds of rules and heuristics that can assist practitioners in devising better influence programmes and strategic communication initiatives. The innovation of using advances in behavioural economics to better understand influence is laudable, and more of this kind of thinking is needed. But as Steve and Andrew will readily admit, whilst both are professional military officers they are not psychologists, and consequently there has been a bit of 'groping around in the dark' to find the most relevant theory for the battlefield. Science, however, can offer a great deal more to assist military influence practitioners, and in this final chapter I will outline some of the relevant material from which behavioural conflict can benefit.

There is a sense that up until now we have been largely getting it wrong, focusing too heavily on messages and attitudinal change, within the framework of a reductionist science – that is, a science built on a simplistic notion of cause and effect, and one that is limited in its capability of dealing with complexity. Failure is the only possible outcome if this continues. In aiming to avoid this eventuality, highly relevant research from the social and behavioural sciences is being successfully applied to better understand foreign audiences and to construct measurable behavioural influence. The theme of the science advanced here is that of group behaviour in complex environments, which, as we shall see, is an area of study that is receiving intense interest – both within and outside academia – and that is yielding near-revolutionary findings. The purpose of this chapter, then, is to describe some of the science of human behaviour and complexity, but also to describe the scientific process and the nature of scientific thinking, and explain how to proceed in integrating all that into a workable methodology for military operations.

The science of the times

The behavioural sciences are coming of age. A July 2010 *New Scientist* front cover proclaimed 'The Greatest Experiment Begins', referring to the recent developments in data collection on human behaviour afforded to us by the advances made in powerful computing and the Internet. Academic accounts of psychology place its birth as a scientific discipline at just over 100 years ago, but it had a sketchy past as it struggled to come of age in the twentieth century. Only now really, over the last twenty years, since the convergence of brain imaging technologies, network-based modelling, and the refined laboratory methods of experimental psychology, has psychology gained the status of a serious science. Still progress continues as the behavioural sciences undergo immense change. As a result, the old models of human behaviour are becoming outdated, and more accurate ones are replacing them.

Part of the difficulty has been in grappling with the complexity of human behaviour. Many people are familiar with statements like 'the human brain is the most complex object in the known universe' (true) and 'there are more connections between the neurons in the human brain than there are atoms in the entire universe' (also true). Now, take that complexity and multiply it by six or seven billion to account for the world's population: that's the complexity of human behaviour. If a single individual contains unfathomable complexity in her head, then putting a few heads together can surely only make matters worse. This is true to a degree, but the science of human behaviour actually shows that individuals within social groups can behave in remarkably uniform ways. Like the flocking of birds, there are patterns of behaviour shared by the members of the group, and, despite the complexity, the behavioural sciences are decoding these patterns.

A new model of human motivation

Understanding human motivation – what drives people, why they do what they do – is integral to conducting effective influence. Unsurprisingly, simplistic accounts of motivation, such as Maslow's now infamous Hierarchy of Needs,[309] barely scratch the surface of the problem. There are, however, two developments in the study of motivation that are highly relevant *right now* to the model of influence expounded in this book.

The first of these concerns the underlying nature of all human motivation. Ever since Darwin, the assumption for many people has been that nature is 'red in tooth and claw', and that therefore each person must be out for himself. From 'selfish gene' theory to the tenets of capitalism, we have been bombarded with exhortations that human beings are in competition with each other, and that the individual must therefore fight for survival within this wretched world. No scientist or politician has perhaps stated it more assuredly than Gordon Gekko in the film *Wall Street*: 'The point is, ladies and gentleman, that "greed" – for lack of a better word – is good. Greed is right. Greed works. Greed clarifies, cuts through and captures the essence of the evolutionary spirit.'

As convincing as this may sound, and as borne out in human affairs as it appears to be, greed does not entirely capture the essence of the evolutionary spirit. There has been a remarkable shift in our understanding of human psychology over the last two decades, and its essence is this: we are a social species, with a brain that is hardwired for social co-operation, and it was through this co-operation that hu-

---

309   A. H. Maslow, 'A Theory of Human Motivation' (*Psychological Review*, 1943, vol. 50, pp. 370–396).

man societies developed. We are, so to speak, the social species par excellence.[310] The social view of human groups does not preclude the display of behaviours that seek to maximise the lot of individuals, but calls into question the extent to which selfish interests are powerful motivating forces, given other alternatives.

Descartes' famous proclamation, that heralded the dawn of the scientific revolution, 'I think therefore I am', may now be considered moribund, as we realise that we exist and think only as part of an intricate socio-cultural nexus, shaped by a devastatingly powerful evolutionary past. John Donne's quotation that heads this chapter is something of an understatement.

The other development in our scientific understanding of human motivation is that the relationship between performance and reward is not as simple as had been believed. In neoclassical economic models of motivation, the predominant theory was that human performance improves in line with greater reward, such that more money will motivate people to work harder, for example. This now seems to be in doubt. Recent findings by senior economists have shown that higher reward will lead to greater performance on tasks that are *mechanical*, but that, as soon as the task involves some cognitive effort, such as doing calculations, then higher reward often leads to *reduced performance* on the task.[311] The finding was so surprising to the Ivy League economists that they reasoned that the reward must not have been high enough to motivate Harvard undergraduates. So they replicated the study in India, where some of the rewards were equivalent to a month's salary, and they found just the same result. There is a very interesting RSA lecture on the web by Dan Pink that explains this in more detail, and it's animated, so quite good fun. Some of the other conclusions he reaches about human motivation make the video worth a look.[312]

These two revelations – that (a) humans are motivated by social need, not just individual greed, and (b) that a greater reward does not necessarily motivate people to perform better – are clearly important for military units attempting to conduct behavioural influence. Making the assumption that rewarding individuals to behave in the manner of our wishes, if not considered in the broader context of what is socially right and acceptable, will likely fail. It means that we will have to get smarter at understanding what people want and need, and apply this understanding judiciously. Chapter 4, for example, discussed some of the inadequacies of the *Homo Economicus* model. In the light of the social view of motivations presented here, the economic postulate of human decision-making – that we seek

---

310   In the 1990s, neurophysiologists at the University of Parma, Italy, identified neurons in the primate cortex that fired when the animal picked up a piece of food, but also when the monkey saw a person pick up a piece of food. The researchers argued that these specialised neurons had 'mirror' properties and were responsible for recognising the actions and intentions of others. More recently, research on humans has strongly suggested that mirror neurons are the foundations of understanding the intentions of other people and for empathising with them, which is the basis of social interaction.

311   Dan Pink, *Drive: The Surprising Truth about what Motivates Us* (Canongate, 2010).

312   http://www.youtube.com/watch?v=u6XAPnuFjJc

to maximise personal material gain – is weakened further. Some writers, such as Jeremy Rifkin in his book *The Empathic Civilisation*,[313] have even gone as far as to suggest that the epithet *Homo Empathicus* is more apposite.

We must be cautious of making generalised assumptions such as characterising humans as 'economic', 'empathic', 'selfish', 'greedy', and so on. If there is one lesson learnt about human motivation it is this: motivations are contextual. Context determines what people strive for and what drives them, not a one-size-fits-all model dreamed up by men in white coats. Maslow's Hierarchy places food and shelter at the very bottom of his pyramid, yet some people actively starve themselves in the name of ideology.

Networks of complexity

If you accept that human behaviour, especially in its social context, is horrifically complex – and I sincerely hope that you do – then you might also accept that a simple scientific account based on a simplistic scientific model will be inadequate for the job. Reductionist formulations resembling the laws of thermodynamics or the equation for photosynthesis would prove absurd in the modelling of human social behaviour. That does not mean that we must despair and throw in the towel. On the contrary, it means we must rise to the challenge, and meet each day with anticipation and vigour. Hard though the task is, great leaps are being made.

As technology improves, so too does our view of reality and the metaphors we use to describe it. The icon of the twentieth century was the atom, the very epitome of individuality in its solitary spin, all matter being reduced to it alone. But the atom is the past. We are beginning to see the failings of the nuclear family, the isolation of ourselves, the dangers of reducing the world to its bare building blocks. The new metaphor is the network, the interconnectedness of all things. The intricate complexity of ecosystems, the dependence of people on social integration, and, of course, the power of the social technologies that the Internet has ushered in: all are the beginnings of a profound realisation that nothing exists independently, and that to imagine otherwise is to fail in the new emerging economies of the twenty-first century. The Net is messy and complex, a web of cause and effect, difficult to understand and impossible to contain. It requires a new set of analytical tools, a new way of seeing and working.

The interconnectedness of all things is also apparent in the changing nature of communication. Manuel Castells, arguably the world's leading communication expert, explains in his recent work *Communication Power*[314] how communication is transgressing the one-to-many process to a many-to-many process of mass *self-communication*. The balance of power is spreading from the top to the bottom,

---

313 Jeremy Rifkin, *The Empathic Civilization: The Race to Global Consciousness in a World in Crisis* (Polity Press, 2010).

314 Manuel Castells, *Communication Power* (Oxford University Press, 2011).

and it is no longer the case, therefore, that a message from the top reaches its audience unadulterated. We are only beginning to grasp the ramifications of this shift.

One of those ramifications is the inadequacy of the old marketing model and the advertising industry it supports. Marketing is increasingly turning to science to provide solutions amid the transformation wrought by the communications revolution. The military must keep pace. In the light of the complexity model of human behaviour expounded here, it is clear that reliance on the marketing approach for strategic communication must be abandoned. For one, marketing deals with differentiation when the behavioural outcome is known. In other words, it aims to persuade you to buy more of a particular product than another similar product. This scenario bears little resemblance to the reality of conflict, where predefined behavioural outcomes are devilishly hard to specify in messy environments of human interaction, and consequently highly sophisticated measures of effectiveness (MOE) are essential. Marketing is simply not equipped to deal with problems and situations of this nature. Marketing gurus can add some sheen, the glitz and the glamour, but that is no substitute for the real business of applying rigorous, evidence-based, scientific thinking.

Scientific thinking

In *On the Psychology of Military Incompetence*[315] by the late experimental psychologist Norman Dixon, the foreword by Brigadier Shelford Bidwell briefly looks at the role that science has played in military affairs, and we find that whilst science had been useful to warfare, it had only 'provided weapons to kill but not the essential apparatus for command and control. Scientists were still only asked for *tools*. No one then dreamt of asking them the question "How shall we do it?"' Bidwell goes on to say that only by the Second World War were talented scientists brought in for the 'purpose of pure *thinking*. The application of the behavioural sciences followed exactly the same cycle one war later.' Bidwell is encouraging when he says that by making use of the science of stress and motivation, psychologists made extremely valuable contributions. Being myself a psychologist and behavioural scientist, I think that Brigadier Bidwell is an extraordinarily insightful man.

Science has garnered the impression that it's not to be messed with. To many people it seems the very antithesis of creativity: not woolly and unfounded, but solid and hard, something we can rely on. Science, supposedly, is fact, not fiction. However, in truth, *real* science is neither as factual as we have sometimes believed, nor is it devoid of the creative impulse. The great twentieth-century physicist Richard Feynman (who famously demonstrated on US TV why the space shuttle *Challenger* malfunctioned) considered that the scientific process consisted

315   Norman F. Dixon, *On The Psychology of Military Incompetence* (Futura, 1976).

of *experiment* and *imagination*. Experiment is the method used to test scientific ideas and to show their validity. Imagination is the faculty that directs the intellect to what is important to know, to verify, and to how to begin to even tackle the experimental problem.

Science, then, is a way of thinking. It is not merely prescriptive solutions or a set of theories, but a method we must adopt. Too many people in the influence game want quick-fix solutions, without realising that the solutions need first to be identified. A doctor can prescribe the medicine only after a diagnosis has been made, and it is the process of diagnosis that requires the intelligence and training that make a good doctor.

Feynman talked of 'cargo cult science'[316] by which he elucidated the distinction between scientific thinking and that of pseudo-science. An interesting anecdote of his brilliantly exemplifies, in my view, what science is really all about. In 1937 a psychologist named Young conducted a set of experiments on seeing whether rats could learn to enter a maze through one door and to locate food behind a different door. The respective locations could be different, but were always related, such that the door with the food behind it was always three doors down from the door through which the rats entered. But rather than learning this relationship between doors, the rats kept going to the door where the food had been the time before. But Young questioned how it was that the rats were finding that same door. There appeared to be nothing distinctive about the door, and the corridors all looked the same with no distinguishing features. Young ensured that all features were uniform on the doors, even down to the textures. He used chemicals to wipe out the smell of the food. He made certain that there was no light streaming in to the maze from the lab that the rats might use as cues. He tried to eliminate all the features that might assist the rats in locating the previous door. Yet still they went to it. In the end he discovered that the rats were using the sound of the floor to locate the door – and so he laid sand on the floor to mask the sounds, and the effect vanished. This is science: it aims to find the exact conditions that are responsible for an effect. Not what you think is happening, but what is actually going on.

To ask questions like these, to be genuinely interested in finding out the real cause of an effect, requires the diligent use of our critical and analytic abilities. Systematic observation and painstaking recording of data and events are necessary to

---

316   Richard Feynman, Caltech commencement address, in which he explains his term 'cargo cult science', which comes from the cargo cults of the South Sea Islanders. He says it here in his own words: 'In the South Seas there is a cargo cult of people. During the war they saw airplanes land with lots of good materials, and they want the same thing to happen now. So they've arranged to imitate things like runways, to put fires along the sides of the runways, to make a wooden hut for a man to sit in, with two wooden pieces on his head like headphones and bars of bamboo sticking out like antennas–he's the controller–and they wait for the airplanes to land. They're doing everything right. The form is perfect. It looks exactly the way it looked before. But it doesn't work. No airplanes land. So I call these things cargo cult science, because they follow all the apparent precepts and forms of scientific investigation, but they're missing something essential, because the planes don't land.'

eliminate alternative explanations of phenomena. This process allows prediction such that the scientist can say something in advance about what is likely to happen under a set of pre-specified conditions.

Science guides the manner in which information is collected, too, which is crucial. Proper scientific research is not concerned with collecting as much information as possible. It's concerned primarily with collecting the right kind of evidence, that which has high diagnostic value. We're not being inductive, finding out all we can about an audience – we're being deductive, finding the information necessary to conduct good influence. It is a method rather than a set of prescriptive steps or products that can be used, and it aims at providing genuinely useful insight.

Influence is not a science of its own and thus requires a co-ordinated effort across a range of disciplines. Weapons systems need the input from physicists, chemists, engineers, computer scientists, and so on; and influence is no different in its complexity, drawing from the range of behavioural and social sciences, mathematical modelling and system dynamics, economics, communication and information sciences, and advanced research methods, to name a few of the many disciplines that are proving relevant.

Wood for the trees

Let us just take stock. This is a confusing mix of new behavioural science, new models of complexity and networks, ways of thinking and the nature of the scientific process. It all seems like an enormous upheaval from our established modus operandi. There is no need for doom and gloom though, nor for despair. Acknowledging confusion is, so said Socrates, the first step to wisdom.

The first point of encouragement is that the complexity has been recognised, and attempts are being made to construct models that can represent the environment of human behaviour in conflict scenarios. David Kilcullen's complex adaptive systems model of COIN that he set forth in 'Countering Global Insurgency' is a commendable and a much-needed step in the right direction. System dynamics and forms of mathematical behavioural modelling will be indispensable to influence campaigns in future conflicts.

The second reason for optimism is that the need for the integration of contemporary behavioural science into influence is also recognised. Andrew and Steve's description of the utility of behavioural economics for theatre is unprecedented, and again to be commended (see Chapter 4). As yet, the wealth of relevant science has not been made use of, and the *process* of scientific *thinking* has not been taken full advantage of, but nevertheless we should be heartened.

Whilst not out of the woods, we no longer just see trees. There is still a good deal of uncertainty over what scientific approaches to take, and there is no co-ordinated assessment of what is working in the field and which theoretical approaches are proving most successful. To bring influence up to speed, widespread co-ordination is needed between allies. We cannot risk having different scientific approaches to influence, in the same way that we would not run an airport without a central control tower. The planes would all fly into each other.

An holistic model is needed that is capable of full compatible integration of research, data and thinking. This is a systemic issue, and beyond my area of authority, but I do know that the science of influence will fail without this commitment. In addition, we need a fully operational systematic methodology that coheres, structures and co-ordinates all influence strategy. This will require the full submission of non-kinetic effects to the strictures of science, the consummation of the marriage between academia and the military, and ensuring that the work of the former is made field-expedient for the latter. As we have seen above, we know most of the building blocks. The remainder of this chapter will suggest some ways that we might put them together.

Target Audience Analysis

Steve and Andrew have already mentioned Target Audience Analysis[317] (TAA; see Chapter 6), and they rightly identify it as the very cornerstone of influence, strategic communication, psychological operations and related disciplines. Unfortunately, in the military domain no consensus exists on what it is, or precisely how it should be done. In keeping with the theme of this chapter, if TAA is to be genuinely useful for military influence, it must be a scientific process and must conform to sound scientific principles.

It has been far too common to conflate TAA with cultural understanding. Undoubtedly, cultural understanding is elemental to TAA, and without a solid understanding of the values, customs, beliefs and history of a target population, influence would be, in almost all cases, impossible. But TAA goes much further. At the very least, TAA must seek to discover the motivations, both individual and social, of a group, and grasp how those motivations are played out against the social norms of the group. Insight into how to get young men to join the Afghan National Police (ANP), for example, will require this level of analysis. Cultural knowledge is simply inadequate for tasks of this nature. Research conducted in Kandahar revealed that a significant proportion of young men would like to join the ANP to protect and serve their country, but their individual wishes are thwarted because they feel they'd be ostracised from their families and tribes should they follow their desire.[318] Whilst understanding the tribal structures and

---

317   A caveat – TAA is currently the familiar term, and I will adopt it here. However, I am working on a new perspective that sees groups not as 'target audiences' but as 'participants' in creating desirable behavioural outcomes. The concept of TAA may need to undergo serious revision.

318   Research conducted by Strategic Communication Laboratories, UK, in Kandahar, Summer 2010.

customs of Afghanistan is important, that alone would not provide the necessary insight into the ANP dilemma.

If TAA is to be fully scientific, then it must collect data in a constrained fashion. That means, rather than collecting piles of information, the process should be streamlined to gather data that has high diagnostic value. A decision system is diagnostic if the data collected is more supportive of one hypothesis over another. This is the manner in which a doctor diagnoses his patients. He would be a poor practitioner if in response to your symptoms of a fever, a sore throat and a rash he only took your temperature – hundreds of illnesses have associated high temperatures. On the other hand, inspecting the rash by pressing a glass to it and seeing if it disappears is a sure-fire way to diagnose meningitis (if it doesn't disappear, you've probably got it). This process is accurate and conservative, but it requires that the practitioner has knowledge of what to look for, and understands the decision process that tests genuinely useful hypotheses. However, if a doctor collected all possible medical information before making a diagnosis, her patient would die waiting.

Good influence science must avoid doing what the FBI did during the first fifty-one days of the Texas Waco siege disaster: they collected so much information that they had to ignore the vast majority of it and just fall back on past practice.

The diagnostic approach to information gathering for TAA will be most effective if the data collected is indicative of group-level traits rather than those of individuals. The difference is stark. It means that, rather than researching aggregates of individuals, which often yields unrealistic scores (no one has ever had 2.4 children), research must aim at discovering group-level traits that are endorsed and shared by its members *with respect to the group*. This means that, regardless of whether a young man would tick a box to say that more than anything else in the world he wants a new sports car, we need to ascertain whether this would still hold if all of his peers were getting new sports cars – would he still be persuaded by the prospect of a new car if he would no longer be the toast of the town? This aspect of influence is so important, and yet is almost universally overlooked. We aim to influence *groups* (or certainly that is the case in Afghanistan), and yet we research *individuals* qua *the individual*.

Recall the above-mentioned example of the ANP: many individuals would like to join it, but they cannot and will not do so because, with respect to the social group, their decisions are greatly affected. Like the flock of birds, group behaviours emerge as a result of how individuals make decisions based on the decisions of the group.

To obtain results of this quality requires a level of research sophistication that vastly supersedes that of the standard polling and survey measures typical of 'social science' marketing companies. Audiences are not static 'things' but dynamic processes, and the unwarranted obsession with metrics that is behind the survey method is failing to capture the nuances inherent in complex societies embroiled in challenging circumstances.

Afghanistan constitutes by far the largest research project ever undertaken by humankind. The CERN particle collider may be the most expensive, but Afghanistan is the most extensive, and despite having accrued millions of data points, unimaginable amounts of paper with ticks and crosses and circles, and knowing almost everything about the culture, we still do not know how to solve the 'communication problem'. The reason is that we are collecting the wrong kind of data and we're not getting the science right. There is too much bogus quantification. The recent 2010 Asia Foundation poll reported that an astonishing 84 per cent agree with the statement 'the ANP are honest and fair'.[319] No peaceful and stable country in the Western world would get a score like that for their police force! In contrast, qualitative data collected in Maiwand province in Kandahar in September 2010 showed that disillusionment with, low confidence in, and fear of the ANP is rife.[320] These qualitative findings formed the basis of a situational model that was then further tested in the field using a quantitative questionnaire. The questionnaire was designed according to strict criteria that allowed several competing hypotheses to be tested with regard to ANP corruption and retainment. This mixed-methods approach, of exploring deep and wide through extensive qualitative research, and then refinement and formal hypothesis testing through quantitative research, is the very minimum needed to tackle problems of the complexity prevalent in Afghanistan.

Obtaining data of the quality argued for here depends on a level of research rigour rarely embraced by military forces. The basis of all subsequent research must rest on a solid qualitative foundation, and to do this requires researchers of the highest order. The research conducted by Strategic Communication Laboratories has always relied on indigenous, intelligent, and fully trained cohorts who are people experts and who understand how to ask questions in a manner that elicits top-quality information from interviewees. This is not a strength of their approach, but an absolute necessity. In Dr Emily Spencer's chapter 'The People Puzzle' in *The Difficult War: Perspectives on Insurgency and Special Operations Forces*,[321] she argues for the need to utilise researchers who have cultural intelligence (CQ), so that they may build rapport with their interviewees and establish the mutual respect and confidence that allows accurate information flow. This is preceisely what is needed.

---

319   On 9 November 2010, the Asia Foundation released findings from *Afghanistan in 2010: A Survey of the Afghan People* – the broadest public opinion poll in the country. Conducted by the Asia Foundation's office in Afghanistan, the 2010 survey polled 6,467 Afghan citizens across all thirty-four provinces in the country on security, development, economy, government, corruption and women's issues to assess the mood and direction of the country. In-person interviews were conducted from 18 June to 5 July 2010 with a multi-stage random sample of Afghan citizens eighteen years of age and older, both women and men, from different social, economic and ethnic communities in rural and urban areas.

320   Research conducted by Strategic Communication Laboratories, UK, in Kandahar Summer 2010.

321   Emily Spencer, *Difficult War: Perspectives on Insurgency and Special Operations Forces* (Dundurn Group Ltd, 2009).

A key skill, therefore, is to relate to the audience in a deep way, and to try and see things from their perspective. This marketing guy once said to me: 'I don't just think that TAA is a good thing, I *know* it is. You've got to fit the message to the audience, right?' Wrong. If you ever find yourself trying to 'fit' the message to the audience, you're on the wrong track. Just because Afghans say they lack food and shelter does not mean that they will be persuaded by arguments promising better food and shelter. This is an egregious assumption, and would be to the detriment of your message campaign from the outset. Far more persuasive than words promising food and shelter would be the action of, say, rebuilding a mosque, especially one destroyed by Coalition forces in the first place. An event like this would be far more influential than yet another message amongst thousands of others.

We might characterise this approach as *audience-centric*, as opposed to the more conventional *audience-focused* one. To be audience-focused is to see the audience as separate from us, somewhere over there, the target of our desires, whereas to be audience-centric means that we strive to see things from their viewpoint in order to understand how the 'right' solution would look to them. This is difficult, for it demands a Copernican shift of perspective, but without that we will inevitably get our messages wrong.

The audience-centric approach advocated here has been adopted by the British government in support of domestic policy. In a 2008 paper by Conrad Bird (the current Joint Action Leader in the UK's Cabinet Office), entitled 'Strategic Communication and Behaviour Change: Lessons from Domestic Policy',[322] Bird recognises the primary need to put 'genuine understanding of audience behaviour at the heart' of strategic communication, and to him that entails 'interactive, collaborative and experiential' participation *with* the audience in 'pursuit of joint outcomes'. Bird cites an example from a recent Department for Transport 'Think' campaign that worked with teenagers to produce a campaign aimed at improving attention when crossing the road. One advert was posted on YouTube and within five days of appearing had been seen by 29 per cent of all teenagers in the UK. Can we conceive of this degree of co-creation with Afghan audiences? Can future campaigns adopt this strategy? I believe they must.

Research parameters

The previous section specified aspects of the scientific process of TAA that are essential to ensuring that it is rigorous and structured, and that it provides a firm foundation for data-collection and research focus. The following section addresses the question of what exactly the research should focus *on* and the kinds

---

322   Conrad Bird, 'Strategic Communication and Behaviour Change: Lessons from Domestic Policy', in J. Welsh and D. Fearn (eds) *Engagement: Public Diplomacy in a Globalised World* (London: Foreign and Commonwealth Office, 2008, pp. 107–119), available at http://www.fco.gov.uk/en/about-us/publications-and-documents/publications1/pd-publication/

of data that need to be collected to conduct influence. Four of the key questions addressed in TAA are:

- *Groups:* How do groups identify themselves and what dynamics govern how the group operates?

- What *issues, beliefs* or *norms* are most salient and frame a group's understanding of its behaviour?

- *Behaviour:* What social structures or incentives motivate or constrain available behaviours?

- *Communications:* How can the pertinent groups be most easily reached?

Looking through this set of questions, it is apparent that the behaviour of groups in a social context, and their attendant motivations, constitutes the bulk of our research efforts for TAA. Earlier in the chapter we discussed the importance of human behaviour to the influence methodology being developed, but it is necessary to emphasise the behavioural approach further. It has been conventional to measure attitudes as a basis for devising persuasive communication, under the erroneous assumption that if a person holds a favourable attitude towards something (say, they 'like America'), then their behaviour(s) will reflect this underlying attitude (not attack American soldiers, for example). On the contrary, the science just does not support this view, and in many instances runs counter to it.

After decades of research into the causal drivers of human behaviour, psychologists have concluded that the three most important variables are the *intention* to carry out a behaviour, the *environmental constraints* on whether it is possible to carry out that behaviour, and the *skill* or *ability* of the individual to execute the behaviour. If these three factors are in place, then the planned behaviour will probably occur.

The first of these factors, the intention, obviously arises for a whole host of different – and competing – reasons, such as the force of law, emotional reactions, reward and punishment, and social norms, to name just a few. Despite the myriad variables that affect our behaviour, there still exists a prevalence of attitude measurement as a predictor of a person's actions. But attitudes are a poor predictor of behaviour, and there is a corpus of scientific research that demonstrates that position (see David Myers's *Social Psychology*, Chapter 4, 'Behaviour and Attitudes', for a quality overview of this topic[323]). In Britain, for example, attitudes towards wearing seat belts were very negative *until after drivers began wearing seat belts*. Research that controlled for the effect of advertising on attitudes about seat belts showed that the *act* of wearing the seat belt resulted in a more favourable attitude

---

323   David Myers, *Social Psychology* (McGraw-Hill, 2009).

towards it, rather than a favourable attitude to the seat belt resulting in the act of wearing it. Behaviour change often leads to attitude change.

There are numerous explanations for the change in seat-belt wearing behaviour, such as people obeying the law, being motivated to stay alive, their kids nagging them to wear one (a powerful force, actually – my daughter tells me off when I leave the tap running when brushing my teeth), and the pressure of social norms (certainly a major factor in the UK drink-driving campaigns). Whilst there are complex interconnections between these factors and attitudes, they are fuzzy, and not at all the neat packet of information that survey studies seek to collect. The intent to carry out a behaviour and the motivations that drive it are contextual, and the function of TAA is to discover how these factors play out in the real world.

If there is one thing to remember from this chapter, it is the following: the role of the influence scientist is to determine *under what circumstances a desired behavioural outcome will occur*. Attitudes may be a part of the puzzle, but so will a detailed array of other factors. The oft-cited example of the children throwing stones at US soldiers in Iraq perfectly exemplifies what I am arguing for. The kids stopped throwing stones because they were more motivated to play football, and consequently they acquired more favourable attitudes to the soldiers who had given them footballs. The change had nothing to do with a message campaign that attempted to change kids' attitudes towards stones, soldiers, the US, or anything else for that matter. It was all purely down to the circumstances that were created: the distraction of playing football. As it turns out, many Iraqi children were not particularly anti-American, they just wanted something to do.

The challenge for influence researchers is to find out the underlying cause(s) of the non-desired behaviour and fashion the mechanism by which it could be changed. This is no easy feat. They must begin by ensuring that the behavioural outcome (the target behaviour) is clearly defined. They must then ask what is causing the current behaviour, and determine if any of these causes can be interfered with. For instance, is it an habitual behaviour, is it associated with other behaviours, and how does it conflict with other behaviours, beliefs and attitudes? Can the conditions be created for the desired behaviour to emerge? Will it be socially accepted and propagated? If the current behaviour is rewarded, can the situation be altered such that it becomes punished? This is demanding work and requires of the researchers diligent diagnostic thinking and a scientific mind.

Social forces

Anthropologist Gregory Bateson was the first Westerner to properly study the native inhabitants of Papua New Guinea. In 1935, whilst observing the Latmul people engaged in a tribal ritual dance, he observed the following:

Women watched for the spectacular performances of the men, and there can be no reasonable doubt that the presence of an audience is a very important factor in shaping the men's behavior. In fact, it is probable that the men are more exhibitionistic because the women admire their performances. Conversely, there can be no doubt that the spectacular behavior is a stimulus which summons the audience together, promoting in the women the appropriate behavior.[324]

Bateson's work in many fields of social science led him to develop the idea of the 'ecology of mind', and he was one of the pioneers of cybernetics in the 1950s, which was essentially an early attempt at modelling complexity in social interactions. The passage above could be expressed perhaps like this: the behaviour of person X affects person Y, and the reaction of person Y to person X's behaviour will then affect person X's behaviour, which in turn will effect person Y, and so on. Bateson called this the 'vicious circle', which fits with his idea of the ecology of mind as a constant interplay, as action and reaction, between the individual mind and the ecology (both the physical and social environment) in which it is embedded.

We saw in the previous section that the link between mental constructs, such as attitudes, and intended behaviour is weak. However, there is a rich literature and consensus showing that social norms powerfully predict behaviour.[325] A social norm is defined as 'a behavioural expectation or cue within a society or group', and describes how people act according to what the majority would do in a given situation. Essentially, norms govern the degree to which members of a group will conform to the standard codes of behaviour within a group, such as wearing a suit to work. The stronger the norms in a group or society, the more highly will people conform.

A year-long field experiment in Rwanda conducted by Harvard psychologist Elizabeth Levy Paluck neatly encapsulates the power of social norms. Published in the *Journal of Personality and Social Psychology* in 2009,[326] Paluck addressed the question of whether the media can reduce inter-group prejudice and conflict. Given the tensions between the Hutu and Tutsi ethnic minority in Rwanda, it was an ideal live laboratory for carrying out research that would be ecologically valid and have future real-world application. Radio is the most important form of mass media in Rwanda, and so Paluk's study tested the impact of a radio soap opera featuring messages about reducing inter-group prejudice, violence and trauma in two fictional Rwandan communities. Specifically, the research tested

324   Quoted in David Lipset, *Gregory Bateson, the Legacy of a Scientist* (Beacon Press, 1982).

325   Again see Myers, *Social Psychology*, and also Elliot Aronson, *The Social Animal*. Both books have undergone ten editions, a good testament to their influence in the field of psychology.

326   E. Paluk, 'Reducing Intergroup Prejudice and Conflict Using the Media: A Field Experiment in Rwanda' (*Journal of Personality and Social Psychology*, 2009, vol. 96).

three questions: Does the mass media have the capacity to affect (a) personal beliefs, (b) the perception of social norms, and (c) behaviour (open communication and co-operation)? Paluk's conclusion was unequivocal: 'listeners' perceptions of social norms and their behaviours changed with respect to intermarriage, open dissent, trust, empathy, cooperation, and trauma healing. However, the radio program did little to change listeners' personal beliefs.' There are important lessons to learn from this study that may be immediately and directly applicable to Afghanistan, itself a place with group/ethnic tensions and that is dependent on radio for mass communication.

The understanding of behavioural change within social groups is being revolutionised by the development of network models. A social network model is basically a collection of nodes that represent individual actors or groups and the links between them that represent relationships between the people within the network. They can be very simple or highly complex, depending on the numbers of nodes and links, but also on the types of relationships that are represented and the kinds of properties attributed to the nodes. Some links can be mathematically weighted to indicate the strengths of relationships. The concept is based on the idea behind the famous phrase 'six degrees of separation', that suggests that all the people in the world are connected by a very short pathway of links.

These social network models can be used to provide insight into all sorts of interesting features of social groups that would otherwise be very difficult to observe. In mapping relationships of interdependency like kinship, financial and sexual, or even more, psychosocial relationships of knowledge and beliefs, scientists can identify where 'hubs' of activity reside in these networks and how behaviours and information are transmitted through the system. Very complex network models can be dynamic and allow predictions based on current data to forecast possible future states of the system.

Decades of work on social networks by Nicholas Christakis, Professor of Medical Sociology at Harvard Medical School, has been used to understand and predict the dynamics of epidemics, as well as how other things spread through complex networks. Christakis's work, popularised in his book *Connected*,[327] with his colleague Fowler, also demonstrates how happiness, smoking behaviours and obesity, to name a few, spread through the connections that people have with each other, such that, if your friend's friend is unhappy, the probability that you will also be unhappy is significantly increased. The application of social network theory has been used in Afghanistan and it should be put to wider use in helping solve influence problems and the spread of information amongst audiences.

A newly developed concept called 'nudge plus networks'[328] takes the idea of 'nudging' from behavioural economics and conjoins that with contemporary

---

327   Nicholas Christakis and James Fowler, *Connected: The Amazing Power of Social Networks and How they Shape Our Lives* (Little, Brown and Company, 2009).

328   Presented in a paper by Paul Ormerod called 'N Squared: Public Policy and the Power of Networks' (August 2010).

network theory. Nudging, made popular by Cass Thaler and Richard Sunstein in *Nudge: Improving Decisions about Health, Wealth and Happiness*,[329] was touched upon by Steve and Andrew in Chapter 4, and it is the notion that people's decisions about all aspects of their lives can be gently nudged by a variety of techniques that help to reframe the choice architecture in a fashion that promotes one choice over another. Combining nudging with an intricate understanding of network models means that one can identify crucial links and busy hubs in the network as the focus for where nudging could best occur, so that behaviour change or information transfer cascades through the network. This is a tantalising prospect with regard to what the influence practitioner may be able to achieve in the near future.

Although it is true that a message will be better received if it is developed through evidence-based TAA, the future is not primarily about tailoring messages – it will be about nudging, shoving and shaping behaviours through a variety of communication means, of which conventional messages will be only one. We will require a detailed and quantifiable understanding of the behavioural, psychological and social environment, and the forces and pressure that create that. This cannot be performed by hackneyed marketing techniques: this is the domain of advanced social science. Finding the messages that exert strong normative pressures is crucial.

Measurement of effectiveness (MOE)

Target Audience Analysis is focussed on doing the right campaign. Data is gathered about the audience in order to determine where influence would be best applied and which levers are best pulled to change group behaviour. On the basis of TAA, potential intervention strategies are constructed that will form the heart of a communication or behavioural influence campaign. If TAA conforms to the scientific principles laid out in this chapter, and if the research yields data of the highest quality, then I grant you confidence in your proposed campaign, but I cannot guarantee its success. TAA may ensure you do the right campaign – but how do you know if you're doing the campaign right? It's all very well being cocksure that your campaign is scientifically valid and pleased with yourself because it has been rolled out perfectly and looks impressive. But what comfort is that if there is no acceptable method of evaluation?

MOE is not a nice idea …

MOE is imperative. Without it we are sticking up a wet finger in the wind. Science is useful because it enables quantifiable verification of interventions. In the

---

329   Cass Thaler and Richard Sunstein, *Nudge: Improving Decisions About Health, Wealth and Happiness* (Penguin, 2009).

laboratory, scientists probe nature's secrets via the experimental process, which explores the effect of the intervention of a variable on the outcome of the system. A chemist will observe and measure the properties of a beaker of solution as a different substance is added to it a small drop at a time. A physicist bombards sub-atomic particles with other sub-atomic particles and measures the size, mass and energy of newly created fragments. The influence practitioner must meticulously measure the effects of a campaign on the behavioural and attitudinal changes of its intended audience. If this is not performed then there is no way of knowing whether there is any accompanying change in the audience, and if there is, exactly what caused it. As an example, did a campaign to reduce poppy growing in Afghanistan actually have an effect on the observed reduction of poppy plants, or was the reduced growing due to some other variable, such as the incentive to grow wheat because of changes in international affairs, as we saw in the example of 40 Commando that opened this book? The complexity of the human behavioural and communication environment (especially in theatres of conflict) means that simplistic MOE is just not able to handle the data. We need a fully integrated, robust and data-driven MOE that is interwoven with the entire influence process from start to finish.

The story in Chapter 6 of the *Sada-e Azadi* newspaper provides a decent case in point, in that enormous sums of money were spent on writers and thousands of copies were printed, and yet the papers were barely even distributed and hardly ever read. An anecdote relayed to me by a retired officer told of a Polish helicopter that was responsible for dropping leaflets to Iraqis. After several drops the soldiers became bored and booted several bundles of leaflets out of the side door of the aircraft and into a lake below. Not quite the leaflet dropping NATO had in mind no doubt, but the numbers would have been high.

MOE is not concerned with quantities of this kind, as they are extremely poor indicators of actual change on the ground. MOE is solely concerned with cause and effect. This is not easy, and is well recognised by the military. Lieutenant Commander William S. Murray, writing in *Parameters* in 2001, understood that the 'fundamental relationship that bedevils MOE … is that of causality'. Murray's statement is embedded in a section of his paper 'The Will to Measure', that discusses the Kosovo conflict. He says that 'analysis of the number of sorties flown might have informed interested parties how well airmen kept their planes flying, but it did not provide a sense of whether Yugoslavian leaders were ready to accede to NATO demands'.[330]

Conducting MOE that is sensitive enough to detect genuine and meaningful change in audiences requires that it captures a wide variety of data and integrates that into a statistical model which compares the current situation with that of a baseline, i.e. the situation before the campaign was launched. As a minimum this model must collect both external behavioural data taken from measurable observations and audience-based data that reflects both behavioural and percep-

330   William S. Murray, 'A Will to Measure' (*Parameters*, Autumn 2001, pp. 134–147).

tual change from their perspective. The data must be related to the behavioural change objectives of the campaign in a hierarchical fashion. Because this model integrates both audience indicators of change and external indicators it is termed an 'audience-based measure of effectiveness' (AB-MOE).

The challenge in building this AB-MOE model is in identifying the best indicators of meaningful behavioural change. All too often we hear that the Afghan people must be persuaded to 'support' the Coalition, or to 'reject' the insurgency. And all too often the only criteria for whether the Afghan people 'support' the Coalition is whether they respond favourably on a survey study. But if the people are not 'supporting' the Coalition, then what is it that they are doing to give this impression? They must be *behaving* in a manner that is reflective of lack of support. What are those behaviours and how can we measure them? The research to identify those measures can be done as part of the TAA process, and then reassessed after the campaign intervention.

There are numerous potentially informative and measurable indicators of success, such as the number and categories of people waving as patrols move through a village; the frequency with which rural families eat meat; offers to have cups of tea; the presence and variety of exotic fruits and vegetables on market stalls; what farmers are planting; what people are talking about; their movements; people on the streets at night (and those loitering in the day); letters of complaint; information provided to the police – and so on. Although inventive, all are proxy metrics of attitudes and behavioural change. Soldiers can be trained as primary gatherers of information, and on patrols data can be gathered and logged at the end of the day and stored for future use. This practice will help to alleviate the current problems that make data management and handover to new troops very difficult. There needs to be consistency such that each new troop coming in does not have to begin anew. Social scientists must work without delay on codifying a list of measures that are useful for commanders. To that end, work in Afghanistan – that I have been involved in – is underway on behavioural indicators for ANP support and local behavioural indicators of economic improvement.

Holistic systems

For MOE to be executed in the manner explicated above it will be necessary to utilise the most advanced technology for both data gathering, database management and computational modelling. In *Countering Global Insurgency*, David Kilcullen advanced a complex adaptive systems approach to COIN, and the same is demanded in influence. Systems approaches differ from conventional linear models in that they are organised around complexity. Kilcullen argued that the COIN environment is akin to a living organism. I like to think of the informational–behavioural environment as resembling the Amazon rainforest: it is a frantically interwoven ecosystem of ideas, opinions, actions and twists. And, just as with an ecosystem, what happens in one sector of the environment affects what happens in another. If an insect is wiped out, the whole system can collapse – or take aeons to recover.

Systems science emerged out of the need to understand behaviours (not necessarily human ones) without recourse to the inadequacies of the classical mechanistic model. One of the founders of systems science, Ludwig von Bertalanffy, puts it thus:

> The analytic, mechanistic, one-way causal paradigm of classical science assumes that reality can be quantifiably analyzed; that a whole can be understood in terms of its parts; and that the nature and function of a substance or an organism can be comprehended by reducing it to its material externally observable components.[331]

Bertalanffy was questioning this view, having begun to conceive of a different way of understanding nature in terms of wholes, not of parts. So too it is necessary to understand the informational–behavioural environment in terms of the totality of the system, that no part is independent of the whole. Like the flock of birds, the behaviour that emerges is greater than any sum of the parts. Leaflets dropped in one region can affect perceptions in another region. Newspaper articles written for a London paper can affect behaviour in Kabul. A strategic communication initiative by a rapid-response team may completely destroy the effects of a NATO year-long radio campaign. For these reasons, the entire influence process in the military sphere must be conceived in the holistic framework.

To conduct influence operations within an holistic framework requires a scientifically sound systematic methodology that is used by allied troops and continuously monitored and updated by trained experts. Collaboration and central control are pivotal to the success of future behavioural conflict. Presently, however, there are too many disparate organisations and individual enthusiasts, and as a result Coalition efforts are rendered somewhat lawless, wild and uncontainable. Attractive though that may sound, we need somehow to civilise the process.

Proper strategic campaign planning, scientific TAA, behavioural influence analysis and MOE are crucial. These phases of the process must be grounded and aligned in an overarching methodology that is applicable to military conflict everywhere, is field-expedient, and is operationally feasible for soldiers to use. In summary, it must:

- Measurably influence behaviour, not just change attitudes.
- Focus on groups, not individuals.
- Employ deductive diagnostic science, not inductive information gather-

---

331   Ludwig von Bertalanffy, *General Systems Theory* (George Braziller, 1968).

ing (solution-driven, not guesswork).

- Provide a framework for formal planning and research, using multi-method field-based research.

- Be grounded in behavioural science, not creativity.

- Be holistic and systems oriented, not narrow or reductionist.

- Be hypothesis driven.

- Be audience-centric, not message-centric.

- Provide intrinsic MOE, not supplementary measures.

The scientific approach advocated in this chapter will be important for developing this capability.

The ghost of influence future

Influence has been recognised as integral to future military operations, but I fear that if we continue in the current vein, without basing influence on proper scientifically derived TAA and MOE, then we are destined to fail. I have argued that a change in course is needed, that we must begin to approach this task differently. The standard model of TAA misses some crucial aspects of what a science of influence should be. It focuses on cultural understanding instead of diagnostic science, it is audience-focused instead of audience-centric, and it takes an attitudinal approach rather than a behavioural one. Yet I have presented some contemporary advances in the behavioural sciences that can be integrated into military TAA immediately and can begin to avert the current future inevitability. In short, we need to bring about a paradigm shift in behavioural conflict that will recast the direction we take and ensure that proper science is used to achieve success.

To assist in this goal we need: multinational field research; TAA field handbooks regularly updated with the best scientific knowledge; civilian scientists to go on PsyOps courses and for PsyOps to come on civilian science courses. We need research scenarios that mimic field operations, gaming situations, systems models; we need to learn lessons from returning soldiers, databases built with influence techniques and message performances, question databases, Ops centres specifically designed for PsyOps; we need established and systematic methodologies, validated questionnaires and interview schedules, behavioural intelligence experts, new computational analysis tools – and more. We can do all this now, and better is to come. The social and behavioural sciences are being revolutionised by technology, and the military should make full use of that.

Yet we must also realise that we hold great power, and with that comes great responsibility. As a science reaches maturity, the knowledge acquired presents ethical dilemmas to those encumbered: evolutionary theory, nuclear physics and genetics have all had their controversies, even though they can be enormously beneficial to humankind. How we deal with the newfound knowledge of the behavioural sciences will dramatically shape events in future conflict. The challenge of the Coalition's withdrawal from Afghanistan will require keen judgement in the deployment of influence science. Let's evade the ghost of influence past and look to the future with renewed insight.

Postscript: the sounds of battle and Soviet factories

We wrote this book in two chunks; the first, smaller, chunk when we produced our Defence Academy paper in late 2009.[332] It was a consequence of the work we had completed prior to Andrew's deployment, during the deployment itself, and then much more thought on expanding the ideas we had generated, embraced, amended and discarded. The second chunk of the book was written in late 2010 and early 2011. Whilst Andrew had left the army by this time, Steve was (and is) still serving, and the book's writing was punctuated by regular trips back to Afghanistan and, as time moved on, experience of the conflict in Libya, to which the UK applied the name 'Operation Ellamy'. In November 2010, Steve returned to Task Force Helmand (TFH) headquarters in Lashkar Gah. It had grown significantly and the operations room, from where all UK military activity was planned and controlled, was a sea of staff officers and PCs. In fact, any visitor would be forgiven for thinking that the soundtrack to the wars of the twenty-first century was not so much gunshots and explosions but the furious pounding of computer keyboards. What, one can only wonder, do the fifty or so majors, captains and assorted other ranks sitting behind computer terminals actually do? In the last days of the Vietnam War it was calculated that the US army's various intelligence organisations were producing 2.5 tonnes of paper a day. Today, this would probably represent the work of minutes if it were all printed out and collated. Warehouses would quickly fill up. As we saw in Chapter 4, in April 2011 Steve visited ISAF HQ in Kabul, his first visit to the capital. His visit coincided with both the start of the Taliban spring offensive and the death of Osama Bin Laden. Tension hung heavy across the city. ISAF HQ is at its geographic heart but, surrounded as it is by twenty-metre-high walls, and lacking any kind of readily accessible viewing platform, it might just as well be in Bangkok, Baltimore or Bognor Regis. Within its walls representatives from forty-nine nations live a not uncomfortable life, able to frequent fast-food outlets and coffee shops, and to sit amongst manicured lawns and pleasantly landscaped gardens. The sight of an Afghan is rare. In an inner compound is the Operations Centre, from where pan-country activity is co-ordinated; or it was once, for in 2009 the Intermediate Joint Command (IJC) was established at Kabul Military Airport to allow ISAF to focus on strategy, and to take the burden of day-to-day operational command. If the operations room

---

332   'Behavioural Conflict: From General to Strategic Corporal: Complexity, Adaptation and Influence' (Defence Academy of the United Kingdom, 2009). This can be downloaded at: http://www.da.mod.uk/colleges/arag/document-listings/monographs/091216%20FINAL.pdf/view

in TFH is impressive, the one in IJC is mind-blowing, with cinema-size ceiling to floor projector screens and tiered banks of staff officers working behind the ubiquitous PCs. Some 900 staff officers, mainly but not exclusively US personnel, live and work in IJC. Like Helmand, the prevailing sound is the click-click-click of computer keyboards. Once again it is difficult to understand what each and every desk officer does, although it clear that they do it for between twelve and sixteen hours per day, seven days per week. To support both organisations, an entire bureaucracy has become entrenched with budget managers, accountants and processes. One British contracts officer told Steve that the average time for a contract to be let within ISAF was 426 days.

Steve visited ISAF to support some ongoing work in strategic influence, and during his visit was asked to present some ideas on behaviourally based pro-grammes. Steve offered up three: the first would aid the Afghan security force's personnel retention; the second would offer alternative livelihoods to young men of fighting age; and the third would aim to disrupt narcotics distribution – but non-kinetically and, importantly, after the farmers had been paid their share by the drugs barons. All three were measurable, all three were focused entirely on non-kinetic interventions (so no collateral damage) and all three would need de-tailed TAA's to be undertaken. There was no end of enthusiasm for the concepts, but the reality was that all three fell outside conventional thinking and planning. None of them would have a senior US champion – a prerequisite to secure any funding at all – and all three would test the bureaucracy to its limit. At the time of writing, all three subsequently failed to be taken up. One senior US officer, clearly enamoured by the ideas, asked why he was being presented the proposals – why not just do it? Steve explained that he had presented the ideas at Task Force level and, whilst finding enthusiasm for them, was also told that it should be pushed to Regional Commands for approval. Regional Commanders liked the ideas but felt it needed operational approval, and that IJC should agree it. IJC also liked the ideas, but suggested that it was a change in strategy and therefore needed ISAF HQ approval. ISAF in turn saw its value but ... 'this is an operational issue. Have you tried the Regional Commands?' The senior US officer grimaced, but did not demur from the rather stark, explicit, assessment of ISAF.

Yet a plan to pay young Afghan men of fighting age a wedding dowry of up to $6,000, introduced by a rather sharp-eyed contractor to a senior US flag officer, seemed to gather rather more interest. The plan, which if extended to the whole of Afghanistan would cost the US taxpayer over $5bn per year, was utterly immeas-urable (the deal being that young men would take the dowry having first prom-ised not to join the insurgency), and would see huge injections of unearned cash into small micro-communities, with all the attendant second- and third-order ef-fects that that would bring. Despite reasoned arguments as to why the scheme was ill-advised, the US commander nevertheless decided it was something he wished to pursue, and he directed that both time and funds be allocated to it. Thankfully, some months later the idea was quietly dropped.

In June 2011, Lieutenant Mike H.,[333] Royal Navy, was seconded to Italy to assist with NATO operations in Libya. A week or so after arriving in Naples, he penned an email of his first impressions:

> My overriding impression of being in a NATO HQ is the similarity between it and the USSR Command Economy or British Leyland [a now defunct British car manufacturer] circa 1970s, in terms of the overriding drive to 'do stuff' – now! – whether or not that 'stuff' is harmful to the organisation or not. Even if folk recognise that an effect is not being measured the central push to keep the inputs goings takes precedence over all other concerns. People accept that we need to do TAA, but also readily accept that we have no time to do it and it is better to just 'do stuff' than have to wait until the point at which we know what effect our activities might have. People are judged on what they are seen to output, not on the effect that that output might ultimately have. Indeed, in many cases that ultimate effect has not yet been agreed or even articulated. People are also aware that if they are not prepared to keep producing the outputs they will be moved on and somebody more compliant will be brought in to do so. A Command driven organisation (or economy) is effective in complicated environments (standard war) but in complex human environments does not even allow the feedback required to be successfully measured before moving onto the next output. It is like constantly throwing stones into a pond and wondering why you can never see what's going on beneath the surface.

In short it is reminiscent of all 'we' subsequently came to learn about Soviet production lines. Russian consumers had long learnt to check the date on the product paperwork. If it was towards the end of the month, it should be avoided because they knew that at that point everybody would be rushing to meet their production targets and taking short-cuts (e.g. hammering screws in instead of screwing them, gluing fabric instead of stitching, leaving out components, not bothering to test), whereas something made during the more leisurely first three weeks of the month would be more likely, but by no means guaranteed, to work.

In June 2011, the former British Ambassador to Afghanistan, Sir Sherard Cowper-Coles, published his memoirs of his time in Kabul. In it he wrote: 'everyone fell in to the same trap: of substituting acquaintance for knowledge, activity for understanding, reporting for analysis, quantity of work for quality.'[334] He goes on to relay a discussion with a more junior officer, a friend of his son, who, he states, told him that: 'many senior officers are covering up failings or trying to achieve short-term solutions which actually lead to longer-term failings.' We are not for

---

333   For security purposes the officer's full name has been excluded.
334   Sherard Cowper-Coles, *Cables from Kabul* (Harper Press, 2011, p. 52).

one minute suggesting any Machiavellian intent – far from it. Instead what we see are senior officers doing their best in increasingly difficult circumstances; circumstances in which they are acutely aware of the sacrifices that young soldiers, sailors and airmen are making on the ground. That said, we are of the view that, in the critical area of influence, the UK's Armed Forces, for too long, have been too willing to allow the wrong people to be in the wrong place doing the wrong thing at the wrong time. We argue that this level of disorganisation has now become systemic, and therefore cultural, making it 'OK' to 'muddle through'. This is now incredibly difficult to resolve. One problem is that for military officers to publicly talk down a mission would be unforgivable, and would betray the efforts of those men and women at the very sharp end of the conflict. But 'we' do need to understand, more clearly, how the Armed Forces are performing in today's battles. In June 2011, an unseemly debate broke out in the British press over the sustainability of military operations in Libya. The head of the Royal Navy, Admiral Sir Mark Stanhope, was reported by the British media as expressing concern over the mission's sustainability, whilst politicians and, eventually, the Chief of Defence Staff, told the media that there was not a problem and the mission could continue indefinitely without detriment. The issue attracted considerable attention. Michael Clarke, Director-General of the Royal United Services Institute publicly commented that:

> he [UK Defence Secretary Dr Liam Fox] slapped down the top brass for their muttered carping about the effects of the Libya operation on their forces. Military leaders warning about the strains the Libyan operation puts on the forces, he said, were in effect giving comfort to the enemy when 'lives are at stake'. Qadhafi [sic] must get 'only one message' from the British. This is as close as a defence minister is likely to come to accusing his top brass in public of unwitting treachery.[335]

Former Royal Navy Admiral, Terry Loughran, told the BBC that: 'we've now reduced … to such a low level that this maritime nation can no longer sustain a tinpot operation like Libya.'[336] Such observations follow on from the retiring US Secretary of Defence, Robert Gates's comments regarding the future of NATO – 'NATO has become a "two-tiered" alliance poorly equipped to deal with challenges, and with members either unable or unwilling to carry out agreed missions' – and do not bode well for the future of Western defence forces and the complexity of operations in a world of expanding populations and dwindling resources.

We started this book with a quotation from Roosevelt's 'Man in the Arena' speech. Unashamedly we repeat a small part of it here:

---

335   http://www.rusi.org/analysis/commentary/ref:C4E10D753A41ED/
336   BBC Radio 4 PM Programme ,14 June 2011.

The credit belongs to the man who is actually in the arena, whose face is marred by dust and sweat and blood, who strives valiantly, who errs and comes up short again and again, because there is no effort without error or shortcoming.

We know, unequivocally, that the people who really understand the problems are those at the sharp end dealing with them, who are unencumbered by issues of politics, not the generals stuck in HQ bubbles and not the politicians and civil servants stuck in government offices. They are young, junior, soldiers and very often their words are lost when more senior but less experienced officers speak. Generals and politicians are hindered not just by remoteness from the problem but by the entire bureaucracy that purports to exist to support them, but which seems at times to govern and control them. Andrew recalls his many visits to the UK Ministry of Defence, and other Whitehall departments, where a series of earnest and important individuals all spent valuable time explaining the nature of the problem in Iraq and Afghanistan. Yet, weighed down by bureaucracy and the limits of UK political and military direction, they were rarely able to describe what the solution might look like. We know that at the root of all the problems 'we' face, both in Afghanistan and Libya today and in other conflict zones yet to emerge, is behaviour. 'Our' behaviour, the behaviour of 'our' adversaries and the behaviour of the population in which 'we' fight each other. Knowing how to understand it, how to change it and how to measure that change comes not from working behind keyboards but from getting faces marred by dust and sweat, by erring, and by learning from those mistakes, very quickly and very efficiently.

There is evidence that this learning process, at least in the UK, is now under way. The UK's Psychological Operations Group is set to almost double in size, the Defence Cultural Unit has been expanded, and greater attention is being paid to other military enablers. In early summer 2011, the UK's doctrine centre issued JDN3/11, a guide to decision-making and problem-solving in the human terrain. Simultaneously, the UK military academy at Sandhurst established its Communication and Applied Behavioural Science course, designed to provide young officer cadets with an insight into what motivates people, how teams work and how to find ways of communicating more effectively. All of these are important steps forward. However, they owe their genesis not to an institutional acceptance that change is needed, but to the personal interest and drive of people such as General Sir David Richards, who has experienced these very problems at first hand in Sierra Leone and Indonesia, and Lieutenant General Paul Newton, the British Army's Commander of Force Development and Training, the man charged with reorganising the British Army for the future. But they are only very small steps and, as we see from the revolutions in North Africa, giant leaps are being made by others. It is with therefore some nervousness that we both look to the future and the West's ability to cope in the face of increasingly complex problems and ever more agile actors.

> Our very survival depends on our ability to stay awake, to adjust to new ideas, to remain vigilant and to face the challenge of change.
>
> Dr Martin Luther King

List of readings

Books

Armistead E, *Information operations: Warfare and the hard reality of soft power*, Brassey's, 2004.

Armitage R and Nye J, *CSIS Commission on Smart Power*, Center for Strategic and International Studies, 2007.

Arquilla J and Borer D, *Information strategy and warfare: A guide to theory and practice*, Routledge, 2007.

Arquilla J and Ronfeldt R, *In Athena's camp*, Rand Corporation, 1997.

Arreguin-Toft I, *How the weak win wars: A theory of asymmetric conflict*, Cambridge University Press, 2005.

Atwan A, *The secret history of Al-Qa'ida*, Saqi Press, 2006.

Badsey S, *The media and international security*, Routledge, 2000.

Bahador B, *The CNN effect in action: How the news media pushed the West towards war in Kosovo*, Routledge, 2000.

Bakr Naji A, *The management of savagery: The most critical stage through which the Umma will pass*, Harvard University Press, 2007.

Barber N, *The war of the running dogs: The Malayan emergency 1948–1960*, Weybright and Talley, 1971.

Barnett R, *Asymmetrical warfare: Today's challenge to US military power*, Brassey's, 2003.

Bell M, *The truth that sticks: New labour's breach of trust*, Icon Books, 2007.

Berlo D, *The process of communication*, Holt, Rinehart, and Winston, 1960.

Bernays E, *Propaganda*, IG Publishing, 2005.

Bobbitt P, *Terror and consent: The wars for the 21st century*, Allen Lane, 2008.

Borovik A, *The hidden war: A Russian journalist's account of the Soviet war in Afghanistan*, Grove Press, 1990.

Brown J, *Techniques of persuasion: From propaganda to brainwashing*, Pelican Books, 1964.

Burnham P (Editor), *Research methods in politics*, Palgrave, 2008.

Buzan B, *People, states and fear*, Longman, 1991.

Buzan B, *Security: A new framework for analysis*, Lynne Rienner Publications, 1997.

Carruthers S, *Winning hearts and minds. British governments, the media and colonial counter-insurgency 1944–1960*, Leicester University Press, 1995.

Carruthers S, *The media at war*, Palgrave Macmillan, 1999.

Castells M, *Communication power*, Oxford University Press, 2009.

Cavelty M, Mauer V and Krishna-Hensel S, *Power and security in the information age*, Ashgate, 2006.

Chevedden P, *The Islamic view and the Christian view of the Crusades: A new synthesis*, Blackwell, 2008.

Childs H, *Public opinion: Nature, formation and role*, Van Nostrand, 1965.

Cimbala S, *Military persuasion in war and policy: The power of soft*, Praeger, 2002.

Cobley P, *Narrative — The new critical idiom*, Routledge, 2001.

Cohen F, *World War 3: Information warfare basics*, ASP Press, 2006.

Cohen F, *World War 3: We are losing it and most of us didn't even know we were fighting in it – Information warfare basics*, Fred Cohen Publishing, 2006.

Collier P, *The bottom billion: Why the poorest countries are failing and what can be done about it*, Oxford University Press, 2007.

Corman S, Trethewey A and Goodall H, *Weapons of mass persuasion: Strategic communication to combat violent extremism*, Arizona State University Press, 2008.

Corman S, Trethewey A and Goodall H, *A 21ˢᵗ century model for communication in the global war on terror*, Arizona State University Press, 2009.

Cottam R, *Competitive interference and 20ᵗʰ century diplomacy*, University of Pittsburgh Press, 1967.

Daily B and Parker P, *Soviet strategic deception*, Hoover Press, 1987.

David G and Keldin T, *Ideas as weapons: influence and perception in modern warfare*, Potomac Books, 2009.

Davison C, *Dubai: The vulnerability of success*, Hurst and Co, 2008.

Defence Evaluation and Research Agency, *Public opinion and casualty levels: A historical analysis study*, United Kingdom Ministry of Defence, 1999.

Dyer M, *The weapon on the wall: Re-thinking psychological warfare*, Johns Hopkins University Press, 1959.

Eichenberg C and Capitanchik D, *Defence and public opinion*, Routledge, 1983.

Engelke M, *The counter-counterinsurgency manual (Notes on demilitarizing American society)*, Prickly Paradigm Press, 2009.

Evans G and Newnham J, *The Penguin dictionary of international relations*, Penguin, 1998.

Fergusson J, *A million bullets*, Bantam Press, 2008.

Finn C, *Effects based warfare*, Joint Doctrine and Concepts Center, 2004.

Fox W, *The super-powers: The US, Britain and the Soviet Union – Their responsibility for peace*, Harcourt, 1944.

Frank A, Anne *Frank: The diary of a young girl*, Bantam Press, 1993.

Francis D, *Rethinking war and peace*, Pluto Press, 2004.

Fraser M, *Weapons of mass distraction*, St Martin's Press, 2003.

Galula D, *Counterinsurgency warfare: Theory and practice*, Praeger, 2006.

Garnett D, *The secret history of PWE*, St Ermin's Press, 2002.

Gigerenzer G and Selten R, *Bounded rationality: The adaptive toolbox*, MIT Press, 2002.

Gladwell M, *The tipping point: How little things can make a big difference*, Back Bay Books, 2000.

Goldstein F, Findley, Benjamin F (Editors), *Psychological operations: Principles and case studies*, National Defense University Press, 1996.

Gramsci A, Hoare Q, Nowell-Smith G (Editors), *Prison notebooks: Selections*, Lawrence & Wishart Ltd, 1998.

Grau L (Editor), *The bear went over the mountain. Soviet combat tactics in Afghanistan*, National Defense University Press, 1996.

Grey S, *Operation snake bite*, Penguin Viking Press, 2009.

Gundlupet V, *Comparative political studies 2*, Cambridge University Press, 2007.

Hammes T, *The sling and the stone: On war in the 21st century*, Zenith Press, 2004.

Herman D, *The Cambridge companion to narrative*, Cambridge University Press, 2007.

Howe E, *The black game: British subversive operations against the Germans during the Second World War*, Futura, 1982.

Jamieson K and Aday S, *The Oxford companion to the politics of the world*, Oxford University Press, 2001.

Johnson-Cartee K and Copeland G, *Strategic political communication. Rethinking social influence, persuasion and propaganda*, Rowman and Littlefield, 2003.

Jowett G and O'Donnell V, *Propaganda and persuasion*, Sage, 1999.

Key V, *Public opinion and American democracy*, Knopf, 1961.

Kimmage D and Ridolfo K, *Iraqi insurgent media: The war of images and ideas*, RRFE, 2007.

Kintner W and Kornfeder J, *The new frontier of war*, Henry Regnery Company Press, 1962.

Knightley P, *The first casualty: From Crimea to Vietnam: The war correspondent as hero, propagandist and myth maker*, Harcourt, 1975.

Kuhn T, *The structure of scientific revolutions*, University of Chicago Press, 1962.

Lapping B, *End of empire*, St Martin's Press, 1985.

Larson E, *Casualties and consensus*, The Rand Corporation, 1996.

Lashmar P and Oliver J, *Britain's secret propaganda war*, Sutton, 1998.

Leonhard R, *Principles of war for the information age*, Presidio Press, 2000.

Linebarger P, *Psychological warfare*, Duell, Sloan and Pearce, 1954.

Lipmann W, *Public opinion*, NuVision Publications, 2007.

Livingston S, *Clarifying the CNN effect: An examination of media effects according to type of military intervention*, Harvard University Press, 1997.

Lloyd M, *The art of military deception*, Leo Cooper Books, 1997.

Lonsdale D, *The nature of war in the information age: A Clausewitzian future*, Frank Cass, 2004.

Lord C & Barnet F, *Political warfare and psychological operations: Rethinking the US approach*, National Defence University Press, 1989.

Lowe R and Spencer C, *Iran, its neighbours and the regional crises: A Middle East programme report*, Chatham House, 2006.

Luhmann N, *Social systems*, Stanford University Press, 1995.

Lukes S, *Power: A radical view*, Palgrave Macmillan, 2005.

Marr A, *My trade: A short history of British journalism*, Pan, 2005.

Martin W, *Recent theories of narrative*, Cornell University Press, 1986.

Melissen J, *Innovation in diplomatic practice*, Palgrave Macmillan, 1999.

Melissen J, *The new public diplomacy: Soft power in international relations*, Palgrave Macmillan, 2005.

Morgenthau H, *Politics among nations: The struggle for power and peace*, Knopf, 1978.

Mueller J, *War, presidents and public opinion*, John Wiley Press, 1973.

Mulvenon J, *The People's Liberation Army in the information age*, RAND Corporation, 1999.

Munkler H, *The new wars*, Polity Press, 2005.

North R, *Ministry of defeat: The British war in Iraq 2003–2009*, Continuum, 2009.

Newcourt-Nowodworski S, *Black propaganda in the Second World War*, Sutton Press, 2005.

Nye J, *Soft Power: The means to success in world politics*, Public Affairs, 2004.

Oncu A, Bucher T and Aytac O, *Strategic communication for combating terrorism,* Private pressing by NATO COE-DAT, Ankara, Turkey, 2010.

Osinga F, *Science strategy and war,* Routledge, 2006.

Payne K, *The battle of ideas: Media strategies in the struggle against militant Islam,* Reuters Institute, 2008.

Radvanyi J, *Psychological operations and political warfare in long-term strategic planning,* Praeger, 1990.

Ramo J, *The age of the unthinkable,* Little, Brown, 2009.

Rankin N, *Churchill's wizards: The British genius for deception 1914–1945,* Faber and Faber, 2008.

Reeve S, *The new jackals: Ramzi Yousef, Osama Bin Laden and the future of terrorism,* Deutsch Press, 1999.

Rid T, *War and media operations: The US military and the press from Vietnam to Iraq,* Routledge, 2007.

Roger L, *The Oxford history of the British Empire vol. IV,* Oxford University Press, 1999.

Schmidtchen D, *The rise of the strategic private: Technology, control and change in a network enabled military,* Australian Ministry of Defence, 2007.

Shannon C and Weaver W, *The mathematical theory of communication,* University of Illinois Press, 1949.

Sheenan J, *Reel bad Arabs: How Hollywood vilifies a people,* Olive Branch Press, 2001.

Smith R, *The utility of force: The art of war in the modern world,* Penguin, 2006.

Sobel R, *The impact of public opinion on US foreign policy since Vietnam,* Harvard University Press, 2001.

Stafford D, *Churchill and the secret service,* Abacus, 1995.

Stiglitz J and Bilmes L, *The three trillion dollar war: The true cost of the Iraq conflict,* Penguin Books, 2009.

Stocker G and Schopf C, *InfoWar,* Springer Verlag GmbH, 1998.

Taber R, *The war of the flea,* Potomac Books, 2002.

Tatham S, *Losing Arab hearts and minds: The coalition, Al-Jazeera and Muslim public opinion,* Hurst and Co, 2006.

Telhami S, *The stakes: America and the Middle East – The consequence of power and the choice for peace,* Oxford University Press, 2003.

Thomas T, *The Russian armed forces at the dawn of the millennium,* US Department of Defence, 2000.

Thornton R, *Asymmetric warfare,* Polity Press, 2007.

Thussu D and Freedman D, *War and the media*, Sage, 2004.

Tzu S, *The art of war*, Filiquarian Publishing, 2006.

Journal Articles and Papers

Ahrari E, Military strategic perspectives on the PRC: New frontiers of information based war, *Asian Survey*, vol. 37, no. 12, 1997.

Ajzen I and Fishbein M, Attitude-behaviour relations: A theoretical analysis and review of empirical research, *Psychological Bulletin*, no. 84, 1977.

Allport F, Towards a science of public opinion, *Public Opinion Quarterly*, vol. 1, no. 1, 1937.

Amr and Singer, To win 'The war on terror' we must first win the 'war of ideas': Here's how, *Annals of the American Academy of Political and Social Science*, no. 618, 2008, p. 212.

Atkinson M, De Vries A, *Communication and interpretation of blue intent. Final Report 07/08 Version 1.1*, DSTL – classified document.

Atkinson S, *Returning science to the social*, UK Defence Academy Shrivenham Paper, July 2010.

Babst S, *Reinventing NATO's public diplomacy*, Research Division, NATO Defense College, November 2008.

Barcott R, Anthropology in conflict: An exchange, *Survival*, vol. 20, no. 3, Jun–Jul 2008.

Barry D, Strategy retold: Toward a narrative view of strategic discourse, *Academy of Management Review*, April 1997.

Baum M, How public opinion constrains the use of force: The case of Operation Restore Hope, *Presidential Studies Quarterly*, vol. 34, no. 2, 2004.

Beavers G, Defining the information campaign, *Military Review*, November–December 2005.

Bell M, The death of news, *Media, War and Conflict*, vol. 1, no. 2, 2008, pp. 221-231, Sage Publications.

Bertram C, Soft power: The means to success in world politics, Book review, *Survival*, vol. 1, no. 47, 2005.

Betz D, The virtual dimension of contemporary insurgency and counterinsurgency, *Small Wars and Insurgencies*, vol. 19, no. 4, 2008.

Black J, Review: How the weak win wars, *Journal of Military History*, vol. 71, no. 1, Jan 2007.

Blandy C, *Provocation, deception, entrapment: The Russo-Georgian five day war*, UK Defence Academy ARAG Paper, March 2009.

Blandy C, *Georgia and Russia: A further deterioration in relations*, UK Defence Academy ARAG Paper, July 2008.

Blankley and Horn, Strategizing strategic communication, *WebMemo* no. 1939.

Blechman B, Soft Power: The means to success in world politics, Book review, *Science Quarterly*, vol. 119, no. 4, Winter 2004.

Bockstette C, *Jihadist terrorist use of strategic communication management techniques*, George C Marshall Centre Occasional Paper Series, no. 20, December 2008.

Bolt N, Betz D and Azari J, *Propaganda of the deed 2008: Understanding the phenomenon*, Whitehall Report 3-08.

Bradfield E, Strategic interactions, *Harvard International Review*, Summer 2005.

Burnham G, Lafta R, Doocy S, Roberts L, Mortality after the 2003 invasion of Iraq: A cross-sectional cluster sample survey. *The Lancet*, vol. 368, no. 9545, pp. 1421–1428.

Calabrese D, *Environmental policies and strategic communication in Iran: The value of public opinion research in decision making*, The World Bank, Working Paper 132, 2008.

Campbell S, *Muslim public opinion and propaganda: Implications for US policy*, Fletcher School of Law and Diplomacy.

Cioppa T, Operation Iraqi freedom. Strategic communication analysis and assessment, *Media, War and Conflict*, vol. 2, p. 25, 2009.

Combs R, *Assessing strategic effectiveness in the war on terrorism*, US Army War College Paper, 2006.

Corman S and Dooley K, *Strategic communication on a rugged landscape: Principles for finding the right message*, Consortium for Strategic Communication Report 801, January 2008.

Corman S and Schiefelbein J, *Communication and media strategy in the Jihadi war of ideas*, Consortium for Strategic Communication, 2006.

Cox J, *Information operations in Operations Enduring Freedom and Iraqi Freedom – What went wrong?*, School of Advanced Military Studies Paper, 2006.

Crede A, Social, cultural, economic and legal barriers to the development of technology-based information systems, *Industrial Management and Data Systems*, vol. 1, 1997.

Criston D, Soft power: The means to success in world politics. Book review, *American Economist*, Fall 2005.

Cull N, *Public diplomacy: Lessons from the past*, Center on Public Diplomacy, University of Southern California, 2007.

Darley W, The missing component of strategic communication, *Joint Forces Quarterly*, no. 47, 2007.

Darwish A, Angering hearts and losing minds, *The Middle East*, August–September 2005.

Dauber C, The truth is out there: Responding to insurgent disinformation and deception operations, *Military Review*, Jan–Feb 2009.

DCDC, *Global strategic trends programme 2007–2008*. Third edition. UK Ministry of Defence.

Delfanti A, Too much power to the networks, *Journal of Science Communication*, vol. 08, no. 04, 2009, R01.

Deutsch R, The droning of strategic communication and public diplomacy, *Military Review*, September–October 2007.

Dodd T, Creating the right image, *Jane's Defence Weekly*, 18 June 2008.

Donnelly C, *Some realities of defence economics*, Defence Academy of the United Kingdom – Unpublished paper.

Dorronsoro G, *The Taliban's winning strategy in Afghanistan*, Carnegie Endowment, 2009.

Douglas F, *The year after Zarqawi: Strategic narratives, peripheral operations and central visions*, US Naval War College, 2008.

Eder M, Toward strategic communication, *Military Review*, July–August 2007.

Eichenberg R, Victory has many friends: US public opinion and the use of military force, *International Security*, vol. 30, no. 1, Summer 2005.

Evans A and Steven D, The new public diplomacy: A theory of influence for 21st century foreign policy, *DEMOS*, 2008.

Fergusson N, What is power? *The Hoover Digest*, no. 2, 2003.

Finocchiaro M, Gramsci: An alternative communism?, *Studies in Soviet Thought*, vol. 27, 1984.

Fisher and Broeckerhoff, *Options for influence: Global campaigns of persuasion in the new worlds of public diplomacy*, British Council, March 2008.

Fleck J, *Limited war theory in Vietnam*, National War College, Fort McNair, 1994.

Foreman J, Defeat in the information battle space, *National Review Online*, 17, March 2007.

Fowler S, How information operations enable combatant commanders to dominate today's battlefield, *Armor & Cavalry Journal*, March–April 2008.

Fuchs C, Some reflections on Manuel Castells' book "Communication Power", *tripleC*, vol. 7, no. 1, 2009, pp. 94–108.

Furia P and Lucas R, Determinants of Arab public opinion on foreign relations, *International Studies Quarterly*, 2006, no. 50.

Gompert D, *Heads we win: The cognitive side of COIN*, Rand Corporation, 2007.

Gordon P, Can the war on terror be won? How to fight the right war, *Foreign Affairs*, vol. 86, no. 6.

Gowing N, *Skyful of lies and black swans: The new tyranny of shifting information power in crises*, The Reuters Institute, University of Oxford, 2009.

Greenberg K, What the torture memo tells us, *Survival*, vol. 51, no. 3, June–July 2009.

Gregory B, *Public diplomacy and strategic communication: Cultures, firewalls and imported norms*, Paper prepared for APSS, August 2005.

Gundlupet V, Review: How the weak win wars, *Comparative Political Studies*, Cambridge University Press, vol. 40, 2007, p. 916.

Halloran R, Strategic communication, *Parameters*, Autumn 2007.

Herz M, Some psychological lessons from leaflet propaganda in World War II, *Public Opinion Quarterly*, Fall 1949.

HM Government, *UK policy in Afghanistan and Pakistan: The way forward*, Cabinet Office, April 2009.

Hoagland J, Soft Power: The means to success in world politics. Book review, *The New Republic*, 17 May 2004.

Holliday S, Strategic communication changes: It's time to call evil doers evil, *American Diplomacy*, August 2007.

ICG, Taliban propaganda: Winning the war of words?, *Asia Report*, no. 158, 24 July 2008.

Ichihara M, Making the case for soft power, *SAIS Review*, vol. XXVI, no. 1, Winter-Spring 2006.

Ikenberry G, Soft power: The means to success in world politics, Book review, *Foreign Affairs*, vol. 83, no. 3, May-June 2004.

Jensen M, Review: How the weak win wars, *International Studies Review*, no. 8, 2006.

Jones J, Strategic communications: A mandate for the United States, *Joint Forces Quarterly*, no. 39, 4th Quarter 2005.

Jordan J and Horsburgh J, Analysis and evolution of the global Jihadist movement propaganda, *Journal of Terrorism and Political Violence*, vol. 18, no. 3, Fall 2006.

Josten R, Strategic communication: Key enabler for elements of national power, *IOSphere Magazine*, Summer 2006.

Kelly J and Etling B, *Mapping Iran's online public: Politics and culture in the Persian blogosphere*, Harvard Law School Research Paper 2008-01.

Kipp J, The human terrain system: A CORDS for the 21st century, *Military Review*, September–October 2006.

Korolyvov A, Features of information warfare of the future, *The Military Diplomat Magazine*, vol. 1–2, 2009.

Krastev I and Leonard M, *New world order: The balance of soft power and the rise of herbivorous powers*, European Council on Foreign Relations, October 2007.

Kulakov O, *Lessons learned from the Soviet intervention in Afghanistan: Implications for Russian defense reform.* NATO Research Papers, NATO Defence College Rome, no. 26, March 2006.

Ladbury S, *Testing hypotheses on radicalisation in Afghanistan – Independent report for DFID*, DFID / CPAu (Kabul) 14 August 2009.

Leng R and Wheeler H, Influence strategies, success and war, *Journal of Conflict Resolution*, vol. 23, no. 4, December 1979.

Levitt M and Jacobson M, Highlighting AQ's bankrupt ideology, Washington Institute for Near East Policy, *Policy Watch*, May 7, 2008.

Lewis J, Television, public opinion and the war in Iraq: The case of Britain, *International Journal of Public Opinion Research*, vol. 16, no. 3, 2004.

Lin O, Understanding why the inferior defeats the superior, *Pointer*, vol. 34, no. 4, 2009.

Livingston S, The influence of personal influence on the study of audiences, *American Academy of Political and Social Science*, vol. 608, November 2006.

Lord C, On the nature of strategic communications, *Joint Forces Quarterly*, no. 46, 2007.

Lynch M, Blogging the new Arab public, *Arab Media and Society*, February 2007.

Mack A, Why big nations lose small wars: The politics of asymmetric conflict, *World Politics*, vol. XXVII, no. 2, January 1975.

Mandel R, Reassessing victory in warfare, *Armed Forces and Society*, no. 33, 2007.

Mullen M, Strategic communication: Getting back to basics, *Joint Forces Quarterly*, no. 55, 4th Quarter 2009.

Murphy D, The trouble with strategic communication(s), *IOSphere*, Winter 2008.

Murphy D, *Strategic communication in domestic disasters*, Center for Strategic Leadership Issue Paper 8-06, August 2006.

Murphy D, *New media and the warfighter*, Center for Strategic Leadership Issue Paper 3-08, March 2008.

Murphy D, *Information operations and winning the peace*, Center for Strategic Leadership Issue Paper 14-05, December 2005.

Murphy D and White J, Propaganda: Can a word decide a war?, *Parameters*, Autumn 2007.

Neumann P and Stevens T, *Countering online radicalisation: A strategy for action*, King's College ICSR, 2009.

Nissen T, *The Taliban's information warfare*, Royal Danish Defence College 2007.

Nye J, Old wars and future wars: Causation and prevention, *Journal of Interdisciplinary History*, vol. 18, no. 4, Spring 1988.

Nye J, The American national interest and global public goods, *International Affairs*, vol. 78, no. 2, Apr 2002.

Nye J and Art D, To what ends military power?, *International Security*, vol. 5, no. 2, Autumn 1980.

Paddock A, *Psychological and unconventional warfare, 1941–1952: Origins of a special warfare capability for the United States Army*, Army War College Paper, Carlisle Barracks, 1979.

Pasanen Y, The implications of virtual deception, *Air and Space Power Journal*, April 1999.

Paul T, How the weak win wars Book Review, *Perspectives on Politics*, vol. 5, no. 1, March 2007.

Paul T, Why big nations lose small wars: The politics of asymmetric conflict, *World Politics*, vol. XXVII, no. 2, Jan 1975.

Payne K, Waging communication war, *Parameters*, Summer 2008.

Petersen J, Lippmann revisited, *Journalism*, vol. 4, no. 2, 2003, pp. 249–259.

Rahman T, Pashto language and identity formation in Pakistan, *Contemporary South Asia*, vol. 4, no. 2, July 1995.

RCMP, *Words make worlds*, Royal Canadian Mounted Police, 2009.

Record J, External assistance: Enabler of insurgent success, *Parameters*, vol. 336, pp. 336–50.

Record J, Review: How the Weak Win Wars, *Survival*, vol. 48, no. 1, Spring 2006.

Ringsmose J, When great powers lose small wars, *Global Security*, vol. 22, no. 3, pp. 411–418.

Romarheim A, Definitions of strategic political communication, *NIIA*, no. 689, 2005.

Romilly M, *Campaigning: A lost art?*, UK Defence Academy, unpublished.

Sanders M, *Using strategic communication more effectively in the global war on terror*, US Army War College Paper, 2006.

Serookiy Y, Psychological-information warfare: Lessons of Afghanistan, *Military Thought*, no. 1, March 2004.

Simmons G, Mass media and the battle for public opinion in the global war on terror, *Perceptions*, Spring–Summer 2008.

Smith D, Corbin M and Helman C, *Re-forging the sword: Forces for a 21st century security strategy*, Center for Defense Information, 2001.

Smith S, General Templer and counter-insurgency in Malaya: Hearts and minds, intelligence and propaganda, *Intelligence and National Security*, vol. 16, no. 3, Autumn 2001.

Smith-Windsor B, Hard power, soft power reconsidered, *Canadian Military Journal*, Autumn 2000.

Soriano M, Terrorism and the mass media after AQ: A change of course, *Athena Intelligence Journal*, vol. 3, no. 2, 2008.

Straus T, *The war for public opinion*, The Institute of Communication Studies, 2001.

Sullivan P, War aims and war outcomes: Why powerful states lose limited wars, *Journal of Conflict Resolution*, vol. 51, no. 3, June 2007.

Tatham S, Tactical strategic communication! Placing informational effect at the centre of command, *British Army Review*, no. 147, Summer 2009.

Tatham S and Mackay A, *Behavioural conflict: From general to strategic corporal. Adaption, complexity and influence*, UK Defence Academy Shrivenham Paper, December 2009.

Tatham S, *Strategic communication: A primer*, Ministry of Defence, 2008.

Taylor P, Strategic communications or democratic propaganda?, *Journalism Studies*, vol. 3, no. 3, 2002.

Thomas T, Russia's reflexive control theory and the military, *Journal of Slavic Military Studies*, vol. 17, no. 2, 2004.

Tversky A and Kahneman D, Judgement under uncertainty: Heuristics and biases, *Science*, New Series, vol. 185, no. 4157, Sep. 27, 1974, pp. 1124–1131.

UNICEF, *Strategic communication for behaviour and social change in South Asia*, 2006.

Unnamed, China's web army: PLA's secret weapon, *Strategic Affairs*, December 2006.

Unnamed, The power of persuasion: A conversation with Joseph Nye, *Harvard International Review*, Winter 2003.

Vaughan J, Cloak without dagger: How the IRD fought Britain's cold war in the Middle East, 1948-56, *Cold War History*, vol. 4, no. 3, April 2004.

Viola J, *What is the proper role of public opinion in the decision to use military force as an element of national power?*, US Army War College paper, 2006.

Walch R, Soft power: The means to success in world politics. Book review, *America*, August 2–9, 2004.

Wicker A, Attitudes versus actions: The relationship of verbal and overt behavioural responses to attitude objects, *Journal of Social Issues*, vol. 25, issue 4, Autumn 1969.

Wilford H, The IRD: Britain's secret cold war weapon revealed, *Review of International Studies*, no. 24, 1998.

Williams M, The weaponisation of oil in the messages of Osama Bin Laden, *The Journal of Military and Strategic Studies*, vol. 10, no. 20, Winter 2007–08.

Windsor M, Strategic communication: Key to success in Afghanistan and future conflicts?, Unpublished internal MoD discussion paper, August 2009.

Yin R, Case study research design and methods, Third edition, *Applied Social Research Methods Series*, vol. 5, 2003.

Yoshihara T, *Chinese information warfare: A phantom menace or emerging threat?*, Strategic Studies Institute, 2001.

Younger K, Public opinion and British foreign policy, *International Affairs*, vol. 40, no. 1, 1964.

Yu Lin O, Understanding why the 'inferior' defeats the superior, *Pointer*, vol. 34, no. 4, 2009.

Zaharna R, The network paradigm of strategic public diplomacy, *Foreign Policy in Focus*, April 2005.

Zaharna R, American public diplomacy in the Arab and Muslim world: A strategic communication analysis, *Foreign Policy in Focus*, November 2001.

Index

Lightning Source UK Ltd.
Milton Keynes UK
UKOW02f0329170813

215411UK00003B/7/P